IRISH ARCHITECTURAL AND DECORATIVE STUDIES
Volume X, 2007

for Desmond FitzGerald, Knight of Glin

IRISH ARCHITECTURAL AND DECORATIVE STUDIES

THE JOURNAL OF THE IRISH GEORGIAN SOCIETY – VOLUME X, 2007

IRISH ARCHITECTURAL AND
DECORATIVE STUDIES
The Journal of the Irish Georgian Society
Volume X, 2007

Published by the Irish Georgian Society
© Irish Georgian Society and the authors, 2007.
All rights reserved.

ISBN 978 0948037 290 hb / 566 pb

This annual journal continues the publishing
tradition of the Irish Georgian Society's *Bulletin*
(38 volumes, 1958-1997).

Edited by William Laffan

Produced for the Irish Georgian Society by Gandon
Editions, which is grant-aided by The Arts Council.
Design   John O'Regan (© Gandon, 2007)
Production   Nicola Dearey
                                Gunther Berkus
Printing   Nicholson & Bass, Belfast
Distribution   Gandon and its overseas agents

GANDON EDITIONS
Oysterhaven, Kinsale, Co Cork
tel +353 (0)21-4770830 / *fax* 021-4770755
e gandon@eircom.net / www.gandon-editions.com

The Irish Georgian Society gratefully
acknowledges the grant-aiding of this book by
THE PAUL MELLON ESTATE
and an anonymous Irish donor

cover	William Osborne Hamilton, *A view of Lota, the seat of Robert Rogers Esq 1772* (detail) (courtesy William Laffan)
frontispiece	*The Obelisk near Castletown, 140 feet high* – an engraving of the Conolly Folly (1740) from the Noble and Keenan map of Kildare, 1752

THE IRISH GEORGIAN SOCIETY

The Irish Georgian Society aims to encourage an
interest in and the preservation of distinguished
examples of architecture and the allied arts in
Ireland. Further information – and membership
application details – may be obtained from:

THE IRISH GEORGIAN SOCIETY
74 Merrion Square, Dublin 2
tel +353 (0)1-6767053 / *fax* 01-6620290
e-mail info@igs.ie / *web-site* www.igs.ie

IRISH ARCHITECTURAL AND DECORATIVE STUDIES

THE JOURNAL OF THE IRISH GEORGIAN SOCIETY – VOLUME X, 2007
EDITOR: WILLIAM LAFFAN

———

Desmond FitzGerald,
Knight of Glin

————

THIS, THE TENTH VOLUME OF *IRISH ARCHITECTURAL AND DECORATIVE STUDIES*, IS
dedicated to Desmond FitzGerald for his 70th birthday. The launch of
Volume X rather pleasingly falls in early 2008, the 50th anniversary of the
founding of the Irish Georgian Society by Desmond and Mariga Guinness.

Desmond FitzGerald, the 29th Knight of Glin, is a scholar of international
repute. He studied in Canada and at Harvard, and worked for eleven years at the
Victoria & Albert Museum, London, before returning to Ireland. Desmond is married to Olda FitzGerald, and has three daughters, Catherine, Nesta and Honor. He
farms at Glin Castle, which he has restored to its former splendour and which houses his collections of Irish paintings, furniture and the decorative arts. The Knight
serves as a governor of the National Gallery of Ireland, and sits on the boards of the
Irish Architectural Archive, the Irish Landmark Trust, Irish Heritage Properties and
the Castletown Foundation. He is passionate about the history, and future, of Irish
country houses, parks and gardens, and has been one of the instigators of the new
Irish Heritage Trust. Desmond acted for many years as Christie's representative in
Ireland, and has been involved in the Irish Georgian Society from its earliest days,
now serving as its president. Among many other accolades, he was awarded a
Doctorate of Letters by Trinity College, Dublin, to whom, with Prof Anne
Crookshank, he donated an important archive of photographs on Irish art. More
recently he was honoured as a 'Hero of Conservation' by the Belfast Buildings
Preservation Trust.

Here, however, it is specifically the Knight's contribution to Irish scholarship
that is celebrated, the depth and breath of which is manifest in the bibliography of
his publications which is listed here for the first time. Desmond's researches have
been pioneering, his writing always fresh and lively. Pioneers in scholarly research
inevitably run the risk of their publications becoming outdated by subsequent find-
ings. Hardly ever has this been the case with the Knight, and on the rare occasion
that it has, he has been the first to admit 'we got that wrong!' The arguments in
almost all of his publications have stood the test of time. It is quite simply impossi-

ble to even begin the study of Irish painting without engaging with the several volumes he has co-authored with Prof Crookshank. This applies equally to his architectural researches. To quote from a re-evaluation by John Logan of the architect Davis Dukart, published elsewhere in this volume:

> What is now known of Dukart owes much to two pioneering 1967 articles by Desmond FitzGerald, Knight of Glin. He proposed a basic chronology, a seminal set of attributions and an assessment of Dukart's achievement, particularly as an architect of country houses in a distinctive, late Palladian manner. Subsequent studies have added detail and proposed further attributions (and de-attributions), but the general chronology of Dukart's career and FitzGerald's assessment of his significance remains largely unaltered.

The impact that his scholarship has made is, however, far greater than a list of works, no matter how impressive, can convey. The Knight has been a seminal figure in the scholarship of our art, architecture, landscape and material culture. He has inspired and encouraged research in a wide variety of areas, and many of the subsequent generations of scholars have taken his writings as the starting point for their own. Time and again, young, and not so young, scholars cite his work as the standard, often the only, source on a given topic of eighteenth-century Ireland. Closely related to this is the Knight's generosity with his scholarship, again a point that does not come across in a simple list of publications. He always takes time from his busy schedule to answer the many detailed enquiries he receives, be it from students or distinguished overseas professors. He is a tireless lecturer, here and in America, promoting Irish scholarship and learning at every opportunity. By this, as much as by his own writings, he has directly moulded the remarkable vitality of scholarship that currently exists in the study of the Irish visual arts.

Far from being a summation of the Knight's scholarship, the bibliography that follows is very much a work in progress. Desmond is as busy as ever in pursuing his scholarly goals. In the last year or so, in addition to the magnum opus on Irish furniture, he has written on the neglected artist Michael Ford, whose only surviving portrait he identified, and on the shameful neglect of Vernon Mount in Cork. He is currently hard at work co-ordinating a volume on the village and castle of Glin.

As usual, things can rarely be put better than by Prof Roy Foster. At the launch of *Painting Ireland* he paid tribute to the Knight:

> He isn't a professor, though if he had stayed at Harvard he would no doubt have become one. However, he would probably have published much less and much less excitingly, and we would not be in such great debt to him as we are. Desmond FitzGerald would not have been contained by a university

department. By following his own furrow, he has contributed an enormous amount to Irish scholarship.

It is hoped that the essays in this volume dedicated to him, touching on many of his own favourite subjects, will serve as a suitable testimony to his remarkable achievements. All those involved in the study of Ireland's past hope that many further publications will flow from his pen.

— WL

———

BIBLIOGRAPHY – DESMOND FITZGERALD, KNIGHT OF GLIN

BOOKS, CATALOGUES AND PAMPHLETS: SOLE AUTHOR

Juste Auréle Meissonnier and Others, exhibition catalogue (New York 1963)
Georgian Furniture (London 1969)
National Trust Guide to the Temple of the Winds, Mount Stewart (Belfast 1970)
The Norfolk House Music Room (London 1973)
Irish Furniture (Dublin 1978)

BOOKS, CATALOGUES AND PAMPHLETS: JOINT AUTHOR

Desmond FitzGerald, Knight of Glin (DF), Desmond Guinness, Anne Crookshank and James White, *Irish Houses and Landscapes,* exhibition catalogue (Belfast and Dublin 1963)
DF and Maurice Craig, *Irish Architectural Drawings*, exhibition catalogue to commemorate the 25th anniversary of the Irish Architectural Records Association (London 1965)
DF and Anne Crookshank, *Irish Portraits, 1660-1860*, exhibition catalogue (London 1969)
DF and Maurice Craig, *Ireland Observed, A Guide to the Buildings and Antiquities* (1971; 2nd edn. Cork 1980)
DF and Edward Malins, *Lost Demesnes: Irish Landscape Gardening, 1660-1845* (London 1976)
DF and Edward Malins, *Irish Gardens* (Dublin 1977)
DF and Anne Crookshank, *The Painters of Ireland, c.1660-1920* (London 1978)
DF and Patrick Bowe, *Gardens of outstanding interest in the Republic of Ireland* (Dublin 1980)
DF and Anne Crookshank, *Mildred Anne Butler, 1858-1941*, exhibition catalogue (Kilkenny 1981)
DF and Anne Crookshank, *The Watercolours of Ireland, works on paper in pencil, pastel and paint, c.1600-1914* (London 1994)
DF, Anne Crookshank and William Laffan, *Masterpieces by Irish Artists, 1660-1860*, exhibition catalogue (London 1999)
DF and Anne Crookshank, *Ireland's Painters 1600-1940* (New Haven and London 2002)

DF and James Peill, *Irish Furniture* (New Haven and London 2007)
DF and Anne Crookshank, *Ireland's Painters*, reprint with corrections (New Haven and London 2007)

BOOKS: EDITED

Desmond FitzGerald, Knight of Glin (ed.), *Georgian Furniture* (London 1970)
DF and Ralph Edwards (eds), *English Chairs* (London 1970)

BOOKS – CHAPTERS: SOLE AUTHOR

'Some inventories and Irish furniture' in George Stacpoole (ed.), *A Guide to Irish Antiques* (Dublin 1969)
'Summerhill, Co. Meath' in John Harris (ed.), *The Country Seat, essays in honour of Sir John Summerson* (London 1970) 131-37
'The Gandon Stables at Carrickglass, Co. Longford' in John Harris (ed.), *The Country Seat, Essays in Honour of Sir John Summerson* (London 1970) 185-92
'Glimpses of social life in west Limerick in the nineteenth-century', Appendix IV in J. Anthony Gaughan, *The Knights of Glin, A Geraldine Family* (Naas 1978) 99-133
'Introduction' in James Malton, *A picturesque descriptive view of the city of Dublin*, (Dublin 1978) vii-xiv
'Preface' in Klaus Hartmut Olbricht, Helen M. Wegener and Günther Voithenberg, *Irish Houses: history, architecture, furnishing* (Munich 1982; 2nd edn. London 1984)
'Furniture' in Brian de Breffny (ed.), *Ireland: A cultural encyclopaedia* (London 1983) 89-93
'Originality and Bravura' in Kathleen J. Ryan, *Irish Traditions* (New York 1985) 141-45
'Foreword' in Hugh W.L. Weir, *Houses of Clare* (Whitegate 1986)
'A Patchwork of Irish Houses', DF, David J. Griffin and Nicholas K. Robinson (eds), *Vanishing Country Houses of Ireland* (Dublin 1988) 10-32
'A Directory of the Dublin Furnishing Trade, 1752-1800' in Agnes Bernelle (ed.), *Decantations: A Tribute to Maurice Craig* (Dublin 1992) 47-59
'Foreword' in Ida Grehan's *Irish Family Histories* (Schull 1993) ix-xi
'The Limerick Customs House' in Patrick F. Doran, *50 Treasures from the Hunt Museum* (Limerick 1993)
'Russborough – its decoration and furniture, some preliminary thoughts' in Sergio Benedetti, *The Milltowns, a family reunion*, exhibition catalogue (Dublin 1997) 118-26
'Introduction' in *An exhibition of Irish Georgian furniture* (Johnston Antiques, Dublin 1998) 1-7
'Introduction' in *An exhibition of Irish Georgian furniture* (Johnston Antiques, Dublin 2000) 1-13
'An introduction to Irish furniture and interiors' in Brian Austen (ed.), *Irish Furniture* (West Sussex 2000) 2-3
'Cynthia O'Connor: An Appreciation' in Michael McCarthy (ed.), *Lord Charlemont and His Circle* (Dublin 2001) i-vi
'Furniture' in Brian Lalor (ed.), *The Encyclopedia of Ireland* (Dublin 2003) 419
'Foreword' in David Sinclair, *The Land that never was: Sir Gregor MacGregor and the most*

audacious fraud in history (London 2004) ix-xxiii

'Irish furniture at Churchill' in William Laffan (ed.), *A Year in Churchill* (Tralee 2003) 190-97

'Foreword' in Brian Egleston, *Egleston Brothers Photography, 1904-2004, A History of Limerick* (Limerick 2004) 7-8

'Foreword' in the Earl of Roden, *Tollymore, The Story of an Irish Demesne* (Belfast 2005) ix-xii

'Foreword' in *An Age of Elegance*, exhibition catalogue (London 2007)

BOOKS – CHAPTERS: JOINT AUTHOR

Desmond FitzGerald, Knight of Glin and James Peill, 'Fancy footwork' in *Christies Important English Furniture* (London 1997) 116-17

DF and Anne Crookshank, 'Reflections on and memories of Irish Painting' in William Laffan (ed.), *The Sublime and the Beautiful, Irish Art 1700-1830*, exhibition catalogue (London 2001) 28-36

DF and Anne Crookshank, 'Reflections on some eighteenth-century Dublin carvers' in Terence Reeves-Smyth and Richard Oram (eds), *Avenues to the Past: essays presented to Sir Charles Brett on his 75th year* (Belfast 2003) 49-66

JOURNAL PUBLICATIONS – ARTICLES: SOLE AUTHOR

'Palladio delineated, colonial architecture in Malaya', *Straits Times Annual*, 1959

'Glin', *Bulletin of the Irish Georgian Society*, II, 3, 1959, 30-40

'Georgian Limerick', *Bulletin of the Irish Georgian Society*, III, 4, 1960, 33-46

'Europe reflected in Siam', *Country Life*, vol. 130, no. 7, 1961

'Architectural books and "Palladianism" in Ireland', *Bulletin of the Irish Georgian Society*,V, 2 and 3, 1962, 9-35

'Richard Castle, architect, his biography and works', *Bulletin of the Irish Georgian Society*, VII, 1, 1964, 31-38

'An unpublished "Chinoiserie" by Jacques de la Joue, I', *The Connoisseur*, 157, October 1964, 109-13

'An unpublished "Chinoiserie" by Jacques de la Joue, II', *The Connoisseur*, 157, November 1964, 156-61

'New light on Castletown, Co. Kildare', *Bulletin of the Irish Georgian Society*,VIII, 1, 1965, 3-9

'The Norfolk House Music Room', *Victoria & Albert Museum Bulletin*, II, January 1966, 1-12

'Nathaniel Clements and some eighteenth-century Irish houses', *Apollo*, vol. 84, no. 56, 1966, 314-21

'Francis Bindon, his life and works', *Bulletin of the Irish Georgian Society*, X, 2 and 3, 1967, 1-36

'A Baroque Palladian in Ireland, the architecture of Davis Duckart, I', *Country Life*, vol. 142, no. 3682, 1967, 735-39

'The last Palladian in Ireland, the architecture of Davis Duckart, II', *Country Life*, vol. 142, no. 3683, 1967, 798-801

'A New Yorker's unusual collection', *Apollo*, 88, March 1967, 160-70

'Chippendale's place in the English Rococo', *Journal of the Furniture History Society*, IV, 1968, 1-9

'A Sheraton designed bookcase and the Gianellis', *Victoria & Albert Museum Bulletin*, IV, 1968, 9-16

'The Temple of the Winds', *The Connoisseur*, 142, 1968, 206-09

'Irish gardens of the eighteenth-century – the Rococo', *Apollo*, vol. 88, no. 79, 1968, 185-97, 204-09

'The mural from 44 Grosvenor Square', *Victoria & Albert Museum Year Book*, II, 1969, 145-51

'Gravelot and his influence on English furniture', *Apollo*, 40, August 1969, 140-47

'The Irish tour of an eighteenth-century antiquary', *Ireland of the Welcomes*, XIX, 3, 1970, 11-14

'A family of Looking Glass merchants', *Country Life*, 149, 28th January 1971, 195-99

'Irish mahogany furniture: A source for American design?', *The Magazine Antiques*, 99, April 1971, 568-73

'Irish interiors and furniture', *Discovering Antiques*, 49, 1971, 1158-62

'A "Sovereign" row in Naas', *Journal of the County Kildare Archaeological Society*, XV, 1, 1971, 23-28

'Limerick of the Limericks', *Ireland of the Welcomes*, XX, 1, 1971, 35-38

'State of the Arts', *Country Week*, 2nd-8th April 1972, 48-51

'A gallery after the Antique: Some reflections on the age of Neo-Classicism', *The Connoisseur*, 181, September 1972, 3-13

'Lord Orrery's travels in Kerry, 1735', *Journal of the Kerry Archaeological and Historical Society*, V, 1972, 46-49

'A history of the interior of Stowe', *Apollo*, 90, July 1973, 572-85

'A cupboard by Jacob Frères', *Victoria & Albert Museum Year Book*, IV, 1973, 48-62

'The O'Brien houses of Clare and Limerick', *Ireland of the Welcomes*, May-June 1978, 32-35

'The Dublin Del Vecchios', *The Magazine Antiques*, October 1981, 259-82

'Newbridge House', *The World of Interiors*, September 1983, 104-17

'Beau Parc', *The World of Interiors*, September 1984, 80-91

'Dublin directories and trade labels', *Furniture History: The Journal of the Furniture History Society*, XXI, 1985, 258-82

'Home in a Castle', *The Irish Times*, 10th September 1986, 12

'Early Irish trade-cards and other eighteenth-century ephemera', *Eighteenth-Century Ireland*, II, 1987, 115-32

'Castletown, Co. Kildare', *House and Garden* (US), March 1987, 184-96

'Wild Irish furniture', *The Connoisseur* (US), February 1988, 73-76

'The ruins of Ireland', *Observer Magazine*, 12th February 1989, 37-42

'Is it a symbol of Irish art', *The Field*, October 1990

'The treasures of Glin Castle', *The World of Hibernia*, Spring 1996, 154-72

'Irish Furniture at Florence Court', *Apollo*, vol. 141, no. 422, 1997, 16-20

'The marquetry decoration of early 18th century Irish Furniture', *Irish Arts Review*, XIII, 35, 1997

'Some thoughts on collecting at Glin', *Antique Interiors International*, 1999, 48-51

'Collector's focus, Irish Furniture, 1740-1800', *Apollo*, October 2005, 63-66

'Some thoughts on Russborough', *Irish Arts Review*, XXII, 4, 2005, 120

'Tarbert House, Co. Kerry', *Irish Arts Review*, XXIII, 3, 2006, 106-09

JOURNAL PUBLICATIONS – ARTICLES: JOINT AUTHOR

DF and Desmond Guinness, 'The Conolly Folly, the case for Richard Castle', *Bulletin of the Irish Georgian Society*, VI, 4, 1963, 59-73

DF and Anthony Coleridge, 'Eighteenth-century Irish Furniture, a provincial manifestation', *Apollo*, vol. 84, no. 56, 1966, 276-89

DF and Peter Thornton, 'Abraham Roentgen "Englische Kabinett Macher" and some further reflections on the work of John Channon', *Victoria & Albert Museum Bulletin*, II, October 1966, 137-47

DF and Maurice Craig, 'Castletown, Co. Kildare I', *Country Life*, vol. 143, no. 3760, 1969, 722-26

DF and Maurice Craig, 'Castletown, Co. Kildare II', *Country Life*, vol. 143, no. 3761, 1969, 798-802

DF and John Cornforth, 'Castletown, Co. Kildare III', *Country Life*, vol. 143, no. 3762, 1969, 882-85

DF and John Cornforth, 'Irish Portraits and the British School', *Country Life*, vol. 146, 30th October 1969

DF and Shirley Bury, 'A design for a candlestick by George Michael Moser, R.A.', *Victoria & Albert Museum Year Book*, II, 1969, 27-29

DF and Edward Malins, 'Landscape gardening by Jonathan Swift and his friends in Ireland', *Garden History Society Journal*, II, 1, 1973

DF and John Cornforth, 'Kilruddery, Co. Wicklow', *Country Life*, vol. 162, no. 4176, 1977, 882-85

DF and John Cornforth, 'Kilruddery, Co. Wicklow II', Country Life, vol. 162 (4177) (1977) 146-49

DF and Anne Crookshank, 'Ireland's landscape painters', *Ireland of the Welcomes*, November-December 1980, 10-37

DF and Anne Crookshank, 'Irish artists abroad, 1700-1880', *Ireland of the Welcomes*, March-April 1995, 28-34

DF and William Laffan, 'Michael Ford's portrait of Lord Chief Justice Singleton, *Irish Architectural and Decorative Studies*, IX, 2007, 266-84

DF and Donough Cahill, 'Vernon Mount, Co. Cork: a Neo-classical gem in jeopardy', *Irish Arts Review*, Winter 2007

CHRISTIE'S AUCTION SALE CATALOGUES

'Introduction', *Malahide Castle, the property of the executors of the late Lord Talbot of Malahide, 10-12 May 1976* (Christie, Manson & Woods Ltd, London, 1976)

'Introduction', *Newtown Park House, Blackrock, Co. Dublin, 20-23 September 1976* (Christie, Manson & Woods Ltd, London, 1976)

'Introduction', *Clonbrock, Co. Galway, Ireland, 1-3 November 1976* (Christie, Manson & Woods Ltd, London 1976)

'Introduction', *Donacomper, Co. Kildare, Ireland, 25-26 July 1977* (Christie, Manson & Woods Ltd, London, 1977)

'Introduction', *Coollattin, Co. Wicklow, Ireland, 1978* (Christie, Manson & Woods Ltd, London, 1978)

'Introduction', *Charleville, Enniskerry, Co. Wicklow, Ireland, 23-24 January 1978* (Christie, Manson & Woods Ltd, London, 1978)

'Introduction', *Adare Manor, Co. Limerick, Ireland, the property of the Earl and Countess of Dunraven, 8-10 June 1982* (Christie, Manson & Woods Ltd, London, 1982)

'Introduction', *Luttrellstown Castle, Clonsilla, Co. Dublin, Ireland, the property of Mrs. Aileen Plunkett, vol. I, 26-28 September 1983* (Christie, Manson & Woods Ltd, London, 1983)

'Introduction', *Glenaulin, Chapelizod, Dublin 20, the property of the Waterstone family, Ireland, 29-30 April 1985* (Christie, Manson & Woods Ltd, London, 1976)

'Introduction', *Newbridge, Co. Dublin, Ireland, 25 November, 1985* (Christie, Manson & Woods Ltd, Glasgow, 1985)

'Introduction', *Castle Hacket, Co. Galway, Ireland. 3-4 July 1986* (Christie, Manson & Woods Ltd, Glasgow, 1986)

'Introduction', *19 North Great George's Street, Dublin, Ireland, 2-3 November 1987* (Christie, Manson & Woods Ltd, London, 1987)

'Introduction', *Castlegar, Co. Galway, 24-25 May 1988* (Hamilton Osborne King / Christie, Manson & Woods Ltd, Glasgow, 1988)

'Introduction', *Mountainstown House, Navan, Co. Meath, Ireland, 28-29 September 1988* (Hamilton Osborne King / Christie, Manson & Woods Ltd, Glasgow, 1988)

SELECTED BOOK REVIEWS

Geoffrey Wills, *English Looking Glasses: a study of the glass, frames and makers, 1670-1820* (London 1965) in *Apollo*, May 1965, 230

Edward Hyams, *Irish Gardens* (New York 1967) in *The Spectator*, 8th September 1967, 274-75

Charles F. Montgomery, *American Furniture: The Federal Period* (New York 1966) in *Country Life*, vol. 142, no. 3683, 1967

C.P. Curran, *Dublin decorative plasterwork of the seventeenth and eighteenth-centuries* (New York 1967) in *Burlington Magazine*, October 1967, 523, and *Apollo*, July 1968, 69-70

C.E.B. Brett, *Buildings of Belfast* (London 1967) in *Apollo*, July 1968, 70

George Savage, *French Decorative Art, 1638-1793* (London 1969) in *Journal of the Royal Society of Arts*, April 1970, 288

Alistair Rowan, *Buildings of Ireland; North West Ulster* (London 1979) in *The Times Literary Supplement*, 29th February 1980

Catherine Lynn, *Wallpaper in America; from the seventeenth-century to World War I* (New York 1980) in *The Magazine Antiques*, November 1981, 1242, 1244

Rolf Loeber, *A biographical dictionary of architects in Ireland, 1600-1720* (London 1981) in *Apollo*, February 1982

Maurice Craig, *The Architecture of Ireland* (London 1982) in *The Times Literary Supplement*, 11th March 1983

Douglas Bennett, *Collecting Irish Silver, 1637-1900* (London 1984) in *Books Ireland*, December 1984, 230-33

Anne Crookshank, *Irish Sculpture from 1600 to the Present Day* (Dublin 1984) in *Books Ireland*,

December 1984, 231

James Howley, *The Follies and Garden Buildings of Ireland* (London 1993) in *Country Life*, 11th March 1994, 106

Claudia Kinmonth, *Irish Country Furniture, 1700-1950* (London 1993) in *Antiques International*, June 1994, 676-77

National Inventory of Architectural Heritage, *An Introduction to the Architectural Heritage of County Laois* (Dublin 2002) in *Irish Arts Review*, XX, 1, 2003, 129-30

Claudia Kinmonth, *Irish Rural Interiors in Art* (New Haven and London 2006), in *Country Life*, 14th September 2006, 172

Conor Lucey, *The Stapleton Collection, Designs for the Irish Neoclassical Interior* (Tralee 2007) in *Magill*, May 2007, 69-70

———

Authors' biographies

TOBY BARNARD is fellow in history at Hertford College, University of Oxford. He is a fellow of the British Academy and an honorary member of the Royal Irish Academy. His new book, *Improving Ireland?*, will be published in spring 2008.

NICOLA FIGGIS is a lecturer at the School of Art History and Cultural Policy at University College Dublin. She is co-author with Brendan Rooney of *Irish Paintings in the National Gallery of Ireland, Volume I* (Dublin 2001).

ALISON FITZGERALD is a graduate of University College Dublin and the Royal College of Art, London. She currently holds an IRCHSS post-doctoral fellowship in the School of Art History and Cultural Policy, UCD, for her research project 'Craft in Crises? The silver trade in post-Union Ireland'.

DR DAVID LAWRENCE, a historian and photographer of stained glass, has been engaged since 2000 on making a comprehensive catalogue of windows in the Church of Ireland. His book on St Fin Barre's Cathedral, Cork, co-authored by Ann Wilson, was published in 2005. He lives in Wales.

DR JOHN LOGAN is a senior lecturer in the Department of History at the University of Limerick.

CONOR LUCEY is a Ph.D. candidate in the School of Art History and Cultural Policy at University College Dublin. He is the author of *The Stapleton Collection: Designs for the Irish neoclassical interior*, published by Churchill House Press (2007) in association with the National Library of Ireland.

JOHN MONTAGUE is an architectural historian. He is the co-author of conservation plans on St Luke's in the Coombe, and on Henrietta Street. He is currently undertaking a Ph.D. at Trinity College Dublin, as an IRCHSS Government of Ireland Scholar, on the subject of John Rocque's *Exact Survey of Dublin*.

JENNIFER MOORE studied at the Courtauld Institute of Art, University of London. She was head of the History of Art department at the two Francis Holland Schools, London, and taught in the Faculty of Continuing Education of Birkbeck College, London, and at Hollins University, Virginia.

ROBIN USHER studied at Trinity College, Dublin, and holds at Ph.D. in history from the University of Cambridge. He is currently a researcher in Scottish urban history at Oxford, working on notions of 'improvement' and their effects on the built environment in Angus, Perth and Ayr.

———

1 – Peacock automaton and clock attributed to the workshop of James Cox
(State Hermitage Museum, St Petersburg)

Astonishing automata: staging spectacle in eighteenth-century Dublin[1]

ALISON FITZGERALD

IN 1774, DUBLIN NEWSPAPERS ANNOUNCED THE ARRIVAL OF JAMES COX'S CELE-brated Museum of Automata to the city (Plate 3).[2] The accompanying catalogue (Plate 2) described the twelve exhibits in meticulous detail, which, by the standards of any period, constituted a remarkable display (see appendix).[3] There was a buffalo – one of a pair – 'so richly gilt as to appear like solid gold'.[4] Contained in its body was a mechanism that activated music and artificial water. Swans and boats glided on the water, stars moved in time to the music, and there was even a three-headed dragon into whose mouth the artificial water appeared to cascade. Just inside the entrance, two mechanical flautists played 'duets and solos', which, according to the catalogue, were performed 'with the strictest musical truth ... the wind actually proceeding from their mouths and their fingers performing the various graces of every note'.[5] And then there were the peacocks, a life-sized pair, whose feathers fanned out in such a convincingly naturalistic way that they were described by their promoter Cox as a 'miracle of Art' which could not fail in 'exciting general admiration', as they turned their heads, opened and shut their beaks, and displayed their tail feathers 'with a precision actually astonishing'.[6]

The timing of this show coincided with a period when art and entertainment were becoming increasingly commercialised across the British Isles, and there is no doubt that profit was central to Cox's agenda.[7] However, the Dublin exhibition is of particular interest for a number of reasons. Firstly, while the museum was a scaled-down version of the one shown at the Spring Gardens in London between 1772 and 1774, it contained, according to the newspaper advertisements, 'a variety of new, splendid and magnificent pieces'.[8] Although survivals of the extraordinary automata from the workshop of James Cox are rare, there is persuasive evidence for the fact that an automated peacock (Plates 1, 5, 7), now in the collection of the Hermitage in

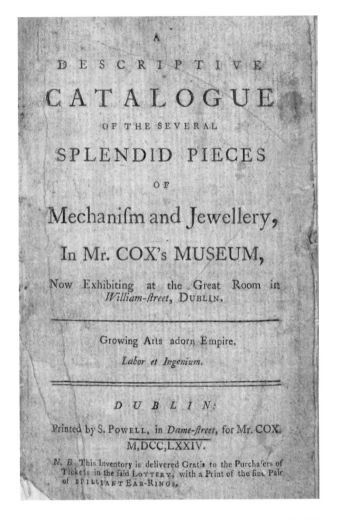

A

DESCRIPTIVE

CATALOGUE

OF THE SEVERAL

SPLENDID PIECES

OF

Mechanism and Jewellery,

In Mr. COX's MUSEUM,

Now Exhibiting at the Great Room in *William-ftreet*, DUBLIN.

Growing Arts adorn Empire.

Labor et Ingenium.

DUBLIN:

Printed by S. POWELL, in *Dame-ftreet*, for Mr. COX.

M,DCC,LXXIV.

N. B. This Inventory is delivered Gratis to the Purchafers of Tickets in the faid LOTTERY, with a Print of the fine Pair of BRILLIANT EAR-RINGS.

2 – Title page of the catalogue for James Cox's museum (Dublin 1774) (courtesy National Library of Ireland)

3 – Advertisement for the Dublin showing of James Cox's museum (SAUNDER'S NEWS-LETTER, 19th-21st January 1774)

Mr. COX's MUSEUM, in WILLIAM-STREET.

THIS Day being the 21ft inft. will be opened for the Infpection of the Public, Mr. Cox's Collection of Mechanifm and Jewellery, confifting of a Variety of new, fplendid, and magnificent Pieces, equal in Elegance, Defign, and Ingenuity, to thofe which have already given fuch general Satisfaction in London. There will be two Exhibitions on faid Day, the firft will begin precifely at one o'Clock at Noon, and the other at feven in the Evening, and each will continue about two Hours. The company are refpectfully defired to be at the Room in Time, as the Curtain will rife and the general Difplay begin at the ftated Hours. The Doors will be open at Half paft 12 at Noon, and Half paft 6 in the Evening.

TO THE PUBLIC.

As it is univerfally allowed that the fine Arts are ho-

4 – Trade card of James Cox, c.1750

(courtesy British Museum)

5 – Rear view of the peacock with the tail feathers fanned
(State Hermitage Museum, St Petersburg)

St Petersburg, is an adapted version of one of the pair that was shown in Dublin in 1774.[9] Interestingly, the promotional language employed in the museum catalogue was revised when it was redrafted for the Dublin viewing. Patriotic references to Britain were toned down; Cox made it clear that he did not plan to take orders as a jeweller in Ireland.[10] Instead he packaged the exhibition as a unique event that would not in any way injure Irish craftsmen. Nevertheless, there are clear indicators that jewellers both in Dublin and in London saw this kind of enterprise as a threat to their livelihoods.

James Cox (*c*.1723-1800) was a London jeweller and entrepreneur (Plate 4).[11] He established an initially lucrative business producing elaborate musical clocks, automata, and jewelled items, primarily for export to the Far East.[12] When the overseas market for these expensive objects declined in the late eighteenth century, his decision to exhibit some of his finest automata in London can be seen as a cleverly calculated exercise in damage limitation. Prior to its arrival in Dublin in 1774, Cox's museum had established itself on the London scene as one of the greatest 'shows' in a city where there was no shortage of choice. Writing to a friend in 1770, the antiquarian and collector Horace Walpole commented that 'the rage to see these

6 – Swan automaton by James Cox, c.1773-74
(courtesy Bowes Museum, Barnard Castle, county Durham)

exhibitions is so great that sometimes one cannot pass through the streets where they are.'[13] At one end of the spectrum there was the Wonderful Pig, who could read, write and do accounts, and at the other the recently established annual fine art exhibitions at the Royal Academy.[14] Cox was clearly aiming to be associated with polite as opposed to popular culture. This is indicated not only by the claims that he made for his museum, but also by the high admission charges. Entrance to the museum in London was half a guinea, and in Dublin one crown.[15] In a similar way to Wedgwood, but with a different agenda, Cox was presenting decorative art objects in the kind of exhibition context more usually associated with fine art. The London exhibition room included portraits of George III and Queen Charlotte by Johann Zoffany, and chiaroscuro paintings of the liberal arts.

By 1773 Cox had secured parliamentary approval to hold a lottery to dispose of the museum exhibits, with prizes valued at £134,000.[16] The fact that the tickets did not sell quickly most likely prompted his decision to tour to Dublin, in an attempt to boost his revenue and attract more subscribers. A silver swan (Plate 6), now in the Bowes Museum, county Durham, was one of the lottery prizes, though it did not feature in the Dublin show.[17] Upon activating its mechanism, this life-sized bird turns its head and preens its feathers before bending down and catching a small fish, which it appears to swallow. The base on which it rests incorporates glass rods, which rotate to give the illusion of moving water, and music accompanies the animation.

Automated animals were not a complete novelty by the late eighteenth century.[18] In 1737 Richard Edgeworth of county Longford paid 2s 2d per person to see 'clockwork statues', and five years later the celebrated duck, created by Jacques de Vaucanson, was a tremendous success when it was exhibited in London.[19] According to the publicity, it was 'an artificial duck made of gilded copper who drinks, eats, quacks, splashes about on the water, and digests his food like a living duck'.[20] This celebrity bird toured Europe, and was even shown as far afield as St Petersburg. In 1792 'a series of moving machinery and paintings', the celebrated *Eidophusikon*, created by Philippe Jacques de Loutherbourg, reached Dublin, where, along with a sunset view of Naples, visitors were treated to 'a view of the Miltonic Hell ... a scene of magnificent horror', animated by sound, movement and theatrical effects.[21]

It was not just the scope and richness of Cox's exhibits that distinguished them, nor the high cost of seeing them, but the additional lure of the lottery. While the original show in the Spring Gardens contained twenty-three exhibits, and the Dublin version twelve, there were fifty-six prizes listed in the published inventory, with a magnificent set of diamond earrings, valued at £5,000, as the top prize. These were illustrated in a print, which was circulated with the tickets in both cities, and, according to Cox, they were 'by far the most capital pair ... on sale in Europe'.[22] Cox made sure that people travelling from Dublin to London could not use the tickets interchangeably. He specified to the nobility and gentry that admission tickets were 'particularly marked' for Ireland, and highlighted the fact that Irish audiences were enjoying a preferential rate.[23] Needless to say, he did not draw attention to the fact that there were much fewer exhibits in the Dublin show. Like his counterpart Wedgwood, Cox was skilled in the manipulation of advertising rhetoric.[24] For a guinea and a half it was possible to buy a lottery ticket that admitted four people to the Dublin exhibition.[25] The venue was the Exhibition Room in William Street, and there were two performances a day, lasting approximately two hours each with a matinee and evening viewing. Despite the fact that so much publicity surrounded Cox's museum, and that he was not averse to engineering puff pieces in the press, it is curious that no information has come to light regarding the prizewinners in his lottery. The lottery was drawn later than advertised, in 1775, and no list of winners was published. Given the value of the combined prizes this seems remarkable. The previous decade, the Bishop of Elphin had been listed in the *Public Gazeteer* as a major winner in the Irish State lottery, and even Mr Magee, a carpenter, who, according to the notice, 'had but 17 days of his apprenticeship to serve' when he received his smaller £50 prize, was mentioned.[26] While a small number of the original prizes from Cox's museum lottery survive, including the silver swan, none of them has a provenance that can be traced back to the period when the lottery was actually drawn.

There was no exhibit in the London show that matched the description of the magnificent peacocks that came to Dublin, the pair described in Cox's own words as ' a miracle of Art'.[27] According to the catalogue, these glittering birds were originally displayed 'within a very rich and sumptuous quadrangular pavilion', supported by gold and white pillars, topped by an elaborate dome and hung with curtains, 'bordered, fringed and tasselled with gold ... to enclose the piece[s] at the discretion of the Spectator'.[28] Visitors could not fail to have been impressed when the curtains were pulled back and the life-sized birds began to move. According to Cox, the whole was 'finished in a manner truly masterly; whether we speak of elegance, magnificence, or ingenuity'.[29]

Recent research has uncovered documentary evidence for two peacocks linked to Cox, one paid for by Catherine the Great of Russia in 1781 and the other sold by Christies as part of Cox's bankrupt estate in 1792.[30] There is persuasive evidence for the fact that the peacock now in the Hermitage was one of the pair shown in Dublin in 1774. The connection with the Russian Empress is not unduly surprising. It was during this period that she commissioned from Wedgwood the exceptional Frog dinner service, with almost a thousand individually painted components.[31] She appears to have paid approximately £1,800 pounds for the peacock, the acquisition of which was facilitated by Prince Grigori Alexandrovich Potemkin. The Duchess of Kingston had been in St Petersburg just a few years prior to the purchase. She was a supporter of Cox and may have spoken favourably of his museum in courtly circles. In November 1778 she wrote to him:

> If you wish to have anything done for you at St. Petersburg, I shall go to the Empress soon – but that you must not mention, I think the things you send there are too rich – no person but the Empress can buy them, they like diamonds of a carrot [sic] or half a carrot each, strung to ear in any shape – pearl bracelets they like much.[32]

The correspondence between Cox and Kingston reveals that the latter facilitated the ordering of personal items for Potemkin.[33] Networks of this kind were invaluable for suppliers of luxury goods, particularly in cultivating markets overseas, and retailers like Cox and Wedgwood depended upon them.

By the time that payment was authorised for the Empress's peacock, Cox was bankrupt, and the payment was made to Frederick Jury, recently identified as one of the principal craftsmen he had employed.[34] Some details of the piece differ from the description in the Dublin catalogue, notably the cockerel and the owl located on the base (Plate 7), but it seems unlikely that Jury made a third peacock at this stage

7 – Detail of the peacock clock showing the owl in its cage (State Hermitage Museum, St Petersburg)
opposite 8 – Thomas Robinson (d.1810), Review of the Belfast Yeomanry by the Lord Lieutenant
(courtesy Belfast Harbour Commissioners)

given the investment of capital, time and expertise involved. More plausible is the argument that Jury modified the Dublin peacock before it went to Russia, working at the direction of some of Cox's assignees. It appears that the advertisements were genuine when they claimed that spectacular new pieces distinguished the Dublin showing of the museum, but Cox's promise that he did not intend to take business away from local craftsman was somewhat disingenuous. He used flattery to suggest that Irish jewellers were in a better position to attract local commissions, and claimed that 'in the course of thirty years extensive trade' he had not only admired, but also encouraged 'the genius of capital workmen from Ireland'.[35] Nevertheless, lotteries that offered goods as opposed to cash prizes did rile shopkeepers, who were expected, at least in the luxury goods trade, to offer favourable terms of credit. Even in the larger market of London, Cox's enterprise was evidently a hindrance to those with fixed-trade interests. In 1774 the London jeweller Arthur Webb wrote to his sister in Dublin commenting, 'I had but an indifferent winter. Cox and his Museum scotch interest for the fixed trade.'[36]

Not surprisingly, the lottery format employed by Cox appealed to certain Irish retailers, particularly those who needed to realise ready money quickly.[37] Although cash prizes would have been the staple of most lotteries, items as diverse as books, looking glasses and even negligees were occasionally retailed in this way in eighteenth-century Ireland.[38] In 1767 the minutes of the Dublin Goldsmiths' Guild (the Company of Goldsmiths of Dublin) recorded the concern of its members about a proposed lottery where many of the prizes were 'to be paid in various goods in the jewellers' and goldsmiths' way'.[39] The Guild argued that the public would be 'greatly imposed upon' and the trade would be damaged if the scheme went ahead. In 1771 'a lottery for the disposal of jewellery, hardware and other valuable goods grafted on the English scheme' was debated by the Guild.[40] Similar reservations were aired, and the Master of the Guild was successful in quashing it. Three years later, the year that Cox's museum came to Dublin, the Goldsmiths' Guild was agitating again, this time about a lottery where the prizes included plate.[41] In fact, two schemes for the sale of plate by lottery were organised in the south-east of Ireland that year.[42] Henry Hatchell, a Wexford goldsmith, was responsible for the Wexford Scheme for the Sale of Plate by Lottery. While Cox's top prize was valued at £5,000, the top prize in the Wexford lottery was worth £25. Nevertheless, approximately five thousand tickets sold, and the odds of winning were roughly five to one. The Kilkenny scheme cost 2s 2d to enter, with prizes including a coffee pot, candlesticks and a plain gold brooch.[43]

Political climates also dictated the way in which goods were retailed. The organiser of the Ladies Lottery in Cork claimed, in 1779, that he was hindered from selling his imported clothes and textiles by what he called 'the present Associations'.[44] While he promised not to import more goods in the short term, he was anxious to realise the value of his stock on hand. For 2s 8d the ladies of Cork or any 'adventurer' had a chance of winning a negligee, nightgown or tablecloth. The Belfast artist Thomas Robinson was also clearly trying to move stock and raise revenue when he proposed a raffle or an effective lottery of one of his most famous paintings in the early nineteenth century. The work, *Review of the Belfast Yeomanry by the Lord Lieutenant* (Plate 8), was begun in 1804, and the artist had hoped to raise money by inviting the nobility and gentry to subscribe to have their portraits included.[45] The painting would ultimately become the property of the subscribers, and the artist would retain the right to engrave it. Evidently, the subscribers were insufficiently enthusiastic; an alternative strategy was a proposed raffle of the painting, with seven other paintings as additional prizes. Second prize was a picture of the Giant's Causeway and third prize *A Picture of Dead Game*.[46] While lotteries were not the most usual way of disposing of luxury goods, the lottery format had sufficiently entered the cultural imagination by 1802 for a farce entitled *Lottery Prize* to be performed at the Theatres Royal in London and in Dublin.[47]

In conclusion, the difficulties, which even enterprising figures like Cox or Robinson faced in disposing of their goods, underscores the competitive realities of surviving in the luxury goods trade. For all his success, Cox ended his career in

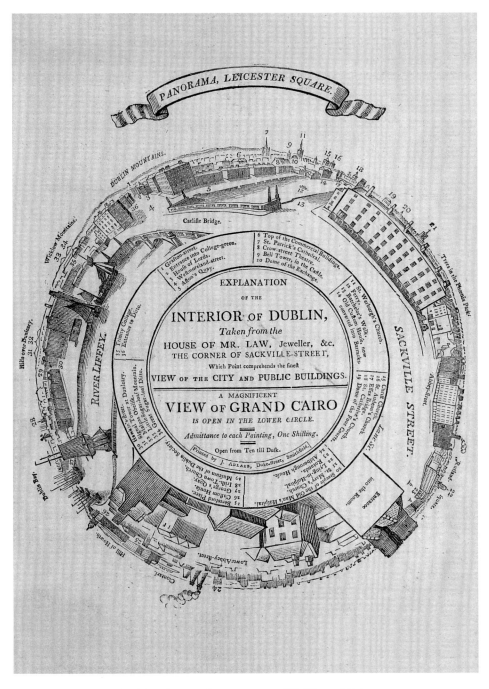

9 – Advertisement for panoramas of Dublin and Cairo,
exhibited in London by Henry Aston Barker in 1809
(courtesy National Library of Ireland)

bankruptcy. The year that his museum came to Dublin, a local jeweller advertised that he had 'secured the services of a workman who principally planned and executed all the jewellery work in Mr. Cox's celebrated museum', underscoring the close links that existed in the supply of patterns, stock, and even craftsmen between the two capital cities.[48] In 1796 the goldsmith William Law advertised his new premises in Sackville Street by highlighting the fact that he had 'some of the greatest curiosities from a celebrated museum' on view in his shop.[49] Law was also instrumental in the execution of a panoramic view of Dublin [taken from the interior of his premises, and] shown in Leicester Square [in London] (Plate 9).[50] In a context where leisure, pleasure and luxury consumption were becoming increasingly interconnected, it is not surprising to find shopping aligned with the 'rage for exhibitions' and polite culture. However, given the complexity of its mechanism, its material worth and its imposing scale, it is remarkable that an eighteenth-century automated peacock could travel from London to Dublin and on to St Petersburg during this period, and survive for its tale to be told.

––––––

APPENDIX

Summary Description of the Exhibits shown in the Dublin Viewing of James Cox's Museum, 1774

Piece the First	A Chariot
Piece the Second	A Buffalo
Piece the Third	A Vase
Piece the Fourth	A Gothic Temple of Agate
Piece the Fifth	A Vase
Piece the Sixth	A Peacock
Piece the Seventh	The Automatons
Piece the Eighth	A Peacock
Piece the Ninth	A large and superb vase of flowers
Piece the Tenth	The Asiatic Temple
Piece the Eleventh	A Buffalo
Piece the Twelfth	A richly Caparisoned Elephant

––––––

ACKNOWLEDGEMENTS

Toby Barnard, Eileen Black, John Loughman, Olga Novoseltceva.

ENDNOTES

The following abbreviations are used:

CGD   Company of Goldsmiths of Dublin

Cox, 1774   James Cox, *A Descriptive Catalogue of the Several Splendid Pieces of Mechanism and Jewellery, in Mr Cox's Museum, Now Exhibiting at the Great Room, in William Street, Dublin* (S. Powell, Dublin, 1774)

[1]   This article is based on a paper delivered at the Eighteenth-Century Ireland Society Conference, Queen's University Belfast, 16th June 2007.
[2]   *Saunder's News-Letter*, 19th-21st January 1774; *Faulkner's Dublin Journal*, 17th-19th February 1774.
[3]   Cox, 1774. The catalogue was also printed by Samuel Law.
[4]   *ibid.*, 14.
[5]   *ibid.*, 22.
[6]   *ibid.*, 19.
[7]   On the commercialisation of leisure and the eighteenth-century 'vogue for viewing', see Richard D. Altick, *The Shows of London* (London 1978); J.H. Plumb, 'The Commercialization of Leisure', in N. McKendrick, J. Brewer and J.H. Plumb, *The Birth of a Consumer Society: The Commercialization of Eighteenth-Century England* (Bloomington, Indiana, 1982) 265-85; David Solkin (ed.), *Art on the Line: The Royal Academy Exhibitions at Somerset House, 1780-1836* (London 1981).
[8]   *Saunder's News-Letter*, op. cit. For the London exhibits, see James Cox, *Descriptive Catalogue of the Several Superb and Magnificent Pieces of Mechanism and Jewellery, Exhibited in the Museum, at Spring Gardens* (London 1772).
[9]   For the most recent and comprehensive commentary on the Hermitage peacock, see Yuna Zek and Roger Smith, 'The Hermitage Peacock: How an Eighteenth-Century Automaton Reached St. Petersburg', *Antiquarian Horology*, 28, 2004-05, 699-720. The authors state that a copy of the Dublin catalogue in private hands is the only known copy in existence. There are, however, additional copies in the National Library of Ireland and the Bodleian Library at the University of Oxford.
[10] Cox, 1774, 3-6.
[11] For further information on Cox, see Clare Le Corbeiller, 'James Cox: A Biographical Review', *The Burlington Magazine*, 112, June 1970, 350-58; Catherine Pagani, 'The Clocks of James Cox: Chinoiserie and the Clock Trade with China', *Apollo*, 141, January 1995, 15-22; Marcia Pointon, 'Dealer in Magic: James Cox's Jewellery Museum and the Economics of Luxurious Spectacle in Late-Eighteenth-Century England', in Neil De Marchi and Craufurd D.W. Goodwin (eds), *Economic Engagements with Art* (Durham and London 1999) 423-52; Roger Smith, 'James Cox (*c*.1723-1800): A Revised Biography', *The Burlington Magazine*, 142, June 2000, 253-361.

[12] According to Cox's catalogue, the pair of automated peacocks shown in Dublin was originally intended for the Palace of the Emperor of China at Peking. Cox, 1774, 21.

[13] Malcolm Baker, 'A Rage for Exhibitions: The Display and Viewing of Wedgwood's Frog Service', in Hilary Young (ed.), *The Genius of Wedgwood* (London 1995) 118.

[14] Altick, *The Shows of London*. See also John Brewer, *The Pleasures of the Imagination: English Culture in the Eighteenth Century* (London 1997); Solkin (ed.), *Art on the Line*, op. cit.; Brandon Taylor, *Art for the Nation: Exhibitions and the London Public, 1747-2001* (Manchester 1999).

[15] The museum opened in London in February 1772, and by June, although weekly receipts were estimated at £500 (approximately a thousand visitors a week), Cox was preparing to halve the admission charge to attract more visitors. See Smith, 'James Cox (*c*.1723-1800): A Revised Biography', 358.

[16] *Museum Lottery, The Act for Enabling Mr Cox to Dispose of his Museum by Way of Lottery* (London [?] 1773); James Cox, *A Descriptive Inventory of the Several Exquisite and Magnificent Pieces of Mechanism and Jewellery, Comprised in the Schedule Annexed to an Act of Parliament, Made in the Thirteenth Year of His Present Majesty, George the Third; for Enabling Mr James Cox, ... Jeweller, to Dispose of his Museum by Way of Lottery* (London 1773).

[17] On the silver swan, see T.P. Camerer Cuss, 'The Silver Swan', *Antiquarian Horology*, 4, June 1965, 330-34; Sarah Kane, 'The Silver Swan: The Biography of a Curiosity', *Things*, winter 1996-97, 39-57.

[18] For a history of automata, see Alfred Chapuis and Edmond Droz, *Automata: A Historical and Technological Study* (London 1958).

[19] National Library of Ireland, MS 1512, 73, 20th February 1512; Chapuis and Droz, *Automata*, 233-42.

[20] *ibid.*, 233.

[21] *The Hibernian Journal*, 3rd February 1792.

[22] This was specified in the print accompanying the descriptive inventory noted above.

[23] Cox, 1774, 5.

[24] For a good survey of eighteenth-century advertising strategies, see Julia Muir, 'Printing Persuasion: Advertising Goods in Eighteenth-Century England', MA thesis (Royal College of Art, London, 2000).

[25] *Saunder's News-Letter*, op. cit.

[26] *Public Gazetteer*, 16th-19th August 1766.

[27] Cox, 1774, 20.

[28] *ibid.*, 21.

[29] *ibid.*

[30] The whereabouts of the second peacock are unknown.

[31] According to the descriptive inventory itemising the goods Cox intended to dispose of by lottery, the earrings had originally been intended for the Empress of Russia.

[32] Yale University, Beinecke Rare Book and Manuscript Library, OSB MSS File 17935, Letter from the Duchess of Kingston to James Cox, 13th November 1778.

[33] *ibid.* The Duchess writes, 'let me know what is done to prince Potompkins book, I understand you have had the necessary Instructions for it from Russia.' See also Letter from the Duchess of Kingston to James Cox, 29th April 1779.

[34] Zek and Smith, 'The Hermitage Peacock', 711.

[35] Cox, 1774, 3.

[36] National Archives, London, MS C108/284/16, Letter from Arthur Webb (London) to Miss Webb (Dublin), 29th August 1774. Webb's own accounts are interesting from the perspective of the jewellery trade in eighteenth-century Dublin and London. The author is currently working on an analysis of these.

[37] For the history of lotteries in an Irish context, see Rowena Dudley, *The Irish Lottery 1780-1801* (Dublin 2005).

[38] See, for example, *Dublin Intelligence*, 30th June 1711, and *The Hibernian Chronicle*, 4th January 1792. I am grateful to John Rogers for the former reference.

[39] CGD, MS 21, f.139, Minutes 15th September 1767.

[40] CGD, MS 21, f.218, Minutes 3rd June 1771.

[41] CGD, MS 21, f.288, Minutes 24th November 1774. On this occasion it was agreed that Guild representatives should try and secure a ticket before openly opposing the perpetrators. Rather than being a participatory measure, this was obviously an attempt to secure evidence to support their case against the scheme.

[42] Edward J. Law, 'Some Provincial Irish Silver Lotteries', *Journal of the Silver Society*, 7, 1995 412-16.

[43] *ibid.*

[44] *The Hibernian Chronicle*, 7th-11th October 1779.

[45] Eileen Black, *Art in Belfast 1760-1888: Art Lovers or Philistines?* (Dublin 2006) 6-10.

[46] Bodleian Library, Oxford, John Johnson Collection, Lotteries 4, *Proposals for Disposing by Raffle of a Picture of the Review of the Yeomanry of Belfast by His Excellency Earl Hardwicke, Lord Lieutenant of Ireland painted by Thomas Robinson*, n.d.

[47] *Lottery Prize of 2,5,3,8; or Pedantic Apothecary Quizzed. A Farce in Two Acts. Performed at the Theatres Royal, London and Dublin* (Dublin 1802).

[48] *Faulkner's Dublin Journal*, 3rd-5th May 1774.

[49] *Faulkner's Dublin Journal*, 1st September 1796. These were unlikely to include any of Cox's items, not least because this was not specified, but also because the item singled out for mention was a 'diamond beetle got in the East Indies'.

[50] National Library of Ireland, MS PD4254TB, *Explanation of the Interior of Dublin Taken From the House of Mr Law, Jeweller* (London 1809). This served as an advertisement for panoramas of Dublin and Cairo exhibited in 1809 at the purpose-built rotunda in Leicester Square, London, by Henry Aston Barker. For more on Barker, see Altick, *The Shows of London*.

1 – Davis Dukart, Castletown, Carrick-on-Suir, Co Kilkenny (begun c.1766)
(courtesy Country Life)

'Dropped into this Kingdom from the clouds':
The Irish career of Davis Dukart, architect and engineer, 1761-81

JOHN LOGAN

D AVIS DUKART OCCUPIES A SIGNIFICANT, THOUGH PARTIALLY OBSCURED SPACE in the history of architecture and engineering in Ireland.[1] Some of the interest in Dukart arises from the mystique attendant on his overseas origins, the scarcity of information on his life and practice, and, not least, the high quality of his work, completed mostly in the 1760s. What is now known of Dukart owes much to two pioneering 1967 articles by Desmond FitzGerald, Knight of Glin.[2] He proposed a basic chronology, a seminal set of attributions and an assessment of Dukart's achievement, particularly as an architect of country houses in a distinctive, late Palladian manner. Subsequent studies have added detail and proposed further attributions (and de-attributions), but the general chronology of Dukart's career and FitzGerald's assessment of his significance remains largely unaltered.[3] The purpose of this paper is to bring all that material together and to add some more to deal in turn with Dukart's public buildings, private architectural commissions and his engineering work.

Even amongst his contemporaries, there was speculation as to Dukart's origins. When giving evidence in 1767 before an Irish parliamentary committee, Dukart revealed that his homeland was a place 'adjacent to the Alps', hillier than any part of Europe, traversed by canals, and 'often visited by the English nobility and gentry'.[4] Soon after, a member of the committee, William Brownlow, described Dukart as a 'Piedmontese', that region then being part of the principality of Savoy, stretching northwards from Nice and centred on its capital, Turin.[5] Dukart may have revealed nothing more, for Brownlow – attentive and well informed – then alluded to the air of mystery that surrounded Dukart: 'He dropped into this Kingdom from the clouds, no one knows how, or what brought him to it.'[6] Three years after Dukart's appearance at the committee, 'La Verite', the pseudonymous author of a rant against foreign engineers in the *Freeman's Journal*, seemed better informed. He related that 'D – s D – t Esq', a builder and engineer, and a 'gentleman adventurer', had been captured on a French privateer during the 'late war' – most likely the Seven Years War (1756-63) – and been brought ashore and imprisoned in the west of Ireland.[7] If La Verite may be believed, Dukart's incarceration was not without its comforts: 'During his confinement he employed himself drawing portraits and little landscapes (being bred a painter) and by selling them to hawkers, procured for himself a comfortable subsistence.'[8]

The earliest known project involving Dukart dates from the later years of the war. In 1761 he was in Cork, where the Corporation, recently empowered to erect a reservoir, paid him £25 to survey the River Lee and to design a scheme to bring water to the city.[9] In November that year he was in discussion with William Colles, the Kilkenny stone merchant, who was keen to have his water pipes used for the project.[10] When the Corporation was given additional powers in 1762 to establish a water company, progress seemed likely.[11] Six years would pass, however, before the reservoir was built or pipes were laid. Whether the work was executed in accordance with Dukart's plan – as has been suggested – or not, is unknown, but it was a local iron-founder, Nicholas Fitton, who got the contract.[12] By then, much would have happened to sour Dukart's relations with Cork Corporation.

Dukart had arrived in Cork at a significant period in its history. An expanding mercantile economy was reflected in the physical expansion of the city. Its amenities were steadily improved, some through private initiative, and others – such as the city reservoir – as public works. All reflected well on the city's Corporation, and it was the need to provide a prestigious residence for the Mayor and a grand space for the enactment of civic ceremonial that led in 1761 to the decision to build a Mayoralty House. News of the project excited interest, not least among local architects, one of whom, John Morrison, presented a plan to the public through the pages of *The Dublin Magazine* in September 1764 (Plate 2).[13] The chosen design should reveal grandeur and economy, he suggested, something that he had aimed for in his own composition, but he would leave it to those who were 'impartial and judicious' to decide whether he had succeeded. The project should raise a spirit of emulation in his fellow countrymen, among whom, he expected, 'a proper design will be found, adequate to the spirit and dignity' of the city.[14] Dukart may not have been a compatriot of Morrison but he felt able to submit a design to the Corporation in February 1765. When it was rejected as too expensive, he set to making revisions. On 6th May 1765, having convinced the Corporation that he could now build a mayoralty house for no more than £2,000, Dukart was awarded the commission. His fee was set at 5% of the total, though it was agreed that in appropriate circumstances

Extend 50 Feet

*2 – John Morrison's proposed elevation for the Mayoralty House, Cork,
in THE DUBLIN MAGAZINE (1764) (courtesy National Library of Ireland)*

he might be awarded a gratuity.[15]

The foundation stone of the Mayoralty House had been laid nearly a year before, on 17th June 1764, at Hammond's Marsh, land not long reclaimed from the River Lee.[16] There Dukart felt confident of securing the building's foundations without recourse to the traditional timber piling.[17] The constricted corner plot dictated what appears at first as a tall rectangular block of three stories atop a low basement. Its seven-bay entrance-front faced north over a narrow piazza; a shorter façade of four bays was hemmed in on the south-west by a tree-lined lane skirting the north channel of the Lee, while the back jostled with the buildings of its recently urbanised neighbourhood.[18] A plan, reconstructed from the 1872 ordnance survey, reveals the house as two contiguous blocks, the larger holding the entrance hall, grand staircase, lobbies and reception rooms; the smaller, the mayor's private apartments (Plate 4).

The Corporation put day-to-day direction of the building in the hands of Charles Sweeny, master carpenter, and Edward Flaherty, master mason.[19] Payments for materials and wages, as approved by the Corporation, would be disbursed through aldermen acting as overseers. By the end of 1765 most of the money had

Mayoralty House, Cork (begun 1764)

3 – Entrance front and north-west elevation (courtesy Cork Public Museum)

4 – First-floor plan (Diarmuid O'Sullivan, 2007)

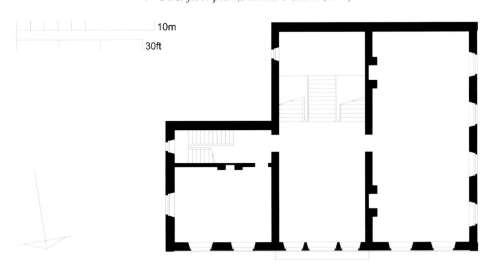

been spent, and in January 1766 the Corporation was forced to borrow an additional £1,000.[20] The upper floors were finished in November 1766 and roofing started.[21] By 23rd May 1767 expenditure had crept to £2,822 0s 1d, and with payments for timber and ironmongery due, the overseers were again forced to seek extra funds. A week later they met to consider allegations that as a result of Dukart's lengthy absences from the city, the masons and carpenters had been left idle and money wasted.[22] Given the substantial overrun of costs, it was easy for the aldermen to conclude that Dukart had submitted an artificially low tender so as to win the commission.[23] As a consequence, and notwithstanding the original agreement that Dukart might be paid a gratuity, the Corporation decided that he was no longer entitled to any additional 'recompense' and posted a notice to that effect at the Exchange.[24]

Stung by what he now regarded as a repudiation of his contract, Dukart responded with his own notice in the *Cork Evening Post*.[25] He argued that, when tendering, he had made it clear that it was impossible to prepare precise estimates where the artificers would be paid by the day and not by the actual work done. Had the management of the project been left to him the building might have been finished 'plain and neat' for the agreed £2,000, or perhaps for an additional 20%, which, he insisted, was as near as he could be expected to calculate. Instead, the workmen had been chosen by the Corporation, and since he considered them inferior and had objected to their appointment, he did not consider himself liable for the consequent waste of money. To the charge that his directions to the overseers had been ambiguous, he replied that they were as clear as might be expected 'from any engineer in Europe'.[26] The fabric of the building was complete by August 1767.[27] Marble chimney pieces were ordered as craftsmen finished the carpentry and the exterior stucco.[28] In January 1768 Patrick Osborne was engaged to decorate the stairway, lobby and drawing room, a commission that continued until November 1769.[29] The overseers were authorised to have a 'proper' entrance and portico fitted at a cost of £11 7s 6d.[30] It was a temporary arrangement, however, and five years later, long after Dukart had departed the city, the house was given its diminutive Doric frontispiece at the cost of £68 8s 2d. The terse entry in the minute book 'pursuant to a plan and estimate before the council' was silent on how much, if anything, the design owed to Dukart.[31] Neither was the verdict of the aldermen on their new Mayoralty House recorded. Notwithstanding the recriminations that marked the end of Dukart's dealings with the Corporation, civic pride alone would hardly have allowed them to concur with the assessment of 'Incertus', another of the *Freeman's Journal* patriot correspondents, that 'our French architect' had given them 'a large monument of his insipid, uncouth taste in the art of designing'.[32] Twenty years later Daniel Beaufort would be no more generous: 'The Mansion House built by Mr Ducart, a very heavy ill contrived one – with strange windows'(Plate 3).[33]

Dukart's ability to step over an ambitious local like Morrison had been demonstrated even more spectacularly when he was awarded the contract for a new Custom House in Limerick. Such a project had been much talked of, as the ruinous condition of the Custom House and Collector's residence on Merchants' Quay in the city's English Town appeared increasingly out of place in a vibrant and prosperous port.[34] A rebuilding on the old site had been proposed, but following an inspection on their behalf by William Brownlow in June 1757, the commissioners of the revenue were prepared to commit to a new building 'in the most substantial and commodious manner' downriver from the English Town and on the edge of South Prior's Land, an estate being developed by the city's Member of Parliament, Edmund Sexton Pery.[35] The commissioners directed their architect, Edward Smyth, to prepare a plan and elevation, and in December 1763, on the recommendation of Pery, the project was put in the hands of Edward Uzuld, the city's most prominent builder.[36] Almost a year would pass before Uzuld's bills of quantity were passed to the commissioners. At their meeting on 22nd December 1764 they approved Uzuld's estimate of £3,073 17s 5d and set his fee at £5 per cent, 'the usual rate to undertakers', and directed that work should commence the following spring.[37] Within the month, however, and without recording a reason for their decision, the commissioners authorised Robert Waller, who, as surveyor general for Connaught, was one of their senior office-holders, to invite Dukart to submit a proposal to superintend the project.[38] His scheme was accepted, and at their meeting on 9th February 1765 the commissioners agreed that Dukart should be offered the contract on the same terms as had been offered to Uzuld. They ordered that Smyth's plan and elevation, together with a schedule of prices for building materials in Limerick, should be sent to Dukart in Cork for his perusal.[39]

In getting the contract to build the Custom House, Dukart had displaced an established and well-regarded local builder; over the next two months his role would mutate further, and he would become the building's architect. At a meeting of the commissioners in early April 1765 Pery presented a plan for the Custom House by Dukart that varied, he suggested, 'in a few particulars' from Smyth's original design.[40] The commissioners agreed to the proposed changes, but in less than three weeks Pery would submit a new plan by Dukart for a building whose materials and embellishment, but especially the disposition of arcaded-wings to a central block, would differ radically from what had been approved.[41] Dukart's design, the commissioners decided, was excessively ornamented for such a building. It would require extraordinary expense and provide a dangerous precedent: other cities 'of equal trade' would expect the same. They were especially opposed to Dukart's proposal for arcaded 'porticos' to the wings. The officials had to be able to look freely onto the adjacent quay, and they believed that the proposed arcade would hamper that. Furthermore, open arcades would encourage the traders to leave their goods lying there. The expense would be needless; a portico to the central block should be sufficient embellishment.[42]

From a position of apparent intransigence, the commissioners began to yield, softened, perhaps, by Pery's offer of the free use of a nearby limestone quarry.[43] They agreed that the proposed wings might be faced with hewn stone and built in the same style as the ground floor of the central block, but they insisted that save for quoins, window sills and entablature in stone, the rest of the building should be in brick, as specified in the original design.[44] Far from being chastened, Dukart kept to his plan, and when he met the commissioners with Pery at the end of April he proposed that all the external walls should be faced with stone. He argued that the additional cost of stone instead of brick would amount to only £212 1s 6d, while stone arcades to each of the side wings would add only £120.[45] Pery had brought a petition from the Limerick merchants to the meeting. They appeared to be fully behind Dukart's plan for arcades, pleading that they were needed 'to preserve their goods from the weather'. Faced with the arguments of architect and merchants, and the formidable presence of Pery, the commissioners retreated and informed the Collector of Custom at Limerick that work should proceed there in accordance with Dukart's plan and elevation (Plate 6).[46]

On 16th June 1765 the Mayor of Limerick laid the foundation stone.[47] Previously unbuilt on, the ground was part of the unfinished Mardyke and still without some of the walls and banking needed to complete a new customs' quay. Away from the river, the site was well below the level of the street leading to the New Bridge and into the English Town. Levels were taken and retaken, and much filling took place before Dukart was satisfied that the building's plinth, if not its vaulted basement, would be above the level of high tide.[48] Work continued briskly during the late spring of 1766. The first storey was almost complete when, at dusk, on 25th June, an 'insolent' mob, its motivation far from clear, broke into the site. Having chased off the watchman, the mob tore down the builder's crane, damaged a number of cut stones and tossed the recently laid courses.[49] A substantial reward was offered to whoever might lead the authorities to the instigators, and thereafter the site was guarded by soldiers from the garrison.[50]

Less easily dealt with was the manoeuvring of the ground landlord, Richard Vincent, who now sought to interest the commissioners in taking additional ground abutting their plot. The commissioners believed this would be an unnecessary purchase until it became clear that without it they would not have proper access from the street.[51] Vincent had also let plots to speculators who hoped to benefit by building close to the Custom House. Among them was Robert Waller, the official who had acted as emissary from the commissioners to Dukart. He now enlisted Dukart in his scheme to build between the south wing of the Custom House and the street.[52] As a result, the Custom House appeared to be in danger of losing its 'principal light', and relations between Dukart and the commissioners worsened when it

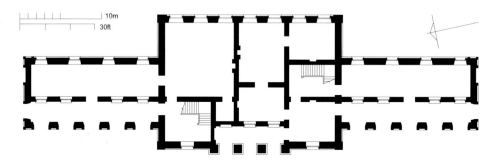

Custom House, Limerick (begun 1764)

5 – *Elevation of the front of the Custom House, now building in Limerick, 1767*
in John Ferrar, An History of the City of Limerick (1767) (courtesy Glucksman Library, University of Limerick)

6 – *Ground-floor plan (Livia Hurley, 2007)*

7 – *Engraving by J. Duff after a drawing by Neville Bath*
in John Ferrar, The History of Limerick (1787) (courtesy Glucksman Library, University of Limerick)

emerged that he had altered the original location of the Custom House to facilitate Waller's scheme.[53] Just as they had been forced to take additional land from Vincent, the commissioners now had to purchase ground from Waller in order to secure their site.[54] The less-than-scrupulous activities of landlord, office-holder and architect had served to lessen the utility and attractiveness of what had initially been an open riverside site.

Every few months the commissioners routinely authorised payments to cover the cost of wages and materials.[55] A demand for additional funds in April 1767, just two years after Dukart had first presented his plan, prompted the commissioners to inquire as to when the Custom House might be completed and what might be its final cost.[56] Dukart informed them that he expected work to continue until the autumn of the following year, but that an accurate forecast of remaining expenditure would prove difficult.[57] By then, £6,511 15s 2¹/₂d had been expended – almost twice what had been agreed – and it was becoming clear to all concerned that much more would be needed.[58] With a growing sense of unease the commissioners now sought economies, and at their November meeting they directed that the inside of the Custom House should be finished 'in a plain, neat and substantial manner', without decoration or ornament.[59] While admitting that he had far exceeded the sum agreed, Dukart now requested more funds to complete essential works: the Collector's private apartments had yet to be fitted out; a specially fashioned brass valve was needed to keep the spring tidewater from the basement; a brew-house with proper utensils had to be set up, and a range of necessary houses built in the yard. Chimney pieces too were needed, and when Dukart inquired as to how much he might spend he was warned that only those in the Collector's eating room and parlour should be in marble; the rest had to be in plain stone.[60]

When engaged on the Cork Mayoralty House, Dukart had to leave day-to-day direction to master craftsmen, an arrangement imposed by the Corporation and one that, he claimed, lead to idleness and work of poor quality. In Limerick he was able to appoint a deputy, initially a Captain Conley, until he was replaced sometime in late 1766 by Christopher Colles, the twenty-six-year-old nephew of the Kilkenny stone merchant who had tried to interest Dukart in purchasing his water pipes in 1761.[61] Direction of the labourers and artisans was put in the hands of William Byrum, an experienced builder appointed on Pery's recommendation at an annual salary of £40.[62] This appeared to be a better arrangement, but Dukart's infrequent visits to Limerick and the delegation of heavy responsibilities to an inexperienced deputy may have rendered a complicated project more difficult.[63] Walter St Lawrence, who had been contracted to cut 'the capitals and other ornament', argued with Colles, and their disagreement led to a suit against Dukart in early 1767.[64] The commissioners informed Dukart that he should employ an attorney and they would reimburse the cost if the case was decided in Dukart's favour.[65] The outcome of the dispute was not recorded, but its architectural consequence was captured when the Corinthian pilasters, depicted in an engraving of 1767, appeared without capitals in an engraving of 1787 (Plates 5, 7). The 1787 engravings also reveal that the inscription GEORGIO TERTIO FEL REG – a formulary for the phrase 'George III of Happy Reign' – proposed for the frontispiece frieze, remained unexecuted. In early summer 1769, with most of the fabric complete, Dukart reported that other parts of the stonework remained unfinished as the masons, though paid as agreed, had refused to do any more work.[66] The commissioners directed that if they persisted in their refusal they should be brought to court. The men submitted that the fault was not theirs but Dukart's, who, having set them 'prophiles', made alterations that obliged them 'to reform their work into other dimensions'.[67] They would finish only if properly compensated.[68] Again, if the case proceeded, its outcome went unrecorded, but the unfinished spandrels of the arcade arches suggest that it was no more satisfactory than before. The stages followed by the masons, from lightly incised marking out, through partially cut circles to finished rustication, provides a vivid record of the carving process, but also an enduring comment on the project's mismanagement (Plate 8).

By late June 1769, Dukart was keen to conclude his dealings with the commissioners, and when he submitted his bill they requested details of what had been paid 'on account of the building' and how much had been paid for his superinten-

8 – Custom House, Limerick: unfinished carving on arcade spandrel (south wing) (2007)

dence.[69] An audit revealed that total expenditure stood at £10,159 13s 3d, of which he had received £439 19s 7¾d.[70] He submitted that he was due more because he had used part of his fee to purchase materials. The commissioners then sent him an itemised account and asked him to indicate what he had paid for.[71] Three weeks later they had not heard from him, and in a rare display of impatience they demanded a full report by 4th September.[72] Dukart's response went unrecorded. Neither is there a note of when his direction of the Custom House formally ceased, but it was most likely between then and the end of December 1769 when Colles casually remarked to his cousin that 'Dukart and his schemes are quite laid aside'.[73]

Just over a year before, when a competition was announced for the design of an Assembly House to stand at the end of the Mardyke, a short distance from the Custom House, Dukart appeared well positioned to give Limerick another noteworthy building.[74] From the middle of August 1768 and into September, the promoters – a loosely bound group of local notables – advertised for subscribers. They also announced that a plan and elevation had been received from Dukart.[75] Edward Uzuld, whom Dukart had displaced as builder of the Custom House, had submitted an elevation, though it was noted that he had yet to forward a plan.[76] All would be available for public inspection (and presumably to encourage potential investors) on the occasion of the upcoming winter assizes.[77] When Uzuld died at his house in the English Town on 10th September, it might have seemed that the way was clear for Dukart.[78] However, when the subscribers met on 30th September to appoint a committee of five to oversee the work, they agreed that it should be to a plan submitted by William Deane Hoare, vicar choral and sub-dean of St Mary's Cathedral and, critically perhaps, one of twenty founding shareholders in the project.[79] An elevation of 1768 survives, but without a signature its authorship – whether by Dukart, Uzuld or Hoare – cannot be established, nor is there anything to show if it was the building as realised and that opened to the public on 11th September 1770 (Plate 9).[80]

Dukart had been given his greatest opportunity to make an impression on Limerick's fabric when Pery employed him in 1765 to draw up a plan setting out the plots at South Prior's Land that he hoped to develop as New Town Pery.[81] The plan was consolidated between 1767 and 1769 by the marking out of the intervening streets.[82] During the 1770s, development was confined mostly to plots on the edge of the Irish Town, but from the early 1780s, when Pery was able to attract a growing number of well-established city merchants as tenants for larger plots to the south and closer to the river, it seemed that his hopes for an extensive and profitable New Town might be realised. Pery's dream had found its earliest and most eloquent expression in 1769 in a map commissioned by Earl Percy, the newly arrived commander of the city's garrison (Plate 10).[83] It recorded the New Town's mostly rectangular plots and streets, framed on the north by the River Shannon and on the south by the road west from the Irish Town. By taking its central axis – what would later

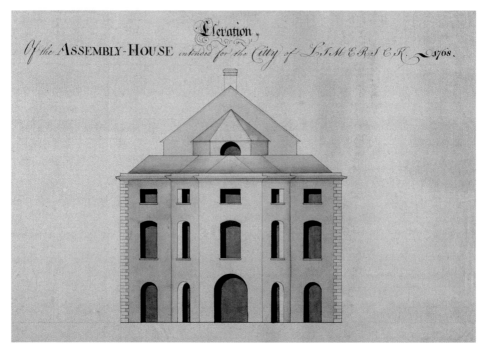

9 – ELEVATION OF THE ASSEMBLY-HOUSE INTENDED FOR THE CITY OF LIMERICK 1768
pen and watercolour on paper, 26 x 37 cm (courtesy Knight of Glin)

10 – Christopher Colles, LIMERICK CITY AND SUBURBS, 1769 (detail opposite showing New Town Pery)
ink and watercolour on paper, 104 x 141 cm (courtesy British Library)

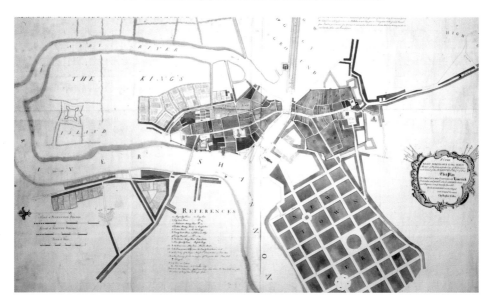

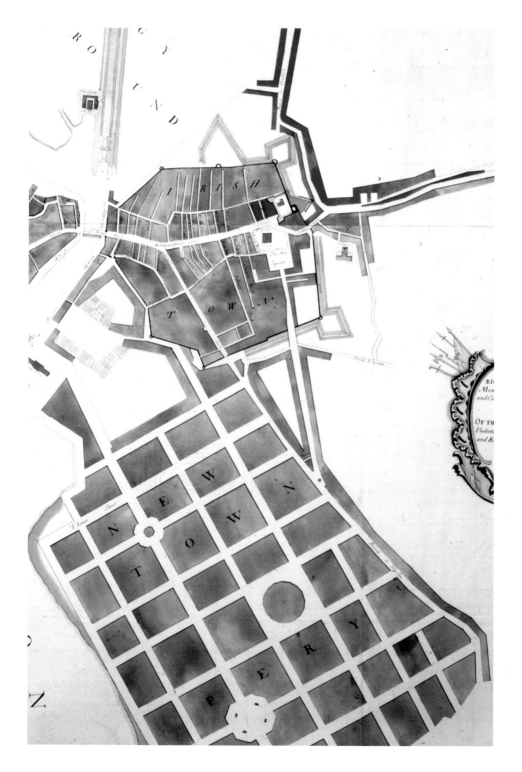

become George's Street – from the line of the Shannon rather than from the New Bridge and the Custom House, the plan skilfully maximised the number of rectangular building plots that could be carved out of Pery's estate. The monotony that might spring from the imposition of such a grid was avoided by the generous provision for open spaces on which the visual success of the baroque city traditionally depended. The smallest of these, an octagon created by scooping out the corners of four contiguous blocks where they met on the main axis, had as its focal point the octagonal church that Pery started building in 1767.[84] Further along the axis a larger octagon provided a grand public space, punctuated by four pedestal-like blocks. Most spectacular of all was the space set aside for a large square with a sixteen-sided plot at its centre. Just how much the plan – fairly described by Christopher Colles, who mapped it, as 'extensive and elegant' – owed to Dukart's determination to infuse a routine survey with a distinctive sensibility, or to the requirements set out by Pery, must remain a matter for conjecture.

Like other contemporary essays in urban planning, New Town Pery was the consequence of the convergence of a number of factors: the constraints imposed by the physical terrain and existing patterns of property ownership, the opportunities thrown up by favourable cycles of trade, and, most critically, the fortuitous circumstances that brought patron and architect together. Within those limits, seigniorial ambition and architectural intelligence combined to produce a plan that, even with some key elements unrealised, would be unsurpassed in any Irish provincial city of the eighteenth century.

───────

IN CONTRAST WITH HIS PUBLIC BUILDINGS IN LIMERICK AND CORK, DUKART'S PRIvate domestic works are poorly documented. If an archive with material for a detailed history of any of them exists, it has yet to reveal its secret. The scraps of information that are available point to Dukart's involvement in just six projects that range from routine renovation and rebuilding to the design of grandly conceived houses.

Dukart was not long engaged on the Cork Mayoralty House when he accepted what may have been his first major private commission, the building of a country seat for Abraham Devonsher at Kilshannig, about fifteen miles north of Cork city (Plates 11, 12).[85] Since the end of the seventeenth century, the Devonshers had been active in the city's mercantile and civic life and in accumulating properties, which included a farm at Kilshannig.[86] When Joseph Wight visited in 1754 he was struck by the air of improvement fostered by Abraham's father, Jonas – a garden brimming with fruit and flowers, handsome avenues, well-kept hedges and ditches, all making a 'great show' in harmony with countryside and village. It provided a memorable lesson on the rewards of virtue: 'hence we can see what money and industry can do, for the above farm was but coarse and hungry land by nature several years ago'.[87] When Jonas Devonsher died in April 1756 it was Abraham's presence at meetings in mourning dress that revealed a worldly vanity to his fellow Quakers.[88] More alarmingly, by recently offering himself as a parliamentary candidate, he had 'very openly and plainly manifested that he is gone from us, and is not one of faith and judgment with us'.[89] Devonsher had set his sights on a seat for Rathcormac, the borough which included Kilshannig. He was returned, it was said, 'by constantly residing and entertaining and drinking with the people'.[90] Thus, political calculation and familial feeling may be discerned in his choice of Kilshannig for his country refuge.

It is not known when Devonsher engaged Dukart to design Kilshannig, but the date 1766 cast on each of the drain hoppers suggests that work might have been underway in 1764 or early 1765.[91] Presented with a generous, open, hilltop site, free of the constrictions that hampered him in Cork and Limerick, Dukart was free to deploy arcaded wings, domed pavilions, office ranges, yards and forecourt in an ensemble that quadrupled the area occupied by the *corps de logis*.[92] Skilled stuccodores, fluent in the language of the European baroque, were called on to turn the ceilings of saloon, library and dining room into a mythical world inhabited by Bacchus, Apollo and Diana. If Devonsher created a mood remote from that of Sunday meeting and city counting house, he may have been alluding to that legacy with medallions enclosing circumspect low-relief portraits.[93] Thus housed, he seemed to retreat. In 1773 the chief secretary noted that he was then living 'a recluse life with a harlot', and amongst erstwhile allies his reluctance to attend Parliament proved an irritant.[94] He lost his parliamentary seat in 1776 following the purchase of Rathcormack borough by William Hull, and that year also saw him making provision from his estate for the support of his wife Mary.[95] He died at his lodgings on Cork's Grand Parade on 22nd April 1783.[96]

Abraham Devonsher – to echo Professor Dickson's phrase – was one of the 'new men', those whose families had amassed fortunes in trade or as soldiers, and established themselves in the early eighteenth century in grand houses near Cork city.[97] Robert Rogers was another. His grandfather had represented Cork in the parliaments of William III and had purchased the Lota estate overlooking the harbour at Glanmire, about four miles east of the city.[98] The younger Robert inherited Lota in 1741, and by then it must have acquired some of the features that by 1750 made it, in Charles Smith's words, 'a pleasant seat adorned with plantations'.[99]

Rogers continued making improvements, and, most likely in the mid-1760s, embarked on the substantial works on which he employed Dukart.[100] The extent of Dukart's intervention, whether a complete rebuilding or a renovation, is indistinct, but a comment from the builder and architect Michael Shanahan some years later provides useful clues.

I never had any dealings whatever with him [Dukart], nor was I ever concern'd where he was employed, but at a Mr Rogers in Lota near Cork – the front of whose house he stuccoed, which totally came off the winter following, the fault of which he attempted fixing upon me, not having my part of the building finished in time, the spring following he stuccoed it a second time, the fate of which Mr Trant [Dunkettle] who lives within a quarter of a mile of Mr Rogers can inform your lordship, also at whose door the fault lay.(101)

One possible interpretation of this is that Dukart was just one of a number of craftsmen engaged by Rogers and that he was responsible only for the stucco work – 'whose house he stuccoed' – while others, including Shanahan, worked on the rest of the building, 'not having my part of the building finished in time'. Another interpretation is that while the overall design of the project lay with Dukart, various builders and craftsmen such as Shanahan were employed for specific tasks. That was

Kilshannig, Rathcormac, county Cork (begun c.1764)

11 – Entrance or south front
(restoration of arcaded wings, pavilions and domes in progress, 2007)

12 – North front (photos Dara McGrath, 2007)
(restoration of arcaded wings, pavilions and domes in progress, 2007)

13 – Lota, Glanmire, Cork (begun c.1764), porch and balcony
(photo Dara McGrath, 2007)

14 – Lota, Glanmire, Cork (begun c.1764)
Detail of first-floor oval window with curved glazing bars (1967) (courtesy Irish Architectural Archive)

how Daniel Beaufort understood it: 'the house is by Dukart', he noted, following a
visit in 1788.[102] By then, Lota had the power to lure visitors on their jaunts out from
the city. Arthur Young had found it 'in the highest perfection' in 1778, and when
William Watmough came in 1785 he was struck by the square central block and the
cut-stone wings: 'the architecture thereof is neat and simple and appears so light,
that it does honour to the architect'.[103] Beaufort too was taken by much of what he
saw – the innovative porch of banded, Doric columns supporting a balcony and the
grand reception rooms (whose rich stucco work closely resembles that by Osborne
at the Mayoralty House) – but he was less impressed by what he characterised as a
general heaviness of design (Plates 13, 14). He also noticed how the plaster continued to give trouble.[104] Dukart's Lota is the house recorded in a series of watercolours
by William Osborne Hamilton in 1772 (Plates 15, 16).[105] It was still intact in the
1830s when, prior to a series of additions that included a pediment and bay windows, its exterior was sketched by Henry Hill (Plate 17).[106]

Dukart had probably finished at Lota and Kilshannig when he undertook the
design of Castletown near Carrick-on-Suir for Michael Cox, Archbishop of Cashel
(Plates 18-20).[107] It was certainly underway in September 1768 when Dukart was

known to have gone south, where 'he had the direction of a palace'.[108] As with the works then progressing in Limerick and Cork, day-to-day supervision was in the hands of a resident builder. At Castletown this was John Nowlan, who was present on 19th August 1774 when a final payment for interior stucco work was made to Patrick Osborne, the stuccodore who had worked alongside Dukart in Cork.[109] Nowlan's own bill of £1,000, 'on account of my attendance at the new building at Castletown', was settled in full by Cox on 4th December 1774.[110]

Cox had been promoted from Ossory as Archbishop of Cashel in January 1754. He was in his mid-seventies when he set about building Castletown, and for someone of his age it might have seemed a wasteful vanity or, at best, a belated protest against the constrictions of his official residence – Edward Lovett Pearce's palace of 1728 – in his cathedral city of Cashel. In truth, the construction of Castletown was an important element in his dynastic calculations, and it can hardly have been coincidental that it was initiated around the time of the marriage of his only son and heir, Richard.[111] Castletown was part of the Cox estate, and the house was conceived as a family seat and not as a primatial palace; its south front would carry the arms of Cox, impaling those of O'Brien of Thomond, the family of Richard's mother Anne.[112] Cox continued to think in dynastic terms for the remainder of his long life. In 1777, spurred on by the conferring of a barony on a fellow archbishop, Richard Robinson of Armagh, he informed Lord Lieutenant Buckingham that he considered himself as entitled to a temporal peerage.[113] For someone who harboured that ambition for his family, possession of a grand house was essential. The palace at Cashel was available to Cox and his family only as long as he held office, and in such circumstances he had to establish his own seat, as would Robinson with Rokeby in county Louth.[114]

Contemporaries may have wondered about possible sources for the design of Castletown. It was almost certainly the barely concealed object of the disparaging comment in La Verite's lampoon on Dukart in the *Freeman's Journal*: 'And soon after, picking from the tattered remains of an old edition of Paladio, in the original Language, a Palace for a R[ight]t R[evere]nd P[rima]te, he was immediately proclaimed all over the west, an Architect.'[115] The suggestion that Dukart was a plagiarist who otherwise would have been incapable of producing a work of merit seemed

---

opposite 15 – William Osborne Hamilton, A VIEW OF LOTA, THE SEAT OF ROBERT ROGERS ESQ 1772
pen and wash drawing, 22 x 39 cm (detail) (courtesy William Laffan)

16 – William Osborne Hamilton, LOTA, c.1772, present location of work unknown
(detail) (courtesy Irish Architectural Archive)

17 – Henry Hill, LOTA NEAR CORK, THE SEAT OF GREEN ESQR
c.1830, sketchbook ink and wash drawing, 13 x 20 cm (detail) (courtesy Cork Public Museum)

*18, 19 – Castletown, Carrick-on-Suir (begun c.1766),
garden front; garden front, arcaded wing, pavilion, dome and cupola (1917) (courtesy Country Life)*

20 – Castletown, Carrick-on-Suir (begun c.1766),
entrance front (1917) (courtesy Country Life)

to leave little room for the argument that a close reading of Palladio and other theorists might be a useful, if not essential, part of an architectural education. FitzGerald may have got closer to identifying a source for Castletown when he suggested in 1967 that its entrance front might have been influenced by William Winde's design of 1703 for Buckingham House in London.[116] Each house rose through four storeys and had a frontispiece of four Corinthian pilasters, a balustraded roof parapet and a Corinthian entablature separating the main floors from the attic story. Except for the use of seven bays at Castletown and nine at Buckingham House, contemporaries might have found the similarity all but complete (Plates 21, 22).[117]

Dukart took on more modest projects. One such was rebuilding a house 'in Co Cork for Mrs Wallis (now Mrs Mercer)'.[118] No more detail of her identity was recorded, but most likely she was Ann, daughter of Emanuel Pigott, MP for Cork city from 1735 to 1760, and his wife Lucy Rogers, a cousin of Dukart's patron at Lota.[119] In December 1763 Ann married Barachias Wallis of Ballycrenane in the parish of Kilcredan near Cloyne.[120] Wallis died in January 1765, and just over a year later she married Captain Richard Mercer of the Royal Irish Dragoons.[121] If Ann Pigott was the patron in question, Dukart would have worked for her at

21 – Castletown, Carrick-on-Suir (begun c.1766), entrance front (1917) (courtesy Country Life)

22 – William Winde, Buckingham House, London (begun 1702): entrance front
in Colen Campbell, Vitruvius Britannicus, or The British Architect, 3 vols (London 1717) I, pl.44

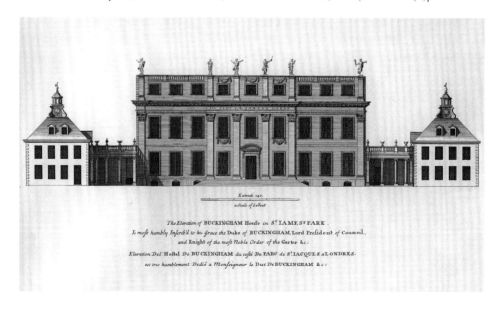

Ballycrenane during the brief period of her widowhood, January 1765 to March 1766. In 1837 Samuel Lewis noted the 'fine' ruins of Ballycrenane, and summarised its history: built by the Carews in the early fifteenth century, destroyed in 1641, restored and occupied by the Wallis family until 1798, when, following bombardment from a boat in Ballycotton Bay, it was abandoned.[122] In 1885 the ruin was reduced to a single story, and by 1991, showing signs of 'much alteration and repair', had become 'fragmentary and ivy clad'.[123] At Castle Mary, just eight miles west of Ballycrenane, Dukart designed 'a difficult roof' for Richard Longfield.[124] Longfield sat in Parliament successively for Baltimore, Charleville, Clonakilty and Cork, a representative career that stretched from 1761 to 1796, when he became the first Baron Longueville.[125] Dukart's fee was eight guineas for what must have been a small job, but he would remain unpaid, unsurprising, perhaps, given his patron's poor luck at gambling and his unrestrained spending on political advancement.[126]

Another rebuilding project came Dukart's way at Brockley Park near Stradbally, Queen's County in 1768. His patron there was Robert Waller's cousin, Robert Jocelyn.[127] Jocelyn had represented Old Leighlin in Parliament from 1745 to 1756 when he succeeded his father as 2nd Viscount. He was appointed Auditor General of Ireland in 1750, and would hold that office until his death in 1797.[128] Jocelyn took

Brockley Park, Stradbally

23 – Engraving after William Pars, 1785
(detail) in Thomas Milton, A SELECTION OF SELECT VIEWS FROM THE DIFFERENT SEATS OF THE NOBILITY AND GENTRY IN THE KINGDOM OF IRELAND (London 1793) xix (courtesy Glucksman Library, University of Limerick)

24 – Entrance front, demolished 1944
(courtesy Irish Architectural Archive)

25 – Brockley Park, Stradbally: staircase with supporting columns, frieze and cornice (demolished 1944)

26 – Lota, Glanmire: staircase with supporting columns, frieze and cornice (c.1965)

(courtesy Irish Architectural Archive)

27 – Castletown, Carrick-on-Suir: arcaded wings and cupolas (1917)
(courtesy Country Life)

possession of his father's house at Donnybrook, county Dublin in 1749, and there-after divided his time between it and Brockley Park.[129] On the morning of 12th December 1767, Brockley was 'entirely consumed'.[130] Thomas Milton wrote in 1793 that a new house was 'built' on the site of the old under the 'inspection' of Dukart.[131] Milton also provided an illustration and a brief description – seven rooms on the first floor, a chapel with four stained-glass windows, portico in front (Plate 23).[132] Brockley may have been altered again in the nineteenth century, and pho-tographs taken sometime before its demolition in 1944 (as well as Milton's print) record little that might link the design of its exterior directly to the builder of Castletown or Kilshannig (Plate 24). However, internal decoration, resembling, in part, that at Lota, suggests that this may have been less a complete project, as Milton seemed to be implying, than a prudent rebuilding (Plates 25, 26).

The study of Dukart's known surviving buildings has resulted in a growing consensus on their essential characteristics. The process got underway in 1913 when Thomas Ulick Sadlier, in his seminal essay on Castletown, wrote that its arcaded wings and cupolas were typical of Dukart's style (Plate 27).[133] In 1967, citing the recurring use of 'straight-edged quoining and heavy semi-circular basement win-dows', FitzGerald brought the analysis a stage further.[134] This was built on by Maurice Craig when, in his 1982 study of the Limerick Custom House, he picked out a frontispiece of fluted pilasters, arcaded wings, panelled piers, arches orna-mented by a tangent circle above, concave weatherings to window cornices, and window architraves broken upwards (Plate 28).[135] To these he added Dukart's use of domed pavilions to terminate an arcade and the deployment of wings in an inward-turning L-plan to partially enclose a yard (as at Castletown) or to fully enclose it with a curtain wall (as at Kilshannig) (Plates 29, 30).[136] Not surprisingly, when a building of the 1760s or 1770s of unknown authorship carries a number of such fea-tures, it can prompt suggestions of a Dukart connection.

These attributions include the five houses – Coole Abbey, just five-and-a-half miles from Kilshannig, Little Island House on Cork Harbour, Castle Hyde near Fermoy, Dunsandle near Athenry, and Woodroffe near Clonmel – proposed by Fitzgerald in 1967.[137] Dr Craig had suggested that Dukart might have had a part in designing the arcaded wings and pavilions at Florencecourt, county Fermanagh, but having allowed himself 'second thoughts' decided that a more obvious source was John Wood's Buckland in Berkshire.[138] In 1972 Edward McParland wrote that the palace at Armagh, usually attributed to Cooley, was started by Dukart.[139] The pres-ence of a bridge in the demesne at Lissan, county Derry, long accepted as by Dukart, led Alistair Rowan in 1979 to speculate that the associated garden works and even the nearby house might also be by him.[140] In 1993 Brian de Breffney won-dered whether the use of 'Mediterranean' features at Castlecor near Ballymahon, county Longford, revealed it to be one of Dukart's first Irish essays.[141] A rumour that

28 – Custom House Limerick (begun 1764): 'frontispiece of fluted pilasters, arcaded wings, panelled piers, arches ornamented by a tangent circle above, concave weatherings to window cornices, and window architraves broken upwards' (2007)

29 – Castletown, Carrick-on-Suir: use of domed pavilion and the deployment of wings in an inward-turning L-plan to partially enclose a yard (courtesy Country Life)

30 – Kilshannig, Rathcormac: use of domed pavilion, the deployment of wings in an inward-turning L-plan, and a curtain wall to enclose a yard (photo Dara McGrath, 2007)

31 – Coole Park, Castlelyons: entrance front

32 – Kilshannig, Rathcormac: north front

(photos Dara McGrath, 2007)

Dukart had a part in the building of Crosshaven House, county Cork, has been recorded, as have the presence of 'Dukartian features' at Ballyowen, near Cashel.[142]

Of all these cases, Coole Abbey carries the strongest visual evidence of Dukart's hand. FitzGerald showed how its entrance break-front is a scaled-down version of the back of Kilshannig (Plates 31, 32).[143] Its window architraves, broken upwards over the openings (as at Limerick, Cork and Castletown); the use of Chinese fretwork carving (as at Limerick and Kilshannig); frontispiece coigns where the stretcher alternates with paired headers (as at Limerick, Cork and Castletown), chamfered (as at Kilshannig) and camber-headed basement windows with keystone and voussoirs (as at Limerick and Cork), all crisply carved, speak the language of Dukart.[144] At Coole, decoration appears to have been confined mostly to the crowded entrance front, while the simple wall arcade on one of the farmyard wings – evoking the round-headed windows in the outbuildings at Kilshannig – went unmatched on the other. It was as if the architect's ambition outpaced his patron's means. In contrast with Castletown and Kilshannig, Coole was much less the villa of a grandee than the home of a gentleman farmer – in this case, Henry Peard.[145] Notwithstanding the compelling cues in its fabric, Coole's designer, like those of the other possibilities, must for now remain anonymous, a point emphasised by FitzGerald when he cautioned against the temptations of undocumented attribution.[146]

––––––

DUKART WAS NURTURING A SUCCESSFUL ARCHITECTURAL PRACTICE IN MUNSTER when, in early 1766, he travelled north to work on the Boyne navigation. Thereafter his ties to Munster loosened and he would return only to consult with patrons and to give directions to deputies and overseers. The works at Limerick, Cork, Kilshannig and Castletown would move towards completion, and following his work at Brockley Park in 1768, Dukart seems not to have taken on any new architectural projects. He was at a turning point in his career, and increasingly he directed his skills towards engineering, particularly where they could be applied to schemes of inland navigation and, later, to coal mining.

Work had started on the River Boyne in 1748 under the Commissioners of Inland Navigation, with the goal of making it navigable from Drogheda, westward, to Slane and Navan. During the 1750s the stretch between Drogheda and Slane was cleared of shoals and rocks, and its banks strengthened. Where the river was hazardous it was bypassed with short lateral canals and locks, mostly to a plan by Thomas Omer, recently appointed as engineer to the Navigation Board. The erection of David Jebb's spectacular corn mill at Slane rendered the completion of an effective waterway all the more pressing, a responsibility entrusted in December 1765 to local commissioners.[147] In April 1766 the commissioners stepped around Omer, and invited Dukart to survey the river and to propose how the work should proceed.[148] Impressed by his report, and notwithstanding the objections of a slighted Omer (whose initial plan, as revised by Christopher Myers, continued to guide the scheme), they agreed that Dukart should be retained as engineer.[149] He was granted an annual salary of £100, but with the appointment of Hamilton Bury as his resident deputy, it was clear that Dukart would spend very little time at Slane. Nonetheless, Dukart remained in the employment of the Boyne commissioners until the end of 1771.[150]

The terms of Dukart's employment at Slane left him free to take on other projects. One was in Dundalk, where, through the patronage of its Member of Parliament, Robert Waller (for whom he had worked in Limerick), and James Fortescue, a Boyne commissioner and MP for county Louth, he was engaged in 1767 to draw up plans and estimates for proposed harbour improvements.[151] Of the £5,397 6s 4d requested, Parliament granted £2,000, which was expended during the spring of 1768.[152]

A greater challenge lay in taking the extension of the Tyrone Canal from its basin at Coalisland to the coal pits at Drumglass. The project would be the final stage of an ambitions scheme to link the Tyrone coal fields to the Irish Sea at Newry, thereby opening the prospect of the easy transport of coal to Dublin. Work had started in 1731 under Edward Lovett Pearce, and by March 1742 boats were able to travel between Lough Neagh and the sea at Newry. By the late 1740s they could make their way on from Lough Neagh, through five miles of the River Blackwater, and then through a newly built canal to Coalisland.[153] Westward from Coalisland the engineers faced a formidable task. Though the distance was but three miles, a canal would have to ascend 150 feet through undulating hills, a project that would require the use of several locks and abundant supplies of water to feed them. It seemed easier to build a road, and to that end Parliament had granted £4,000 in 1753.[154] In January 1760 Thomas Omer was instructed to design a navigation that would take seagoing vessels all the way to the mines, using, where possible, the River Torrent. If he succeeded in that, it would be possible to ship coal all the way from Drumglass to Dublin without the delays and expense occasioned by unloading and loading at Coalisland and again at Newry. Christopher Myers, appointed as Omer's successor in June 1762, had proceeded initially on that basis, but he soon came to the conclusion that the Torrent, fast-flowing and hazardous in winter but contracting to a trickle in summer, could not be successfully adapted to take ships. Neither was there any possibility of sufficient water to supply the very large locks that a ship canal would need. The most practicable course, he believed, would be the construction of a canal for small boats.[155]

It was left to Dukart to bring Myers's plan to realisation. Instead of a conventional canal where boats were moved from one level to another via locks, he proposed a single-level canal, taken across valleys by aqueduct and staunched embankment, and through hilly terrain by tunnel. When the canal reached Coalisland, cargo would be taken from the boats and lowered 150 feet down a shaft to an underground canal that linked up with the basin.[156] The audaciousness of the proposal was sufficient to draw criticism, not least from Omer whose scheme it would supplant, but Dukart's eloquent advocacy before a parliamentary committee in November 1767 gained him support where it counted.[157] Thus encouraged, he proposed an even longer underground canal, perhaps a mile in all, so that four faulty locks on the old canal below Coalisland could be bypassed. Again, with the backing of the local commissioners, he was able to get parliamentary approval.[158] Most critically he had the support of James Fortescue, now a member of the key committee on public works. Together they travelled to England in October 1768 to view the acclaimed aqueduct and underground channel built by James Brindley for the Duke of Bridgewater.[159]

An underground canal would be costly to build and operate. Having asked in February 1768 for £26,802 to get the works started, the local commissioners were given but £5,000, and it became obvious that additional grants would be infrequent and no more generous. Consequently, Dukart was forced to revert to the original canal scheme, but he quickly learned, as had Myers before him, that there would never be a sufficient supply of water for four busy locks. He decided to dispense with locks entirely and use instead a ramp or inclined plane on which containers of coal, having been lifted from the boats, would be eased from one level down to the next. The first plane, close to the mines at Farlough, would cover a drop of fifty feet; another at Drumreagh, sixty feet; and the third, at Gorthaskea, fifty-five feet. A final fifteen-foot plane would bring cargo down to the basin at Coalisland.[160]

In June 1771 Dukart announced that the course of the canal had been marked out and that he was looking for contractors.[161] By the autumn of 1773 most of the work had been completed, and the local commissioners sought an assessment of Dukart's proposal for inclined planes from John Smeaton, the pre-eminent English civil engineer. Smeaton repeated what others had often said: the terrain and water supply was such that any canal project would be fundamentally flawed, 'the circumstances attending it are such that I never could have recommended a canal of any kind'.[162] He advised that the canal should be replaced by a wooden railway. If that was not possible and the inclined planes had to be retained, they should be rendered more efficient.[163] Dukart proceeded on that basis, but when a parliamentary committee reviewed the operation of the canal in 1787 it found that only a few trial boats had ever made the journey from Coalisland to the mines.[164] The channel had dried up and the inclined planes had begun their long decay (Plates 33, 34). Almost as soon as it had been completed, what had become known locally as Dukart's Canal was 'entirely laid aside' and replaced by a railroad for horse-drawn wagons (Plate 35).[165]

The three-arched aqueduct near Newmills is the most enduring manifestation

*Tyrone Navigation, Dry
Hurry, Drumreagh Etra
(begun c.1772)*

33 – North-east face

*34 – Detail of south-west
face, voussoirs and roof*
(1967)

*(courtesy the Controller of Her
Majesty's Stationary Office)*

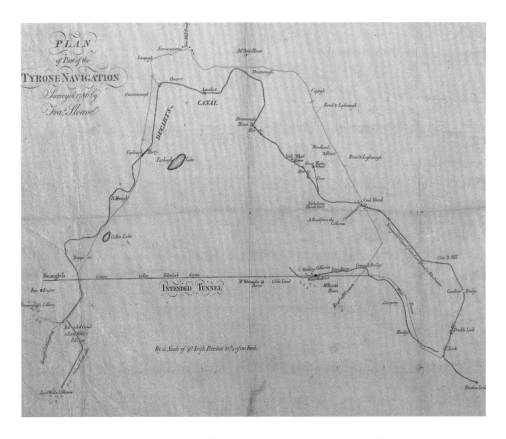

of Dukart's canal engineering skill (Plate 37). An aqueduct had been proposed by Myers in 1767 as part of his plan to take the Coalisland canal westward over the River Torrent to the mines. Dukart became responsible for its design and execution, and it was completed in 1768.[166] Several of the motifs used on his private and public buildings – rusticated keystones, strongly articulated quoins, centred roundels, all sharply and precisely cut – were deployed (Plate 36). Dukart was justifiably proud when, at a parliamentary committee, he announced the completion of the aqueduct 'so happily situated', but he may have overstated its potential when he suggested that it could be used as the starting point for a grand canal southwards, 'without one single lock', through the drumlins of Monaghan and Fermanagh to the Erne.[167] The Newmills aqueduct may have provided the inspiration for a bridge commissioned by John Staples for his demesne – a 'secluded recess of mountainous territory' – at Lissan near Cookstown.[168] The three-arched bridge carries a woodland path, protected by wooden balustrades à la chinoiserie, across a tumbling stream (Plate 38). Although differing in scale, both aqueduct and bridge provided conspicuous demonstrations of Dukart's bridge-building skill, and it might have found further expression when Augustus Hervey, Bishop of Derry, commissioned him to design a bridge

Tyrone Navigation aqueduct over Torrent river, Newmills (1768)

36 – North-west face (1967)

37 – Detail of south-east face (1967)

(courtesy the Controller of Her Majesty's Stationary Office)

opposite

35 – PLAN OF PART OF THE TYRONE NAVIGATION, SURVEYED 1786 BY FRANS. SLOANE

(courtesy Royal Irish Academy [Misc. Maps, vol. I, C 32 1 C])

38 – Lissan Demesne, Cookstown: the bridge, c.1900
(courtesy Trustees of Lissan Estate)

over the Foyle.[169] By February 1769 Dukart had prepared two sets of drawings, one for a stone bridge that might be built for £32,000, and another for a simpler wooden structure.[170] In April he went to Derry to present his plans to the Corporation.[171] The Corporation adopted his proposals and used them in an application for finance to the Irish Society, the body responsible since the Ulster plantation for the economic development of the city and county.[172] Support was not forthcoming, and when a bridge was eventually built in Derry in 1790 it was not to Dukart's design.

Dukart seemed likely to land another canal project in early 1768 when the merchants of Strabane proposed to their landlord, the Earl of Abercorn, that a canal northwards from the town to the River Foyle would enable it to become a port comparable to Derry.[173] They suggested that a plan by Dukart might be used to support a petition to Parliament for funds.[174] Abercorn found the project attractive, not least because of the short distance – two miles – over easy terrain, and he consulted his uncle, William Brownlow, MP for Armagh, about possible engineers.[175] Brownlow believed that Dukart was the most capable of those then practicing in Ireland. His performance before the parliamentary committee the previous November had been impressive; he was an excellent draughtsman and surveyor, 'indefatigable in anything he undertakes'. Should Abercorn decide to go ahead, Dukart's proximity at Coalisland would lessen the cost of employing him. Notwithstanding his endorsement of Dukart, Brownlow advised Abercorn that a man trained in England under Smeaton or Brindley would be better, however: 'The opinion of one of their journeymen would be more attended to than the greatest master in this country.'[176]

Dukart knew that Brownlow was advising Abercorn on the choice of engineer, and he set out his terms to him directly.[177] He would conduct a preliminary survey: the easier the work, the less need to be there and the lower his costs. If the project did not progress, thirty guineas would cover his costs. Should it proceed, however, it would be necessary to employ a deputy at about £100 a year. As to his own fee, he would leave that decision to Brownlow and to Edmund Sexton Pery.[178] Brownlow was irked by Dukart's presumptuousness. He thought that £100 a year for a deputy excessive, particularly if, as Dukart had suggested, he would be merely an 'observer of workmen'.[179] Chastened somewhat, Dukart agreed that if the ground proved trouble-free, an overseer who could work on his own might be got for £40, in which case his own fee would be £150 a year and as much again on completion.[180] However, if the work proved complicated, his fee would have to be £200, and all on the assumption that he would continue working on the Drumglass Canal. He would be at least as good as Brindley or Smeaton, neither of whom, he claimed, would attend such a project for more than one month in twelve.[181] While Dukart haggled with Brownlow, those behind the initial proposal began to consider how it might be extended to provide for a canal westwards to Castlefinn and south to Omagh. Such a project would involve other landowners, in which case Abercorn would be less inclined to take a leading role.[182] Pending the outcome of those deliberations, Brownlow and Abercorn suspended negotiations with Dukart.[183]

Left to himself, Abercorn might have proceeded with the short canal from Strabane to the Foyle, but once a more elaborate scheme led by 'other gentlemen' was mooted, he could only bide his time. When the scheme was resuscitated in January 1774 he let it be known that he would subscribe up to £12,000, provided that it would be no more than one third of the total.[184] In February Dukart was sent for by the town clerk of Strabane to make a survey and to prepare a report for consideration by the gentlemen of Tyrone and Fermanagh at the next assizes.[185] Abercorn's agent, James Hamilton, was present when Dukart presented his scheme, and it struck him that the gentlemen 'did not seem to enter warmly into it'.[186] Hamilton may have been understating the negative reception of a proposal dear to him, but Abercorn was under no illusion as to how his fellow proprietors felt. He believed that Dukart's proposals were so outlandish and extravagant that they killed any enthusiasm that might have been there: 'But the part Dukart has taken, could only tend to make them laugh and to defeat the project entirely: whilst he thought he was merely giving a specimen of his genius and imagination.'[187] Dukart had suffered a stinging public humiliation, but against a background increasingly sceptical of the utility of such schemes and greater parliamentary scrutiny, it would be wrong to conclude that it was his misjudged comments alone that brought the project to a halt.[188]

Dukart had gone north to work as a canal engineer, but like Christopher Myers before him, had been tempted to turn his skills there to mining. In the late 1760s he borrowed heavily and expended £1,250 on a 55% share in the Tyrone Mining Company, an association dominated until then by John Staples of Lissan and James Caulfeild of Drumrea.[189] As well as being the majority shareholder, Dukart now assumed the role of resident manager, and for the next eleven years, from his home at Drumrea at the centre of the Tyrone coal field, mining would provide the principal concern of his professional life.

Initially, there was much to do, not least establishing firm control of a coal field where opportunistic short-term mining by locals had been tolerated in the past. Dukart placed notices in newspapers warning that anyone who had hitherto been mining at Drumglass should desist 'at their peril'.[190] In June 1771 he had to forcibly close an illicit pit.[191] Another challenge was to restore public confidence in the collieries whose output had often suffered adulteration by middlemen and carriers.[192] Financial control too was improved. In December 1770 he announced that he would no longer arrange for the collection of trifling sums about the country, and that all new orders would have to be accompanied by cash.[193] Much of his energy was directed at finding good workmen. Most were manual labourers, by the nature of their work prone to illness and injury and often in short supply. In March 1772 he hoped to recruit forty or fifty skilled miners, and in 1775 he was looking for another thirty.[194] Effective day-to-day management required the skills of an underground overseer, a land steward 'well acquainted with setting and keeping labourers at work', and a chief groom for a stable of forty horses.[195] A carpenter was employed to make and repair coal wagons and build houses for employees.[196] Honest clerks were essential, but were neither easily found nor kept. In 1771 the chief clerk left, taking the account books with him.[197] When Dukart went to Dublin and left a new clerk in charge, he found him no more reliable; he and his assistant were negligent and their drunkenness soon spread down the ranks to the miners.[198]

Dukart came to coal mining at a time of technological innovation. The power of pit horse and collier was being amplified as never before through the use of water power and, increasingly, steam. In November 1769 Dukart informed a Commons committee that he was sinking a shaft over two hundred feet deep to accommodate a pump and a steam engine that would cost £500.[199] By October 1771 the shaft had been completed, and turning his mind to what machines might be installed, books in German and Dutch on mechanics were borrowed from the Dublin Society.[200] Lack of funds thwarted his ambition, however. He was unable to purchase the engine and when the newly sunk pits flooded, they had to be abandoned. Under Dukart the

Tyrone coal field never moved beyond using the simplest technologies. Shovel, rope and pick set a low limit on output, and that was pushed lower still when flooding confined mining to the driest part of the year. When Arthur Young visited – most likely echoing Dukart's own opinion – he noted the 'utter deficiency of capital' there.[201] Without investment in new machinery, output and profits would remain low.[202] A half-century later, Richard Griffith praised the coal itself – 'fully equal to the second quality of coal in England' – and while he admired the detail in Dukart's working notes, still being consulted at the colliery, he was tempted to conclude that the poor performance of the mine was 'owing to a want of system and foresight in the management'.[203] It might be unfair if that criticism were extended to Dukart. Observers were yet without the means to make an accurate assessment of the field's potential, and carried along by the enthusiasm of mine-owners and political interests, tended to be optimistic regarding the value of the Tyrone coal. Ultimately, its relatively poor quality deposited in shallow seams ensured that at no stage would it compete successfully against the rich products of British coalfields.[204]

Throughout the 1770s Dukart remained anchored at Drumrea in a manner that contrasted with his incessant travelling between one job and another in the 1760s. His old energy had been evident as he angled to land the Strabane canal project in 1774, but when he was approached the following year by Sir James Caldwell of Castle Caldwell, near Belleek, to design a navigation from the Erne to the Atlantic, he told him that he now found engineering disagreeable and that he no longer put his name to plans or estimates.[205] He came from a country where mathematics and natural philosophy were esteemed by those of the highest rank, but he found it otherwise in Ireland.[206] His gripe notwithstanding, Caldwell was able to entice Dukart to Fermanagh, but the visit proved fruitless: 'He was not half an hour upon the ground, took no survey of it, guessed the levels, made no enquiry or experiment into the stratum that was to be worked through and in short did nothing, but for very obvious reasons wished that the application might be laid aside.'[207] Dukart might have endured the rancour that marked the final stages of his work in Limerick and Cork, but the intractable problems thrown up by the Drumglass Canal and the public rejection of his proposals for the Strabane navigation may have weakened his spirit. He ventured occasionally to Dublin on colliery business and to meet friends, among them William Colvill, merchant, astute man-about-town, and, since 1777, MP for Newtown Limavady.[208] When Dukart made a will in 1768 he had appointed Colville an executor, and he turned to him again in November 1780 when he added a codicil.[209] By then he may have been in decline, but if so, the first that most people knew of it was when a notice in the *Belfast Newsletter*, dated 3rd February 1781, announced that mining would continue at Drumglass, notwithstanding the recent death of Mr Dukart.[210]

D UKART WAS FORTUNATE TO ARRIVE IN IRELAND AT A TIME WHEN UNPRECEDENT-
ed amounts were being spent on public and private projects. From an
unpromising beginning when he appears to have survived by selling pictures to peddlers, he moved up to surveying and drawing plans and then to take
charge of significant building projects. His skill as a designer resulted in houses at
Kilshannig and Castletown that were pre-eminent at their time in their respective
counties, and he gave Limerick its first almost-modern building. But even as he
completed these, the tide of fashion was on the turn: his work began to appear conservative, even archaic, and it is reasonable to ask if he would have been a serious
contender against those such as Cooley and Ivory, who won the major commissions
of the 1770s. Nonetheless, at his peak in the mid-1760s, Dukart showed that he
could outpace his professional competitors – Morrison in Cork, Uzuld and Smyth in
Limerick, and Omer at the Boyne.

These successes owed much to Dukart's energy and to his technical skill, but
they were also the fruit of his ability to cultivate important patrons. One such was
Robert Waller who was acting for the revenue commissioners when Dukart was
brought in over Uzuld in Limerick. Edmund Sexton Pery was another powerful
patron, and it seems likely that it was his intervention that resulted in Dukart replacing Edward Smyth as the architect of the Custom House. Pery wanted a building
that would embellish his constituency and provide an anchor for his own development of New Town Pery, and he had no scruple in seeing all others pushed aside in
favour of an untested stranger and collaborating with him until they got the grand
building they both wanted. Dukart did well from his association with those who
mattered. His patrons in the decade from 1765 to 1775 – Members of Parliament
such as Brownlow, Devonsher, Fortescue, Longfield, Staples and Waller; the
Archbishop of Cashel and the Bishop of Derry; Jocelyn, an auditor general, and
Pery, a future speaker of the House of Commons – reveal the exclusive and concentrated nature of patronage in eighteenth-century Ireland, as well as Dukart's skill in
landing lucrative commissions.

Dukart's successes animated the envious, the most irksome being those who
disparaged him from behind a pseudonym in the *Freeman's Journal*. While some
used his foreign origins against him, he could turn that to his advantage, especially
in those cultivated circles where knowledge of European ways was valued. Others
would have wondered about his political beliefs – and given the manner of his
arrival in Ireland, they might have had reason to do so – but he gave due attention to
the business of fitting-in. When an edition of Sir John Temple's uncompromisingly
protestant history of the Irish Rebellion was being prepared for publication in Cork
in 1766, he subscribed, alongside his patrons Robert Rogers and Abraham
Devonsher.[211] If his fluent, articulate letters in a clear, confident hand and a number
of well-argued memoranda to parliamentary committees provide an appropriate

measure, he had adapted well to local modes of expression.[212]

When his enemies found an opportunity to attack, he did what others in similar circumstances might have done and looked for a scapegoat: the Cork aldermen who forced incompetent workmen on him; the stonecarver and masons in Limerick who had difficulty following his instructions; the supervisors at Drumglass who took to the drink. Frequently, however, the fault lay with Dukart himself. He was cavalier in his attitude towards other people's money, he took liberties when interpreting the terms of contracts, and when he wanted to alter the details of a design halfway through execution, it was for his subordinates to deal with the consequences. He acted as if his ambition should not be constrained by practicalities. Thus, in 1767, when the building projects at Limerick, Cork and Castletown were each at a critical stage, he felt able to take a different professional path and seek challenging engineering commissions at Slane, Dundalk, Derry, Strabane, Coalisland and Drumglass. Dukart may have overstretched himself, and from the successes of the mid-1760s he had descended by 1774 to a point where shrewd patrons such as Abercorn and Caldwell would come to the conclusion that his involvement in a project would be a liability. It was a dispiriting end to a decade of considerable achievement.

Dukart's professional successes serve to accentuate the extent to which almost everything else about him remains uncharted. In the absence of private letters, diary or portrait, there is a danger that his surviving works will be forced to speak more loudly than they should. His life, as he lived it away from the public space, can be observed only on the odd occasion and then but briefly, as when he made a pathetic plea for the return of a parcel of shirts (plain and ruffled), handkerchiefs, stockings and pillow cases, lost of a winter's evening on the road home from Dungannon.[213] More mysterious still is a laconic report of his acquittal at the 1775 spring assizes in Omagh of a charge of murdering one Charles Coningham, and the return instead of a verdict of manslaughter in self-defence.[214] After Dukart's death, his business partners John Staples and James Caulfeild disposed of his property at Drumrea and settled his debts.[215] His principal creditor, a Dublin attorney Richardson Williams, had acquired Dukart's interest in the Drumglass mines, which, for a consideration of £400, he gave over to Caulfeild and Staples.[216] Bequests, totalling £1,446 15s 0d, had been made to friends in Italy and France, but there was no one in Ireland, or any relative or family member, to whom Dukart felt a similar obligation.[217]

———

APPENDIX: THE WILL OF DAVIS DUKART

Dukart made a will on 24th June 1768 and subsequently added three codicils, the last of which was written on 30th November 1780, a few months before his death. It was proven on 29th March 1786 and administration was granted to Richardson Williams on 27th April 1787. None of these documents appears to have survived. The little that is known of the contents of the will of 1768 may be gleaned from a deed registered on 24th February 1789 which noted that Dukart had appointed James Fortescue, John Townsend and William Colville as his executors in 1768. (RD, 404/166/267540). Rather more is known of the contents of the final codicil from notes taken from it by Thomas Burtchill Sadlier sometime before the destruction of the records of the Prerogative Court at the Four Courts in June 1922. Sadlier's notes are preserved in NLI MS GO 424, 237-8 and are printed here in full:

> Davis Duckart.(Daviso de Arcort) Employed as Engineer for the Newry Canal & the Tyrone and Boyne Navigation. Richd. Longfield owes me 6 Guineas for designing a difficult roof for Castle Mary; rebuilt house in Co Cork for Mrs Wallis (now Mrs Mercer) & Kilshannig, Co Cork, for Abraham Devonsher. Mentions his friends Jas. Fortescue of Ravensdale Park, John Townsend of Castle Townsend & the E. of Bristol, Bishop of Derry. Will in form of letter written to Wm Colvill, whom he appoints Executor. Property at Drumrea, Co Tyrone.
>
> 30 Nov. 1780. pr 29 Mar. 1786.

Sadlier gave a slightly different summary in *The Georgian Society, Records of Eighteenth-Century Domestic Architecture and Decoration in Ireland*, V (Dublin 1913) 72, where the additional information, not included in NLI MS GO 424, may be found: 'There are also legacies to friends in France and Italy, but none apparently to relatives.' The significance of the 1780 codicil is that it is the only document that links Dukart directly to his work at Castle Mary, Kilshannig and Ballycrenane. It also refers to three acquaintants, James Fortescue, Augustus Hervey and John Townsend as his friends, though it is unclear whether this might indicate more than a mutually beneficial business relationship. Dukart appears to have had most dealings with Fortescue, who had an interest in many of the projects on which he found employment. Hervey shared Dukart's interest in building and coal mining, but appears to have had no dealings with him apart from proposing him to design a bridge for Derry. Perhaps a friendship had been forged in Cloyne, prior to Hervey's transfer to Derry in 1768. Even less is known of John Townsend's relationship with Dukart. He was in his early twenties and recently appointed Surveyor of the Revenue for Baltimore when Dukart first enters the record in Cork, and it may have been there, when both were beginning to make their way in the world, that they first met.

ACKNOWLEDGEMENTS

The author wishes to thank the following who, in various ways, assisted his research: Prof M. Bucholz, Mr D. Breen, Mr G. Carty, Ms S. Cherry, Mr N. Clark, Dr M. Craig, Dr B. Cunningham, Ms F. Davern, Mr W. Dilworth, Dr R. Finnegan, Mr D. Falvey, Mr B. Graham, Mr S. Healy, Ms J. Hill, Mr J. Howley, Mr M. Logan, Ms P. McCarthy, Mr M.J. McGuckin, Dr E. McParland, Dr A.P.W. Malcomson, Mr A. Malley, Dr R. O'Donnell, Dr F. O'Dwyer, Mr F.W. Peard, Mr J. Redmill, Mr T. Reeves-Smith, the Earl of Roden, Dr W. Roulston, Dr K. Varnelis. He is grateful for the kind hospitality of owners and custodians at the properties dealt with here: Mr and Mrs Leahy (Ballycrenane), Mr and Mrs Magan (Castletown), Mr A. Nardone (Lota), Ms V. Teehan (Custom House, Limerick), the late Mrs H. Radclyffe-Dolling (Lissan), Mr and Mrs Merry (Kilshannig), Ms S. O'Mahony (Mayoralty House, Cork), Mrs Koowenberg and Mr and Mrs Keane (Coole Abbey), Mr D. Hurley (Castle Mary). Material is quoted or reproduced by permission of the British Library; Cork Public Museum; Environment and Heritage Service of Northern Ireland; Friends Historical Library, Dublin; Glucksman Library, University of Limerick; Irish Architectural Archive; John Rylands University Library, Manchester; National Archives, Dublin; National Archives, London; National Library of Ireland; Public Record Office of Northern Ireland; Registry of Deeds; Royal Irish Academy; Trinity College, Dublin. The author is especially indebted to the director and staff of the incomparable Irish Architectural Archive. Dr T. Barnard kindly provided transcripts of material from his own research in the Bagshawe Papers, and offered answers to some difficult questions; Mr K. Bergin, Dr D. Fleming and Ms J. Moore all supplied a number of references and helped in other important ways, as did Dr B. Whelan. Ms L. Hurley generously shared the fruits of her research on Slane and drew the plan that disentangles Dukart's Custom House from its nineteenth-century additions; Mr D. O'Sullivan did the same for the Mayoralty House. Mr D. McGrath kindly photographed the exteriors of Kilshannig and Lota. The author is especially grateful to Olda FitzGerald, and to Desmond FitzGerald, Knight of Glin, for sharing the fruits of many years' research and thinking about Dukart, and for first suggesting that this paper be written.

ENDNOTES

The following abbreviations are used:

BN	*Belfast Newsletter*
Council Book	Richard Caulfield (ed.), *The Council Book of the Corporation of the City of Cork* (Guilford 1876)
CJI	*Journals of the House of Commons of the Kingdom of Ireland* (Grierson edition)
FJ	*Freeman's Journal*
HIP	Edith Mary Johnston-Liik, *History of the Irish Parliament*, 6 vols (Belfast 2002)
IAA	Irish Architectural Archive
NLI	National Library of Ireland
PRONI	Public Record Office of Northern Ireland
Remembrancer	Francis H. Tuckey, *The County and City of Cork Remembrancer* (Cork 1838)
RD	Registry of Deeds, Dublin
TNA	National Archives, London

[1] Contemporaries gave various forms to his name, including Dukart, Duckart, Ducart, Ducarte, Du Cart and Duchart, a mix that reflected attempts to find an appropriate Anglicisation of the Romanic 'Daviso de Arcot' recorded in a codicil to his will (NLI, MS GO 424, 237-8). Modern scholars are divided between using Ducart and Duckart, but the form Davis Dukart, used consistently by him in autograph letters and accounts (PRONI, D/623/A/38/100, D/623/38/94, D/2798/2/1, DIO 4/13/5/4, T/2519/12/11) is adhered to here.

[2] The Knight of Glin, 'A Baroque Palladian in Ireland: the Architecture of Davis Duckart-I', *Country Life*, CXLII, 28th September 1967, 735-39; 'The Last Palladian in Ireland: the Architecture of Davis Duckart-II', *Country Life*, CXLII, 5th October 1967, 798-802.

[3] Ron Cox, 'Ducart, Davis' in A.W. Skempton (ed.), *A Biographical Dictionary of Civil Engineers in Great Britain and Ireland, I, 1500-1830* (London 2002) 191-92; Maurice Craig, *The Architecture of Ireland from the Earliest Times to 1880* (London and Dublin 1982) 195-96; Anne Crookshank, 'The Visual Arts, 1740-1850' in T.W. Moody and W.E. Vaughan [eds], *A New History of Ireland* (Oxford 1986) 500, 503, 508, 512, 534; Brian de Breffney and Rosemary ffolliott, *The Houses of Ireland* (London 1975); Judith Hill, 'Davis Duckart and Christopher Colles: Architects Associated with the Custom House at Limerick', *Irish Architectural and Decorative Studies*, II (1999) 119-45; Edward McParland, 'Ducart, Davis', *The Dictionary of Art* (London 1996) 9, 341; Frederick O'Dwyer, 'Making connections in Georgian Ireland', *Bulletin of the Irish Georgian Society*, XXXVIII, 1996-97; Ann Martha Rowan, 'Davis Ducart', *Oxford Dictionary of National Biography*, 60 vols (Oxford 2004) XVII, 29-30; IAA, *Biographical Index of Irish Architects*, electronic database compiled by Ann Martha Rowan.

[4] *CJI*, VIII, 17th November 1767.

[5] PRONI, Abercorn Papers, D/623/A/38/82, William Brownlow to Abercorn, 8th August 1768.

[6] *ibid.*

[7] *FJ*, 2nd June 1770.

[8] *ibid.* For contemporary reports on the capture of privateers off the south and west coast of Ireland, see *Universal Advertiser*, 23rd June 1759, 10th July 1759, for which references I am grateful to Dr D. Fleming.

[9] *Council Book*, 751-52. Dukart may also have worked on a scheme to improve the Munster Blackwater navigation around this time. Such a role was alluded to by John Roach, an engineer, who claimed to have worked under Dukart at Youghal but without indicating when that was; see PRONI, Hervey-Bruce Papers D/2798/2/75; John Roach to Bann Navigation Committee, 20th November 1784: 'For the inspection of the committee appointed for the improvement of the navigation of the river Bann, by John Roche who superintended a work of the same kind, under Mr Ducart, at the river at Youghal to the satisfaction of the committee concerned.' The Blackwater project was most likely to have been sometime before the mid-1760s when the focus of Dukart's work shifted from Cork to Tyrone. Parliament voted funds to aid the Blackwater navigation in 1755, 1759 and 1761; *CJI*, VIII, 637.

[10] National Archives, Dublin, Prim Papers, M.87/77, William Colles to Davis Dukart, 2nd November 1761.

[11] *Council Book*, 765.

[12] *Council Book*, 827; Cox, 'Ducart, Davis', 191.

[13] *The Dublin Magazine*, 1764, 501-03.

[14] Despite Morrison's professed patriotism, he was able to find the inspiration for his design in

George Dance's London Mansion House of 1739; see Edward McParland, *Public Architecture in Ireland 1680-1760* (New Haven and London 2001) 7.

[15] *Council Book*, 816.

[16] *Remembrancer*, 149.

[17] *ibid.*

[18] The Mayoralty House finds its first cartographic expression in the 1771 revision of John Rocque's Cork city map of 1759, and somewhat more clearly in Joseph Connor's map of 1774.

[19] *Remembrancer*, 149.

[20] *Council Book*, 815.

[21] *ibid.*, 812.

[22] *Remembrancer*, 149.

[23] *Council Book*, 816

[24] *Cork Evening Post*, 13th July 1767.

[25] *ibid.*

[26] *ibid.*; *Remembrancer*, 149.

[27] *Remembrancer*, 149; *Council Book*, 821.

[28] *Remembrancer*, 150; *Council Book*, 826, 833, 845.

[29] *Council Book*, 819, 823, 836, 839, 842, 843. Osborne was paid £60 13s 3d in October 1768, and £82.1s.0^{1}/2d in November 1769, *ibid.*, 833, 845.

[30] *Council Book*, 826, 837.

[31] *Council Book*, 883.

[32] *FJ*, 4th February 1773. See also, *Sleater's Public Gazetteer*, 4th November 1769.

[33] Trinity College, Dublin, MS 4030, 'Journal of the Reverend D.A. Beaufort', 8th September 1788. Beaufort also provided rough sketches of the windows.

[34] TNA, Cust 1/32/131-34, 6th October 1741; Cust 1/58/87, 16th July 1756.

[35] TNA, Cust 1/60/89, /91, 15th June 1757.

[36] PRONI, T/3087/1/30, John Ponsonby to Edmund Sexton Pery, 27th August 1761; T/3087/1/29, Lord Newport to Edmund Sexton Pery, 27th August 1761; TNA, Cust 1/79/82-3, 24th November 1763; Cust 1/80/43, 28th January 1764. Among Uzuld's works were the New Bridge (1761) and the Lock Mills (1762). For Uzuld's business transactions with Pery see RD, 239/527/16219, 239/528/162913, 239/529/162914.

[37] TNA, Cust 1/84/126, 22nd December 1764.

[38] TNA, Cust 1/85/54, 9th February 1765. For Waller see, *HIP*, VI, 483-84.

[39] TNA, Cust 1/85/54, 9th February 1765.

[40] TNA, Cust 1/86/10, 4th April 1765.

[41] TNA, Cust 1/86/45, 24th April 1765.

[42] *ibid.*

[43] *ibid.*

[44] *ibid.*

[45] TNA, Cust 1/86/44, 19th May 1765.

[45] *ibid.*

[47] John Ferrar, *An History of the City of Limerick* (Limerick 1767) 69. Ferrar gives 9th June 1765 as the date when building commenced.

[48] TNA, Cust 1/88/7, 6th September1765.

[49] TNA, Cust 1/92/140, 13th July 1766.

[50] TNA, Cust 1/92/140, 13th July 1766.

[51] TNA, Cust 1/93/157, 30th September 1766; Cust 1/97/116, 26th May 1767.

[52] TNA Cust 1/95/65, 24th January 1767.

[53] TNA, Cust 1/95/65, 24th January 1767.

[54] TNA, Cust, 1/98/13, 19th June 1767.

[55] TNA, Cust 1/92/37, 3rd June 1766; Cust 1/93/20, 5th August 1766; Cust 1/95/40, 19th December 1766; Cust 1/96/149, 13th April 1767; Cust 1/99/48, 12th September 1767; Cust 1/100/44, 21st November 1767.

[56] TNA, Cust 1/96/122, 4th April 1767.

[57] TNA, Cust 1/96/38, 16th April 1767.

[58] TNA, Cust 1/96/39, 16th April 1767.

[59] TNA, Cust 1/100/44, 21st November 1767.

[60] TNA, Cust 1/101/36, 14th April 1768.

[61] Private collection, Colles Papers, William Colles to Hannah James, 27th August 1766. I am grateful to the Knight of Glin for premission to consult transcripts of the Colles Papers.

[62] TNA, Cust 1/86/10, 4th April 1765.

[63] Private collection, Colles Papers, William Colles to Hannah James, 27th August 1766: 'I have got Kit Colles (whose affairs here were in a desperate way) into an employment under one Mr Dukart, an engineer, in which if he behaves with care I doubt not but he will do very well.'

[64] TNA, Cust 1/95/65, /85, 24th January 1767.

[65] TNA, Cust 1/95/86, 24th January 1767.

[66] TNA, Cust 1/108/140, 22nd July 1769.

[67] TNA, Cust, 1/109/21, 8th August 1769.

[68] ibid.

[69] TNA, Cust 1/108/140, 22nd July 1769.

[70] TNA, Cust 1/109/25, 8th August 1769.

[71] ibid.

[72] TNA, Cust 1/109/84, 30th August 1769.

[73] Private collection, Colles Papers, Christopher Colles to William Colles, 23rd December 1769; TNA, Cust 1/115/131, 10th December 1770.

[74] Limerick Chronicle, 18th August 1768. I am grateful to Jennifer Moore for this reference.

[75] ibid., 18th, 22nd, 25th, 29th August; 1st, 5th September 1768.

[76] ibid.

[77] ibid., 18th August 1768.

[78] ibid., 12th September 1768.

[79] ibid.. Maurice Lenihan, Limerick: Its History and Antiquities, Ecclesiastical, Civil and Military (London 1866) 358-59. Lenihan based his account of the building of the Assembly Room on the Society's minute book, then in the posession of Stephen Hastings. Its present location is unknown.The wording used by Lenihan – 'it was resolved to take a lease of the plot of ground, as described in a plan presented by the Rev. Dean Hoare, which was approved of, from Charles Smyth, Esq., for the term of 999 years, at the yearly rent of five shillings' – is ambiguous. It could be referring to a map of the plot prepared by Hoare, or, equally, to a design by him. However, John Ferrar, The History of Limerick (Limerick 1787) 206-07 also credits Hoare: 'The building which was planned by the Rev. Mr. Deane Hoare, is large and elegant...'

[80] Lenihan, Limerick, 358-59, noted that the building – its lower story of brick, those above in

stone – was commenced on 24th October and finished in August 1770. It was demolished in 1839.

[81] Dukart's role as the maker of the 1765 plan for New Town Pery is documented in the leases granted by Pery. For examples, see RD, 338/182/226771, Edmund Sexton Pery to Patrick Arthur Arthur, 11th November 1781: 'in front to the New Street is the same as is marked and laid out in a map made by Mr David Duchart'; Glucksman Library, University of Limerick, Pery leases, Edmund Sexton Pery to James Fisher, 31st January 1790: 'assigns all that and those the lot of ground marked number one in the plan of the New Town laid down by David Dukart, in one thousand seven hundred and sixty five'; Edmund Sexton Pery to Launcelot Hill, 26th April 1791: 'assigns all that and those the half plot of ground marked number three in the plan of a Newtown laid down by David Dukart in one thousand and seven hundred and sixty five'.

[82] Ferrar, *The History of Limerick*, 89, states that the plots and streets were marked out in June 1769. But see also Royal Irish Academy, Father White manuscript, MS 24 D 21, 191-92 (a transcription by Maurice Lenihan of the original in the possession of the Diocese of Limerick) which states that the streets and squares of the New Town were laid out in 1767.

[83] British Library, Add MS 27391 E. The map is undated but was most likely completed some-time between January and September 1769 when Percy was resident in Limerick. Colles hoped to find subscribers for a printed edition of the map (presumably with the permission of Percy), but it is not known if he was able to bring the project to completion; see *Limerick Chronicle*, 7th August 1769. In 1787 John Ferrar obtained permission from Percy (who succeeded his father as 2nd Duke of Northumberland in 1786) to use 'an actual survey in 1769' as the basis for a new map of the city drawn for him by Claude Joseph Sauthier, then resident in Percy's household; see Ferrar, *The History of Limerick*, xviii. A comparison of the Colles and Sauthier maps reveals that they have identical co-ordinates.

[84] Royal Irish Academy, Father White manuscript, MS 24 D 21, 191-92. In March 1768 Pery was given permission to borrow the scaffolding from the Custom House for use at the church build-ing site; see TNA Cust 1/101/110, 5th March 1768.

[85] Rosemary ffolliott, 'Devonsher of Co. Cork', *The Irish Ancestor*, 2, 1984, 71-74; Friends' Historical Library, Dublin, 'Registry of Births of Cork Monthly Meeting, to 1859'.

[86] NLI, MS 8630, 'Copy deed of the farm of Kilshanick, dated 30th March 1723, Lord Doneraile and Redmond Barry esq, to Jonas Devonshire, Merchant'.

[87] Friends' Historical Library, Dublin, MS E6D, P3, 'Diary of Joshua Wight'.

[88] Friends' Historical Library, Dublin, MM, VIII, F2, 'Testimonies of Disunity (1745-57)'.

[89] Friends' Historical Library, Dublin, MM, VIII, A5, Cork 5, Minutes Men's three weeks meet-ing (1752-56).

[90] Matthew Bodkin, 'Notes on the Irish parliament in 1772', *Proceedings of the Royal Irish Academy*, C, xlviii, 1942, 145-232, 184-88: 185. A reminder of Devonsher's conviviality sur-vives in a glass whiskey square bearing his name and dated 1761; Rosc, *Irish Glass* (Limerick 1971) 8.

[91] *Cork Chronicle*, 14th January 1765, *Cork Journal*, 5th January 1765, and *Cork Evening Journal*, 25th and 28th February 1765, all carry notices from Abraham Devonsher of Kilshannig advertising various properties in Cork. While these suggest that Devonsher was res-ident at Kilshannig in January 1765, they do not necessarily refer to the house in question.

[92] For a description see Desmond Guinness and William Ryan, *Irish Houses and Castles* (London

1971) 77-82.

93 Joseph McDonnell, *Irish Eighteenth-Century Stuccowork and its European sources* (Dublin 1991) 19-20, 56-59; Timothy Mowl and Brian Earnshaw, *An Insular Rococo: Architecture, Politics and Society in Ireland and England, 1710-1770* (London 1999) 245-48.

94 Matthew Bodkin, *Proceedings of the Royal Irish Academy*, C, xlviii, 1943, 145-232, 182-83, PRONI, Shannon Papers, MIC/465/1, Lord Shannon to James Dennis, 12th November 1775.

95 *HIP*, IV, 449-50; RD, 195/67/129060.

96 Friends Historical Library, Dublin, 'Registry of Deaths of Cork Monthly Meeting, to 1859'; *The Hibernian Chronicle*, 28th April 1783.

97 David Dickson, *Old World Colony: Cork and South Munster 1630-1830* (Cork 2005) 79-85.

98 John Burke and John Bernard Burke, *A Genealogical and Heraldic Dictionary of the Landed Gentry of Great Britain and Ireland* (London 1846) 40; Rosemary ffolliott, 'Rogers of Lota and Ashgrove', *Journal of the Cork Historical and Archaeological Society*, LXXII, 215, 1967, 75-80.

99 Charles Smith, *The Antient and Present State of the County and City of Cork,* 2 vols (Dublin 1750) I, 364.

100 To date, no documentary evidence that might enable a dating of Dukart's work at Lota has come to light. However, it was most likely to have been sometime before 1767 when Dukart's attention was fixed on various schemes in the North. The use of various features such as the oval windows with curved glazing bars found at the Mayoralty House raises the possibility that both buildings might have been underway during the same period, spring 1765 to spring 1767.

101 PRONI, Hervey-Bruce Papers, D/2798/2/51, Mick [Michael] Shanahan to Bishop of Derry, 2nd January 1784.

102 Trinity College, Dublin, MS 4030, 'Journal of the Reverend D.A. Beaufort', 10th September 1788.

103 Arthur Young, *A Tour in Ireland with General Observations on the Present State of that Kingdom*, II, part ii (Dublin 1780) 65; James H. Watmough, 'Letters of James H. Watmough to his wife, 1785', *The Pennsylvania Magazine of History and Biography*, XXIX, 1905, 31-43: 34.

104 Trinity College, Dublin, MS 4030, 'Journal of the Reverend D.A. Beaufort', 10th September 1788.

105 See Anne Crookshank and the Knight of Glin, *The Watercolours of Ireland: works on paper in pencil, pastel and paint c.1600-1914* (London 1994) 198-99. Two works by Hamilton depicting Lota have been located: the view reproduced here (Plate 15) and a view of the demesne from the house, now in the Richard Wood Collection. Two others, their present location unknown, are recorded in photographs in the IAA. One shows the house and demesne from Blackrock. The other, depicting the demesne with the house in the foreground, provides the most detailed record of the house at this period (Plate 16).

106 Cork Public Museum, 'Henry Hill Notebook', accessions number 1951.93. For an unsigned lithograph of the house of around 1857, when Lota was for sale through the encumbered estates court, see Mary Cecelia Lyons, *Illustrated Incumbered Estates; Ireland, 1850-1905* (Whitegate 1993) 190.

107 For descriptions of the house, see The Georgian Society, *Records of Eighteenth-Century Domestic Architecture and Decoration in Ireland*, 5 vols (Dublin 1909-13) V; [W.H. Wyndham-Quin], 'Castletown, County Kilkenny', *Country Life*, XLIV, 1131, 7th September

1918, 190-95, and 1132, 14th September 1918, 214-19; Guinness and Ryan, *Irish Houses and Castles*, 219-23; Seán O'Reilly, *Irish Houses and Gardens from the Archives of 'Country Life'* (London 1998) 46-55.

[108] PRONI, Abercorn Papers, D/623/A/38/93, William Brownlow to Earl of Abercorn, 17th September 1768. This is the earliest source to link Dukart directly to the building of Castletown. I am grateful to Livia Hurley for this reference. The earliest printed attribution of Castletown to Dukart is in William Tighe, *Statistical observations relative to the county of Kilkenny* (Dublin 1802) 589: 'Few private houses can shew a more beautiful façade, than the southern front of Mr Coxe's house at Castletown; the architect was Duchart, a Sardinian.' For early references to Castletown as the seat of Cox, see *Cork Journal*, 27th August 1767; *FJ*, 13th February 1768.

[109] The Georgian Society, *Records*, V, 79-80; Brian de Breffny, 'Stucco work by Patrick Osborne at Castletown Cox', *Irish Ancestor*, XIII, 1, 1981, 15-17; Seán O'Reilly, 'Patrick Osborne, an Irish Stuccodore', *GPA Irish Arts Review*, 1989-90, 119-27. A photocopy of the manuscript bill is in the IAA, RP.D.71.1.

[110] IAA, RP.D.71.1. Keogh's payment appears to have been more than twice what Dukart received for his work in Limerick. Byrum, the 'overseer of artisans and labourers' in Limerick, was granted £40 a year on his appointment in April 1765, and received his last payment – £30 for the previous three months – in August 1770.

[111] *FJ*, 25th January 1766.

[112] For the history of the estate, see de Breffny, 'Stucco Work by Patrick Osborne', 15-17. Cox's first wife, Anne Purcell, died shortly after their marriage in 1712, and in 1744 he married Anne O'Brien, daughter of an MP for Youghal, and granddaughter of the 3rd Earl of Inchiquin. She died in 1746 shortly after the birth of their only child, Richard; James B. Leslie, *Ossory Clergy and Parishes* (Enniskillen 1933) 28-29. When Richard married Maria Burton on 21st January 1766, celebrations took place at Cashel Palace; *FJ*, 25th January 1766; for marriage settlement of Maria Burton and Richard Cox see RD, 241/365/159605.

[113] NLI, Heron Papers, MSS 13,036/9, Michael Cashel [Cox] to Lord Buckinghamshire, 13th May 1778; A.P.W. Malcomson, *Archbishop Charles Agar: Churchmanship and Politics in Ireland, 1760-1810* (Dublin 2002) 201-02.

[114] A.P.W. Malcomson, *Primate Robinson 1709-94* (Belfast 2003) 50-51. For life at Castletown, see [Dorothea Herbert], *Retrospections of Dorothea Herbert 1770-1789* (London 1929) 9, 39-40. Following his death, aged ninety, at Castletown on 28th May 1779, Cox was buried in St Canice's Cathedral, Kilkenny. His epitaph, and that of Anne, is transcribed and translated in James Graves and John G. Augustus Prim, *The History, Architecture, and Antiquities of the Cathedral Church of St. Canice, Kilkenny* (Dublin 1857) 323-35.

[115] *FJ*, 2nd June 1770.

[116] Glin, 'The last Palladian in Ireland', 798-802.

[117] Colen Campbell's view in *Vitruvius Britannicus* (1717) 44 was perhaps the most widely circulated of the many contemporary prints of Buckingham House. Others include those by Sutton Nichols (1731), J. Maurer (1746) and John Tinney (1752).

[118] NLI, MS GO 424, 237-8.

[119] *HIP*, VI, 66.

[120] Sir Bernard Burke, *A Genealogical and Heraldic History of the Landed Gentry of Ireland*, 9th edition (London 1899). For Pigott-Wallis marriage settlement see RD, 229/178/1499.

[121] *Cork Journal*, 12th February 1765; *Cork Chronicle or Universal Register*, 31st March 1766. For the Wallis-Mercer marriage settlement see RD, 251/74/160219.

[122] Samuel Lewis, *Topographical Dictionary*, 2 vols (London 1837) II, 73.

[123] Timothy Gleeson, 'Some Account of Castles, etc., in the Neighbourhood of Castlemartyr', *Journal of the Cork Historical and Archaeological Society*, IA, 1892, 179-82; James H. Healy, *The Castles of County Cork* (Cork and Dublin 1988) 98; Denis Power, *Archaeological Inventory of County Cork, volume 2: East and South Cork* (Dublin 1994) 219.

[124] NLI, MS GO 424, 237-8.

[125] *HIP*, V, 117.

[126] Matthew Bodkin, 'Notes on the Irish parliament in 1772', *Proceedings of the Royal Irish Academy*, C, xlviii, 1942, 145-232: 182-83. Beaufort's reaction to the house on his visit in 1788 suggests that Dukart probably did no more than the roof: 'The house is very old and very low and bad.' Trinity College, Dublin, MS 4030, 'Journal of the Reverend D.A. Beaufort', 12th September 1788.

[127] *HIP*, IV, 490-91.

[128] *ibid*.

[129] *ibid*.

[130] *FJ*, 15th December 1767.

[131] Thomas Milton, *A Selection of Select Views from the Different Seats of the Nobility and Gentry in the Kingdom of Ireland* (London 1793) xix: 'The present house was built in the year 1768 under the inspection of Dukart, a gentleman of Italy, who practiced architecture in this country, on the site of a former house that was burnt down.' This is the earliest reference to Dukart at Brockley. See also *Anthologia Hibernica*, IV, September 1794, 185, and William Wilson, *Post-Chaise Companion* (Dublin 1784) 210.

[132] *HIP*, IV, 49, states, without source, that the Donnybrook house was designed by Dukart with ceiling work by the Francini brothers.

[133] The Georgian Society, *Records*, V, 73.

[134] Glin, 'A Baroque Palladian', 735-39: 738.

[135] Craig, *The Architecture of Ireland*, 192.

[136] *ibid*., 195.

[137] Glin, 'The last Palladian in Ireland', 798-802.

[138] Craig, *The Architecture of Ireland*, 195-96.

[139] E. McParland, 'James Gandon and the Royal Exchange Competition, 1768-69', *Journal of the Royal Society of Antiquaries of Ireland*, CII, 1972, 58-72: 68.

[140] Alistair Rowan, *The Buildings of Ireland: North West Ulster – The Counties of Londonderry, Fermanagh and Tyrone* (Harmondsworth 1979) 299, 362.

[141] de Breffny and ffolliott, *The Houses of Ireland* (London 1973) 142.

[142] O'Dwyer, 'Making Connections in Georgian Ireland', 22 (endnote 20).

[143] Glin, 'The last Palladian in Ireland', 801.

[144] Noting that some Dukartian motifs were often present in the repertoire of other architects, Maurice Craig commented: 'Some of these, notably [architraves of the upper windows broken upwards over the openings] have been used by other architects, for example Cassels, but together they say Ducart and only Ducart'. Craig, *The Architecture of Ireland*, 192.

[145] Peard family tree kindly supplied to the author by Mr F.W. Peard.

[146] Glin, 'The last Palladian in Ireland', 801.

[147] NLI, Townley Hall Papers, MSS 14,917-25.

[148] PRONI, Coddington Papers, T/2519/12/11, 'Resolutions of the commissioners appointed for carrying on the Boyne Navigation'. I am grateful to Livia Hurley for bringing this source to my attention.

[149] PRONI, Coddington Papers, T/2519/12/11.

[150] *ibid.*

[151] *CJI*, VIII, 14th November 1767, 184.

[152] *CJI*, VIII, 16th November 1767, clxxiii; *CJI*, VIII, 25th November 1767, 201-02. Dukart does not appear to have been directly involved in 1771 when Parliament was again petitioned for funds to complete the Dundalk harbour works; see *CJI*, 21st November 1771, 438.

[153] *A Letter to the Commissioner of the Inland Navigation Concerning the Tyrone Collieries* (Dublin 1752); 'Publicola', *The Irish Colleries and Canal Defended* (Dublin 1753).

[154] *CJI*, IX, 94, 2nd November 1753.

[155] *CJI*, VIII, part 2, clxxxi, 17th November 1767.

[156] *CJI*, VIII, part 2, clxxx, 17th November 1767.

[157] PRONI, Castle Stewart Papers, D/1618/15/6/34, 'Relative to Mr Dukart's plan of a navigation from Farlough to Derry, 1767'; *CJI*, VIII, clxxxi, 1767.

[158] *CJI*, VIII, appendix, ccxlix, 7th May 1768; *CJI*, VIII, cccviii, 20th November 1769.

[159] *FJ*, 17th October 1768; PRONI, Abercorn Papers, D/623/A/38/100, Davis Dukart to William Brownlow, 19th October 1768.

[160] CJI, XII, appendix, dxxxv-xxxix, 16th April 1787, 'Report from the committee apointed to enquire into the state of the navigation from Lough Neagh to the Collieries in the Count of Tyrone, and of the best methods of working the said Collieries.'

[161] *FJ*, 21st June 1771

[162] John Smeaton, 'Mr. Smeaton's opinion on Mr Jessop's report on the Tyrone Canal', *Reports of the late John Smeaton*, 2 vols (1812) II, 278-79.

[163] *ibid.*

[164] *CJI*, XII, appendix, dxxxv-xxxix, 16th April 1787.

[165] William Chapman, *Observations on the Various Systems of Canal Navigation* (1797) 5-7. See also M.B. Mullins 'An historical sketch of engineering in Ireland', *Transactions of the Institution of Civil Engineers of Ireland*, VI, 1836, 28.

[166] 'An elevation of the navigable bridge on the new Tyrone navigation, designed and executed by David Dukart, engineer in the year 1768, under the inspection of Thomas Penrose', George Breeze, *Society of Artists in Ireland: index of exhibits, 1765-90* (Dublin 1985) 21.

[167] *CJI*, VIII, cccxi, 18th November 1769.

[168] For a description of the house and demesne, see Jeremy Musson, 'Lissan House, Co. Tyrone', *County Life*, 12th March 1998. The earliest documented attribution of the bridge to Dukart is in G. Vaughan Sampson, *Statistical Survey of the County of Londonderry* (Dublin 1802) 411: 'Among persons of the first order I may class Mr. Staples of Lissane ... The river is managed so as to form a beautiful sheet of water, surrounded by stately trees, and a smooth green margin. The water afterwards tumbles over an abstraction, there is beside it a neat bridge, built by the famous Ducart.'

[169] PRONI, Hervey-Bruce Papers, D/2798/2/1O, Davis Dukart to Bishop of Derry, 13th February 1769.

[170] *ibid.*: 'I have made such a progress in my designs of a bridge for the city of Londonderry that I

can with certainty assure your lordship a stone bridge executed in the best manner will not exceed the sum of £32000 – I am also drawing the plan of a wooden bridge but how much this will cost I cannot ascertain as yet. This much I beg you will do me the favour to believe that I shall do my best in both & when all the papers relative to them are ready, I shall have no objection to their being perused and examined by people of taste and knowledge.'

[171] PRONI, 'Corporation of L'Derry Minute Book from 1765 to 1780', LA 79/2A/8B, 83, 13th April 1769.

[172] *ibid.*, 2nd May 1769, 84.

[173] PRONI, Abercorn Papers, D/623/A/38/186, James Hamilton to Abercorn.

[174] *ibid.*

[175] *ibid.*, D/623/A/19/40, Abercorn to William Brownlow, 31st July 1768.

[176] *ibid.*

[177] *ibid.*, D/623/A/38/94, Dukart to William Brownlow, 20th August 1768.

[178] *ibid.* Dukart's suggestion to Brownlow that Pery might have a part in deciding his fee suggests that he had learned that Pery and Brownlow had discussed the canal project and the role that Dukart might play in it.

[179] *ibid.*, D/623/A/38/93, Brownlow to Abercorn, 27th September 1768.

[180] *ibid.*, D/623/A/38/100, Dukart to Brownlow, 19th October 1768.

[181] *ibid.*

[182] *ibid.*, D623/A/19/52, Abercorn to Hamilton, 6th November 1768.

[183] *ibid.*

[184] *ibid.*, D/623/A/21/73, Abercorn to John Hamilton, 18th January 1774.

[185] *ibid.*, D/623/A/42/10, James Hamilton to Abercorn, 25th February 1774.

[186] *ibid.*, D/623/A/42/14, James Hamilton to Abercorn, 25th March 1774.

[187] *ibid.*, D/623/A/21/86, Abercorn to Hamilton, 7th April 1774.

[188] Eoin Magennis, 'Coal, Corn and Canals: The Disposal of Parliamentary Moneys 1695-1772' in David Hayton (ed), *The Irish Parliament in the Eighteenth Century: The Long Apprenticeship* (Edinburgh 2001) 71-86.

[189] *CJI*, VIII, cccviii, 20th November 1769. On 1st November 1753 the Archbishop of Armagh gave a thirty-one-year lease on the mining rights of Drumglass, with provision for the following shares in the royalties or profits: Archbishop of Armagh, eight-fortieths; Archbishop of Tuam, nine-fortieths; Arthur Hill, five-fortieths; James Caulfeild, nine-fortieths; Thomas Staples, nine-fortieths. The purchase of the shares of the archbishops of Armagh and Tuam, and Arthur Hill gave Dukart a 55% share in the company; see RD, 404/166/267540.

[190] *BN*, 29th September 1769.

[191] *FJ*, 25th June 1771.

[192] *BN*, 23rd October 1769.

[193] *ibid.*, 11th December 1770.

[194] *ibid.*, 22nd September 1775.

[195] *ibid.*, 24th March 1772.

[196] *ibid.*, 22nd September 1775.

[197] PRONI, Armagh Registry Papers, DIO 4/13/5/2.

[198] Richard Griffith, *Geological and Mining Surveys of the Coal Districts of the Counties of Tyrone and Antrim in Ireland* (Dublin 1829) 35.

[199] *CJI*, VIII, cccviii, 20th November 1769.

[200] *BN*, 8th October 1771; *Proceedings of the Dublin Society*, 30th May 1771, 18th March 1773.

[201] Young, *A Tour in Ireland*, II, part ii, 91.

[202] For colliery output during the period 1770-78, see PRONI, Armagh Registry Papers, DIO 4/13/5/2.

[203] Griffith, *Geological and Mining Surveys*, 41.

[204] A. Fowler and J.A. Robbie, *Geology of the County Tyrone around Dungannon* (Belfast 1961).

[205] John Rylands University Library, Bagshawe of Ford Papers, B 3/16/82, Davis Dukart to Sir James Caldwell, 25th July 1775. I am grateful to Toby Barnard for bringing this and the following sources in the Bagshawe Papers to my attention.

[206] *ibid*.

[207] *ibid*., B 3/20/13, Sir James Caldwell to Mr Archdall, 29th January 1776; see also Davis Ducart to Sir James Caldwell, 24th October 1775, B3/16/83. Dukart was introduced to Caldwell by James Fortescue in 1770; see *ibid*., B 3/10/5, 995-7, James Fortescue to Sir James Caldwell, 16th August 1770.

[208] PRONI, Armagh Registry Papers, DIO 4/13/5/2.

[209] RD, 404/166/267540; NLI, MS GO 424, 237-8.

[210] *BN*, 6th February 1781.

[211] John Temple, *The History of the General Rebellion in Ireland, 7th ed.* (Cork 1766), subscribers list at front.

[212] PRONI, D/623/A/38/100, D/623/38/94, D/2798/2/1, DIO 4/13/5/4, T/2519/12/11; 'To the right honourable and honourable the committee of the honourable house of Commons: the report of Davis Dukart, Superintendent of the Canal to the Tyrone Collieries', 16th November 1769 in *CJI*, 1769, cccxi

[213] *BN*, 7th December 1773.

[214] *Londonderry Journal*, 14th April 1775. I am grateful to Dr W. Roulston for this reference.

[215] NLI, MS GO 424, 237-8. Dukart's properties most likely included the two parcels of land totalling 14$\frac{1}{2}$ acres at Brackaville recorded in a map 'Coal Island being part of the Estate of Thomas Christy Esqr lying in the County of Tyrone by James Anderson', 18th April 1780, (private collection, county Tyrone). In 1766 Dukart leased 'the rock field', a two-acre property at Glasheen, near Cork, from Thomas Roberts; see RD, 228/572/152525.

[216] RD, 404/166/267540.

[217] The Georgian Society, *Records*, V, 72; NLI, MS GO 424, 237-8.

ILLUSTRATIONS

The following photographic credits arrived too late to be included in the captions:
– A.E. Henson – plates 18-21, 27, 29
– John Logan – plates 8, 28
– Dara McGrath – plates 11, 12
– W.A. McCutcheon – plates 33, 34, 36, 37

———

1 – Mezzotint of Sir James Caldwell
(courtesy Daniel Kinahan)

The artistic and cultural activities of the Caldwells of Castle Caldwell, 1750-1783

TOBY BARNARD

THE CALDWELLS BELONGED TO A SECTION OF IRISH PROTESTANT SOCIETY thought to have contributed much to the material and intellectual worlds of eighteenth-century Ireland. A Caldwell arrived from Scotland during the plantation of Ulster early in the seventeenth century, and settled first in Enniskillen. Soon the family covered its tracks as traders with the acquisition of land. As part of the transformation, the Caldwells moved to Rossbeg, later renamed Castle Caldwell, on the shores of Lough Erne. Ornamented with a baronetcy in 1683, they settled into the modes of well-to-do landowners.[1] However, they were not in the uppermost stratum (of peers), nor did they ever serve as members of the Dublin parliament. Their circumstances, while comfortable, were not easy. Measured by known income – approximately £2,300 in 1770 – they fell below the hurdle, conventionally set at £3,000 per annum, which had to be vaulted to enter the peerage.[2]

Much of the interest of the Caldwells lies in their idiosyncrasies. Although part of the Protestant élite of Hanoverian Ireland, they do not wholly conform to the stereotypes of their order. Some of the family archive survives to tantalise. Intermittently, the eighteenth-century Caldwells' spending, patronage and cultural interests can be illumined. This account, inevitably constrained by the fragmentary records, considers their houses – primarily Castle Caldwell, but also in Dublin – how they were modified, furnished and used. In addition to trying to reconstruct the physical realities of the Caldwells' lives, this essay speculates about the attitudes that inspired or arose from the material worlds.

— I —

James Caldwell (Plate 1), born about 1720, succeeded his father as 4th Baronet in 1744.[3] In 1753 he married Elizabeth Hort, a daughter of the Archbishop of Tuam. Caldwell had received a conventional education – a good school in Dundalk, then Trinity College, Dublin. To complete his preparation, he was despatched on an educational grand tour. Such finishing to give a high gloss to those of his rank was becoming more common, but remained far from universal. In later life, Caldwell would utilise the connections that he had established during his time abroad. Initially, he studied in France, but he also took in Switzerland and northern Italy. Life outside Ireland appealed enough for him to enter the Austrian imperial army. This seems to have been a congenial episode, and, in terms of the lasting links and rewards, profitable. He was made a knight of the Holy Roman Empire and a count. He was also given personal mementoes by the empress, Maria Theresa. Two points are worth extracting from this continental phase. The empire was a Catholic state. Its army, ecclesiastical institutions and territories offered refuge to others from Ireland, but mostly Catholics. Protestants did venture to Vienna and Prague, but seldom made careers there.

Sir James Caldwell thrived in the cosmopolitan world, but other than to exploit his well-placed contacts he was not specific about what he had seen and liked in Central Europe – like county Fermanagh, a borderland, but a rather different one. The all-too-obvious legacy from the imperial sojourn was dissatisfaction with the smaller arena in which, once returned to Ireland in 1749, he now strutted, and the inadequate outlets for and appreciation of his talents. Caldwell developed an obsession. He wanted his imperial distinctions to be matched by similar recognition in Ireland. He craved elevation to the peerage. The craving possessed him. Most of his recorded activities throughout the remainder of his life centred on this obsessive quest. Indeed, the documents that survive have been carefully weeded and preserved by Caldwell – and, it has to be suspected, doctored by him – to back his claims to ennoblement. Reasonably, he might suppose that a hereditary honour from an ancient empire would bring him the Irish distinction that he sought. The Empire was vast and polytheistic. There, unlike in the Ireland of his day, it was possible for those of confessions other than the State religion of Catholicism to serve and prosper. This difference in policy, however, was not one that he ever directly acknowledged.

The impact of Caldwell's long stay in Continental Europe is obvious in some of the arrangements that he introduced onto his Fermanagh inheritance. He was unusual, but hardly unique in his exposure to foreign modes. The ideological and artistic consequences of travel for the *moeurs* of the members of the incipient Irish Protestant ascendancy have yet to be fully explored. The grand tourists from Ireland who have been studied in detail – Edward Lovett Pearce, Lord Charlemont, Joseph Leeson – were those who headed to Italy and the Mediterranean.[4] More numerous and arguably more typical were those who meandered through the Low Countries (popular for education and medical training), the German states, Switzerland and the Empire. This was a point emphasised by the contemporary bookseller, George Faulkner.[5] Caldwell, despite the lengthy period in Austria, always communicated with his acquaintances there in the French language, not (as might have been expected) in German. Caldwell, to judge from the surviving letters and memoranda, noted most keenly agricultural and proto-industrial novelties, the look of places and inhabitants, architectural spectacles, diet and music.

Immersion in Continental ways was combined with familiarity with London and other parts of England, notably Bath and the west of England. It was a visit to kinsfolk in Derbyshire, not the west of Ireland or central Europe, that provoked Caldwell's observation, 'the natives are rather slovenly in their dress, but within doors have everything very neat and are in their way very civil and good natured.'[6] Despite the Caldwells' origins in Scotland, and Caldwell's eagerness to discover his aristocratic antecedents there, he never visited the northern kingdom. Within Ireland, too, his travels seem to have followed well-trodden routes. His circuits were concentrated in the north, Dublin and its environs, with occasional forays into the midlands. He had little or no first-hand knowledge of Munster. Instead he relied on information from correspondents there, such as the younger Sir Richard Cox from Dunmanway, and members of the family who travelled further south.[7]

The range of experiences and influences that Caldwell brought to the business of estate management in county Fermanagh was greatly enlarged by his marriage in 1753. His bride was Elizabeth Hort, the eldest daughter of Josiah Hort, successively Bishop of Kilmore and Archbishop of Tuam. Hort was disliked as yet another prelate imported from England, and castigated for neglecting his duties. It was alleged that he had shouted so loudly at an errant coachman that he lost his voice. This misfortune explained his reluctance to preach; the search for a restorative justified long absences from Ireland.[8] Nevertheless, Hort belonged to a circle of zealous Protestants with a taste for charitable works.[9] In addition, his long occupancy of bishoprics enabled him to improve the family fortunes.[10] Archbishop Hort left his children well educated, steeped in the fundamentals of practical Christianity, and financially secure. Elizabeth was bequeathed £5,000, together with the Horts' house in Dawson Street, Dublin, 'a pretty house large enough for an Irish peer and elegantly furnished', its furniture, silver plate (reckoned to amount to 1,600 ounces) and paintings. She was also to have the jewels that she usually wore; they were valued at £700.[11]

Such were the financial difficulties facing Caldwell that his wife's dowry was quickly treated as an asset to relieve his own embarrassments. In the short term, the

Dublin house was let to a series of tenants (including bishops), for £150 for one parliamentary winter.[12] The tenancies were not altogether satisfactory. Prospective tenants demanded reductions in the rent.[13] Meanwhile, the condition of the house deteriorated.[14] Rather than themselves conducting the troublesome negotiations for short-term lets, the Caldwells made a more permanent agreement with an architect and property developer, Francis Sandys, reputed to be 'so very nick-knack and clever in many things'.[15] Sandys leased the house for 140 years at an annual £66 (Alderman Crampton had offered £60).[16] He reordered, redecorated and furnished afresh the interior, so that by 1773 he could sublet it for six months to Sir Richard St George at a rent of £140.[17] The arrangement did not entirely free the Caldwells from worry about the Dublin house. Furthermore, it created a fresh problem. Where would they stay when they came to town? Caldwell on his own could lodge at an inn, rent rooms or cosher with friends. But in the 1770s Lady Caldwell proposed to bring the family to Dublin, and had to contrive where they might be accommodated respectably and economically. This scheme, as will be seen, involved her in demeaning pleas to grander relations. By this juncture, a combination of factors – the expense of the regime that Caldwell insisted on in county Fermanagh and his own inclinations – recommended a contraction of the country establishment and life in or near the capital. Before these plans could really take concrete form, illness obliged the couple to dip into the cures of Bath. Elizabeth Caldwell died in 1778. Sir James, as a widower, was freer to follow his own fancies, accepting invitations in England (for example, at the Lascelles' Harewood) and inhaling the sea air of Sidmouth in Devonshire.

—— II ——

According to the laws of the time, Sir James Caldwell, on marriage, gained control over much of his wife's property. Yet she did not relinquish interest in the Dublin house that she had inherited, even when she agreed that it must be let. In the mid-1750s, the couple's life was focussed on the estate beside Lough Erne. In part, this was because Sir James Caldwell's attention shifted to the improvement of mansion and lands. Also, the birth of children restricted Elizabeth Caldwell's jaunting. Soon her husband's incurable restiveness would uproot him, turning him into an intermittent absentee. However, during the earlier years of marriage, the couple shared happily in the schemes to modernise, enlarge and embellish house and grounds. In practice, owing to the frequent absences of Sir James Caldwell, much of the planning and superintendence of the works fell to Lady Caldwell. As overseer, she was not just the passive executor of Sir James's orders, she also took decisions about the design and furnishing of the house. In doing so, she drew on her own observations and preferences, and on the suggestions of friends and kindred.

2 – Castle Caldwell
1780, engraving

An early example of Elizabeth Caldwell's access to the aesthetic judgement of a larger circle came in 1752 (before she was married). Having enquired about the repair and possible copying of Hort family portraits, a correspondent in England recommended Nathaniel Hone as 'the best painter here of that sort'. Hone, it was reported, 'is a very fine man, who keeps his coach, the son of an Irish tobacconist, and he means very shortly to go and visit his friends in Ireland, and to stay there about 3 weeks.' Elizabeth Hort was assured that Hone could draw a miniature from the large portrait of her father in the Dublin house.[18] Portraiture soon gave way to the more urgent priority of improving Castle Caldwell (Plate 2). At first, the Caldwells contented themselves with renewing the roof and internal rearrangements. Storm damage also necessitated patching.[19] In 1758 an addition of two rooms to enhance the look of the main façade was considered. Again, there was no shortage of advice. Lady Caldwell's brother, the future Sir John Hort, explained to her the advantages of collecting as many opinions as possible. Once a draft design had been prepared, 'let it lie open in the parlour, explain to all who ask and hear what they have to say from Inigo Jones down to Darley, which may chance to give you twenty little improvements you never dreamt of.'[20]

Within the Caldwells' ambit there was no shortage of advisers – expert, *soi-disant* expert, or ignorant but opinionated. John Hort and the redoubtable Lady Arbella Denny, distantly related to the Caldwells, freely offered guidance.[21] Later, Caldwell listed among his papers copies of the designs for Lord Fairfax's house in York, Sir Francis Dashwood's West Wycombe Park, and Lord Marchmont's seat in Scotland.[22] Dashwood and Marchmont were known to Caldwell, and so acquaintanceship may be enough to explain the presence of those designs at Castle Caldwell. However, another paper by Carr, Fairfax's architect, may indicate that Carr was considered for works at Castle Caldwell, or even consulted.[23] Carr's only recorded link with Ulster, in Armagh, would come later through Archbishop Robinson.[24]

No evidence identifies the main architect of the rebuilding of Castle Caldwell in the early 1760s. This uncertainty may reflect exactly the collaboration of amateurs proposed by Hort to his sister. Practical needs, as well as the grandiose notions of Sir James Caldwell and the wish of the couple to put a distinctive and modern stamp on their home, prompted the building campaign. Castle Caldwell had to house a lengthening train of children, Caldwell's widowed mother and seven servants.[25]

If the identity of the architect is unknown, the 'conductor' of building operations was Whitmore Davis. Described as 'architect and bricklayer' and initially as of Newbliss, county Monaghan, Davis was active in the district.[26] When approached about the Castle Caldwell job in 1762, he was working at Edward Madden's house at Spring Grove, near Clones.[27] It fell to Lady Caldwell, with her husband away first in London and then in Dublin, to negotiate terms with him. Davis submitted a detailed schedule of what he would oversee. The east and south fronts of the ground floor were to be of hammered stone, ten feet high, clear of the vaults. The next floor was to be fifteen feet in height, and the attic seven feet and coved within. Brick would be used for the bulk of the walling, but a chamfered base of cut stone with rusticated quoins and a frontispiece according to the Doric order gave greater presence. The choice of Doric may have paid tribute to Caldwell's military prowess since the order had martial connotations. It would remind of his foreign service and his more recent exploits in raising locally a troop of light infantry. Also there would be cut-stone window surrounds and sills. The cornice would conceal the gutter to deal with rainwater, clearly a worry in the damp locality. Inside, oak was to be used for doors and for the windows, crown glass either from Bristol or Newcastle for the glazing. Davis undertook to complete the building according to the schedule for £840.[28]

Davis, assisted by his son, was to superintend the work of 'common stone layers, stone cutters otherwise masons, bricklayers, carpenters, slaters, plasterers and glaziers'. He boasted 'never work of this kind done so cheap in Ireland'. Soon

enough, winter, with the Christmas holiday and poor weather, interrupted operations. Ominously it was reported in December 1762 that the workmen were dispers-
ing to Dublin for the impending festival.[29] Davis had offered to vary the terms on
which the men were engaged with the changing seasons. While the hours of day-
light were long, they would receive a daily rate; during shorter winter days, the men
would be paid 'by the great', that is for what they actually did.[30] Their departure,
prompted by wintry conditions, meant that building was suspended. This delay gave
Lady Caldwell an opportunity to revise Davis's terms.[31] Originally he had asked to
be paid one guinea weekly, together with a room in which to lodge, diet, an
allowance of ale and specific travelling expenses. This pay was reduced to 18s
weekly. At the same time, the wages of the masons and bricklayers were lowered
from the original weekly 10s 6d to 7s 7d.[32] Elizabeth Caldwell hoped to bring Davis
down to a weekly wage of 12s and the skilled workers to a mere 6s 6d. She
achieved a reduction by inviting others – Robert Wallace and William Moore – to
tender with alternatives.[33] In the event, she stuck to Davis, but was soon wondering
if Wallace would not have been preferable. In the summer of 1763, Lady Caldwell
complained that Davis and the masons had succumbed to what she euphemistically

3 – Whitmore Davis, DESIGN FOR STABLES AT CASTLE CALDWELL
(courtesy John Rylands Library, Manchester)

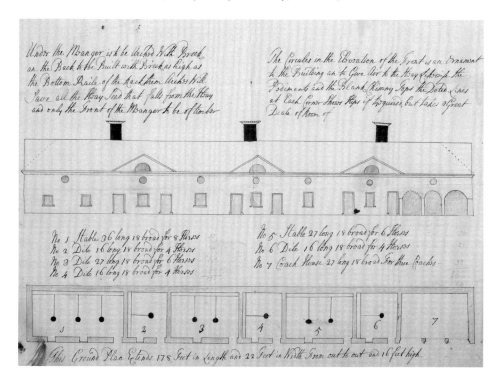

termed 'whiskey fever'.[34] Yet, even with such failings, Davis was entrusted with other projects on the estate, among them a stable block (Plate 3).

Davis brought his own familiar groups of specialist workers to Castle Caldwell. For some tasks the Caldwells engaged others. Their preferred carpenter was from Dublin – Patrick Gernon. His contract required him to execute the commission, 'completely, thoroughly and workmanlike, according to the exact rules of such work done in the city of Dublin'. Gernon was to attend and oversee the work in person. As supervisor he would be paid 15s weekly, over and above payment for specific pieces of work. Gernon, evidently the smart Dubliner, would travel in the stage coach as far as Cavan and then be provided with a horse to ride to Castle Caldwell. It was envisaged that he might also have to journey to Sligo to find suitable timber. He would be paid 4s 10d daily for such trips.[35] It is probable that Sir James Caldwell in Dublin located Gernon. Meanwhile, his wife contracted with the best glazier in Enniskillen.[36]

In the intimate company of landowners with the Caldwells' resources and status, information about the merits and demerits of particular operatives was readily shared. Shortcomings were soon spotted and reported. Within the Caldwells' neighbourhood, the Wards were builders to be avoided, but Alexander Boggs was approved. Yet, the Wards, despite a low reputation, found work at Castle Caldwell, as elsewhere in the north-west.[37] Boggs (also known as Bogg and Bagg) emerges as a more substantial figure, with some claim to be regarded as an architect rather than simply a master mason and contracting builder. He is credited with the design of the church at Belleek, a commission probably entrusted to him by the Caldwells.[38] He also built the barracks and some houses in Belturbet.[39] Boggs, on the strength of Caldwell's recommendation and his work for Mervyn Archdale at Castle Archdale (also on Lough Erne), was employed as clerk of the works at Ardbraccan, where the bishop of Meath, Henry Maxwell, was erecting a mansion. Maxwell deemed Boggs 'an active stirring man'.[40] Indeed, Boggs's reputation ensured his employment by other Church of Ireland bishops in Ulster.[41] The Caldwells, having undertaken their works, added to the store of knowledge within their circle about pitfalls and pleasures in using the different operatives.

—— III ——

With structural work completed, the house had to be equipped and run in appropriate style. Once more, it is difficult to separate the choices of Lady Caldwell and Sir James. Furthermore, the occasional illumination, through bills and letters, may be misleading about which spouse was responsible for specific decisions. Bills for furnishings and artefacts were usually sent to Sir James Caldwell, and it was he who normally paid them. It does not follow that it was he who had chosen the supplier or the particular object. Equally, the guidance that rained down on Elizabeth Caldwell, from her brother and female relations and friends, was not necessarily heeded. During the 1760s, motherhood tended to maroon her at Castle Caldwell. She was eager to keep abreast of changing fashions in dress and furniture. She did not want for advice, some of it unsolicited. A sister commiserated with her in her rural isolation and urged her to plunge anew into the hectic round of Dublin pleasures.[42] Later, her brother, by now settled in Portugal as British Consul, also blamed Castle Caldwell for her declining health, and counselled escape to the sun. Elizabeth Caldwell herself had at first shared her husband's enthusiasms. Gradually, as she was obliged by his gadding to maintain the household in Fermanagh, she lost patience. She wanted the costly establishment at Castle Caldwell scaled down, and for the family to remove itself to Dublin. But there, the Dawson Street residence was no longer available. Lady Caldwell asked her grander connection, Lady Shelburne, if she and her family could stay in Shelburne House on St Stephen's Green while its owners were absent. She was snubbed.[43] Instead, Lady Caldwell contemplated taking a more modest place in Dublin for £70 per annum. Further economies could be practised by bringing essential furnishings from Castle Caldwell.

By 1773 Lady Caldwell believed that her husband's zest for provincial life had abated. He himself had earlier admitted his restlessness. In 1757, after his first extended bout of estate management, he grew bored, and he searched for fresh outlets for his energies. For a time he found satisfying alternatives – raising a militia troop, proffering political advice and writing tracts. In turn, he wearied of the novel activities, and redirected his efforts onto Castle Caldwell. He aimed to make the estate a nonpareil through the entertainments that he offered and the innovations and improvements that he sponsored among his tenants. The projects were all linked to his quest to be raised to the Irish peerage. His elegant manner of living would demonstrate definitively how well qualified he was for the honour.

That manner of living, as will be suggested, owed something to what he remembered from his years in central Europe and more to what he observed of the arrangements of grander neighbours. Less easily distinguished are the preferences introduced by his long-suffering wife. Certainly, Elizabeth Caldwell picked the brains of her correspondents. From Dublin, Lady Arbella Denny guided about wallpapers, sofas, silver and chimney pieces. Lady Arbella, a formidable widow distantly related to the Caldwells, was a stickler for social niceties, many of which were being abandoned by the casual young.[44] On the Caldwells' behalf, she procured looking glasses from Booker and chimney pieces of variegated Egyptian marble from Darley.[45] She sketched designs for sofas and suggested that the horse hair for stuffing them could be had more cheaply in the country.[46] She was imperious in her recommendations about papering rooms. She urged Lady Caldwell to hang one room with a white grounded paper similar to that in her own dressing room at Peafield. Lady Arbella claimed that she had used eleven sorts of paper, at a total cost of approximately £8. She informed her country kinswoman that a fine yellow paper resembling caffoy could be had for eight or nine shillings per dozen. She admired red paper that imitated flock as 'very handsome', but warned that it was hard to match with fabrics such as moreen and serge. Stripes would do well for a bedroom but looked very ugly in the drawing room. Even so, this arbiter of taste conceded that Lord Hertford was said to have furnished an apartment in his London house with it. She further warned her country cousin that, 'a great many people of the first fashion have the paper of their rooms no lower than the sur base'. Others papered below the chair rail: an effect that she felt prettier, since it made the room look finished.[47] She applauded Lady Caldwell's choice of green and white checked fabric in the drawing room since it 'will be much the mode'. She also wrote, 'I much approve of your design of the bookcases with looking glass doors. They will be commodious & cheerful.' She went on to warn that they were likely to cost £40.[48]

Perhaps the most striking instance of the assistance offered by Lady Arbella Denny, both in aesthetic judgement and practicalities, relates to an earlier commission for a silver coffee pot wanted by the Caldwells. It was to be given as a present, perhaps at a wedding between a Gregg and a Walshe. Lady Arbella tried three silversmiths in Dublin.

> I, finding Mr Walsh the dearest, have rejected him. I bespoke a coffee jug to hold something more than a quart from Mr Holmes. It is to come to seven pounds, of which 1 guinea and half is to be for fashion. Mr Walsh would have 3 guineas for fashion & Mr Champian 46s. I am not to take it after 'tis made if I don't like it, but I have given him a Dutch coffee jug that I brought out of England to make it by.

Nearly two months later, Lady Arbella reported that

> the coffee pot I bespoke of Holmes, who is to have 7s 10d per ounce, it all came to £11 & be done in a fortnight. Mr Walsh would have 8s & no less. A smaller coffee pot I am satisfied would be ungenteel to give, so 'tis best at once as Sir James & your ladyship says do it well at first, for that satisfies.[49]

The coffee pot may have been given away. But even in the matter of gifts, those of the first fashion, or aspiring to be of it, trod warily between the genteel and ungenteel. In finishing their own houses, such avatars of refinement and discernment as Lady Arbella Denny and the Caldwells faced even greater opportunities and hazards for impressing or distressing. Little of the detail of the fixtures and fittings at Castle Caldwell can now be reconstructed. The meagre scraps of evidence show conventional choices, with the Caldwells following the prevailing modes. They ordered their mirrors from Booker, their knives and forks with handles stained green from Read's, their books and stationery from George Faulkner – all in Dublin.[50] Families of the consequence of the Caldwells announced their lineage and linkages through the paintings that hung in their houses. Lady Caldwell, as has been mentioned, wanted to safeguard the portrait of her father, Archbishop Hort. Whether or not Hone undertook the work is unknown. In the representation of themselves and their offspring, the Caldwells did not lack advice. Sir James, while dining at Castle Ward, was buttonholed by Lady Clanwilliam. She sang the praises of John Trotter, recently returned to Ireland from Rome. However, Caldwell escaped her clutches without committing himself to Trotter.[51]

The one artist known to have been patronised by the Caldwells was based in London. Sir James Caldwell went to England at the end of 1759 to further his projects, and returned there in 1760. While pursing political and personal objectives, he had time to commission works from Thomas Frye. Of Irish background, Frye had removed to London, where he won fame through his promotion of the Bow porcelain factory. Concurrently he continued to paint portraits, but also scraped a dazzlingly innovative series of mezzotints of male and female heads (Plate 5). Caldwell subscribed to the first dozen of the series. Frye aimed to have two-hundred subscriptions: subscribers would pay one guinea in advance and another guinea on publication. At the same time, Caldwell paid Frye six guineas for his own picture in 'crayons'. Frye also repaired and finished two miniatures for Caldwell (Plate 4).[52]

Interest and even practical accomplishment in painting and drawing were

4 – Bill of Thomas Frye, 1760, 'For repairing and finishing two miniatures', and for Sir James Caldwell's 'picture in Crayon' (courtesy John Rylands Library, Manchester)

Thomas Frye (1710-62)

5 – A YOUNG MAN HOLDING AN OPEN BOOK BEFORE HIM, A LIGHTED CANDLE TO THE RIGHT,

1760, mezzotint from series of 12 (collection of Anthony O'Connor and the author)

6 – SIR JAMES CALDWELL
1760 (private collection)

attributes approved among those of the Caldwells' station. Lady Arbella Denny had an informed interest in this, as in most other matters. Among the Caldwells, one daughter developed talents that were reckoned to surpass the customary. Arbella Caldwell, a goddaughter of Lady Arbella, was frequently praised for her facility in music and painting. She compiled and illustrated a journal of a tour through the north of Ireland.[53] She supplied Arthur Young, the agricultural propagandist, with sketches to remind him of what he had seen on his visit to the north of Ireland and thereby to assist him in writing a detailed account. Her godmother, Lady Arbella, bequeathed her money for drawing equipment. Seemingly the younger woman had unusual culinary skills, and delighted her godmother with the gift of a 'badger ham'.[54] In 1778 Arbella Caldwell recorded her part in a droll masquerade when, at last, she, her siblings and her mother came to stay in Dublin. 'Half the part was acted and for the rest, I went around talking Irish sometimes to those of my own class.'[55] Her joie de vivre made her a favourite. The proficiency in Irish may suggest a growing fascination with indigenous culture among contemporaries. The most conspicuous example was Charlotte Brooke, who had a residual Fermanagh link. Arbella Caldwell's talents led to her copying (or perhaps even forging) documents wanted by her father in his increasingly desperate bid for ennoblement.[56] Alas, no example of Arbella Caldwell's writing or painting has been identified to assess whether her abilities would bear comparison with those of Laetitia Bushe or Mary Delany.

— IV —

Arthur Young, to whom Arbella Caldwell sent drawings, was one of numerous visitors who attested to the pleasures of Castle Caldwell. Young's *Tour* gratifyingly publicised Caldwell's sustained and apparently successful campaign of improvement on his holdings.[57] Indeed, the regime that he had introduced at Castle Caldwell was intended to elicit exactly this kind of praise. Being feted as a model landlord could only strengthen his claim on a peerage. Many of Caldwell's innovations were common to the improvers who abounded by the mid-eighteenth century. Altruism and public spirit combined with mercenary calculations about how best to raise the revenues of estates. In the case of Caldwell, the need to lift his income above £3,000 was an unacknowledged motive in his strenuous exertions. Increases of this magnitude were never achieved.

Less usual in Caldwell's dispositions were three elements. He devised celebratory pageants to reward tenants and workers. The most elaborate, billed 'the jubilee', was advertised to a wider world, not just by processions through his territory, but in printed accounts. Caldwell appreciated the potential of print to bring his achievements to wider notice. Self-advertisement of this sort had occurred before:

7 – Castle Caldwell, c.1880
(Lawrence Collection, courtesy National Library of Ireland)

Richard Purcell at Kanturk and the younger Sir Richard Cox at Dunmanway were obvious precursors.[58]

Music featured prominently in the gala, and also in the private entertainments with which the Caldwells' guests were regaled. Again, this was a constituent of the diversions in other Irish country houses, such as the Edgeworths at Edgeworthstown.[59] Yet Caldwell's recitals and performances differed. He maintained a wind ensemble. He took great pains and spent prodigiously to procure instruments, printed and manuscript music, and a musical director. Traditional melodies may have been interwoven with the imported novelties. Nevertheless, it is the latter that are documented.[60] Caldwell conceded that music-making was a personal indulgence.[61] As he intended, it beguiled visitors, who might be serenaded as they were rowed across Lough Erne towards Castle Caldwell. Sir James hardly rivalled the Esterhazys with their patronage of Haydn, but the effect of his band struck the knowing as more reminiscent of Germany and the Austrian Empire than of Britain and Ireland. In 1777 Owen Wynne of Haselwood (the Wynnes, like the Caldwells, were a family with strong military traditions) enthused over his recent stay at Castle Caldwell, 'your sweet and agreeable place, which for its beauty and situation, I affirm, (in my opinion) far exceeds any place that I ever saw either in England or in Ireland.' Wynne, having praised the regimentation of servants and tenants, concluded

I confess you appeared to me in the light of a worthy German prince, having a regular household well kept up with a proper uniform, every person in their proper station well disciplined and each striving to prove their gratitude to his master by their several exertions.[62]

It is tempting to trace Caldwell's passion for and preferences in music to his Continental experiences. At Castle Caldwell it was integral to the benign and uplifting order. So too were the content and service of meals. In earlier years, Caldwell had been exposed to habits rather different from those which prevailed in provincial Ireland. Yet, he seldom recalled those foreign manners. Instead, it is clear that he was fascinated by the domestic arrangements of the houses into which he was welcomed in Ireland and England. He noted the number of servants and their pay. He commented on the look of houses, whether fashionably new (like Castle Ward) or outmoded and indifferent (Rostrevor). Caldwell was an educated analyst of architecture. This discrimination showed strongly when he tried to persuade the actor, David Garrick, to visit the north of Ireland. In an effort to overcome Garrick's reluctance, Caldwell described the houses that he might see. He deployed his knowledge of the families in the various seats.[63] However, in his surviving observations, he never compared Irish buildings explicitly with those in England, let alone on the Continent.

In writing to his wife, Caldwell took special care to note how meals were served. In particular, the dessert fascinated Caldwell. At Castle Ward, the latest vogue of queen's ware – the lighter pottery pioneered by Wedgwood – had already appeared by 1772.[64] He carped at the limited choice and poor quality of hothouse fruits offered. Implicitly, he was proclaiming the superiority of his own produce. Yet, the 'grapery' at Castle Caldwell was not big enough to allow melons to be grown in 1764. However, by 1772, Caldwell's hothouses were supplying pineapples, peaches, nectarines and muscatel grapes.[65] With a well-attuned ear, he also evaluated the musical accompaniments. Undoubtedly, Caldwell was storing up ideas for what might or might not be tried at Castle Caldwell. On occasion, he clearly felt that the delicacies and music offered by his grand hosts fell short of what his own house could supply. Only one bad fiddle and a bassoon was the withering verdict on a gathering under the auspices of the Ogles at Newry.

These impressions of the domestic arrangements in the establishments at Castle Ward and Ravensdale, and of Lord Clanbrassil at Dundalk, were retailed to Lady Caldwell.[66] No doubt she was delighted to hear from the Fortescues' Ravensdale in county Louth

that the living here is the very highest, much in the French way, few things substantial. It is the fashion to have the dessert laid on after the second course without the cloths being taken away & the bottles and glasses set down after the table is cleared and the cloth taken away and the bottles and glasses set down again. The dessert is made out very fine things: creams, cascurses [custards?], and sweetmeats as they have but very little fruit and that but bad. No pineapples but very fine melons; excellent wines but no great variety.

The following year, dinner at Rochfort, county Westmeath, was described: 'A complete service of plate covers and all: 2 soups 2 removes 9 and 9: a dessert in the highest taste, all sorts of wine – burgundy, champagne.' For Lady Caldwell, vicarious enjoyment of her husband's pleasures palled. Executing his lofty notions at Castle Caldwell had seriously overstrained their resources. Early in 1773 she called halt to his extravagances. Without ready cash she had been unable to pay the postage on the letters that arrived. Indeed, she had been reduced to selling eggs and tobacco left in the house in order to have a little money.[67]

After 1772, the high style maintained at Castle Caldwell was reduced. There was even talk of closing the house as an economy. Lady Caldwell managed to bring the children still living at home to Dublin. Lady Shelburne had refused to assist, but Lady Arbella Denny proved a benefactor, just as earlier she had been a counsellor.[68] The death of Elizabeth Caldwell in 1778 made her husband rely more heavily on his daughters, notably Arbella. He consoled himself with visits to imposing English mansions, tried to recover his own health at Bath and Sidmouth, and persisted in the delusive pursuit of his peerage.[69]

When he returned periodically to Castle Caldwell, a chief concern was to sort, preserve, copy and select the papers that might assist his claim to ennoblement. The routine documentation of domestic spending – so valuable for retrieving detail about house and gardens – would not help, and therefore was largely discarded. As a result, only fleeting impressions of Castle Caldwell in its heyday can be gained. The impediments are increased by the changes wrought by Sir James Caldwell's heir, Sir John Caldwell, who inherited in 1784. The younger Caldwell, aware of his father's foibles, had, during the lifetime of Sir James, occasionally chided him but more often deferred to his fancies. Once in possession of Castle Caldwell, Sir John imprinted the place with his own stamp of toy-fort gothick. This decorative icing shows clearly in the late nineteenth-century photographs of the house.[70] On the ground, solid foundations remind in outline of what James and Elizabeth Caldwell engineered and presided over. What filled the house – the fabrics and furnishing approved and sometimes ordered by Lady Arbella Denny, the silver, the portraits, the musical instruments and scores, the books – have either perished or, dispersed long since, are unrecognised as once having graced this odd Germanic court beside Lough Erne.

———

ENDNOTES

The following abbreviation is used:

JRL   John Rylands Library, University of Manchester

[1]   Two exemplary works set out the essentials about the Caldwells: M. Busteed, *Castle Caldwell, County Fermanagh: life on a west Ulster estate, 1750-1800* (Dublin 2006); J.B. Cunningham, *A History of Castle Caldwell and its Families* (Monaghan [1980]). W.H.G. Bagshawe, *The Bagshawes of Ford: a biographical pedigree* (London 1886) also remains valuable.

[2]   T. Barnard, *A New Anatomy of Ireland: the Irish Protestants, 1649-1700* (New Haven and London 2003) 31; Busteed, *Castle Caldwell*, 31.

[3]   G.D. Burtchaell and T.U. Sadleir, *Alumni Dublinenses*, 2nd edn (Dublin 1935) 127, states that he was seventeen when he entered Trinity College, Dublin, in 1737.

[4]   T. Barnard, *Making the Grand Figure: lives and possessions in Ireland, 1641-1770* (London and New Haven 2004) 310-44; J. Ingamells, *A Dictionary of British and Irish Travellers in Italy 1701-1800* (New Haven and London 1997) 196-99, 593-94, 750.

[5]   R.E. Ward (ed.), *Prince of Dublin Printers: the letters of George Faulkner* (Lexington 1972) 50.

[6]   JRL, B 3/29/2, Sir James Caldwell to Lady Caldwell, 1st February 1757.

[7]   JRL, 3/13/4, Anne, Lady Caldwell to Sir J. Caldwell, 4th November 1749; 3/14/141, Frederick Trench to same, 2nd September 1752; B 3/30/47, Lady Mary Coghill to Lady Caldwell, 7th April [1756?].

[8]   Christ Church, Oxford, Wake MS 14/191, Bishop W. Nicolson to Archbishop W. Wake, 10th April 1724; J. Nichols (ed.), *Letters on various subjects ... to and from William Nicolson, D.D.*, 2 vols (London 1809) II, 599, 607.

[9]   Christ Church, Oxford, Wake MS 14/105, Bishop J. Hort to Archbishop W. Wake, 19th October 1723.

[10] A.F. Hort, 'The Horts of Hortland', *Journal of the Kildare Archaeological Society*, VII, 1912-14, 208-11.

[11] Public Record Office of Northern Ireland (PRONI), D 1634/1, item 6, will of Archbishop Josiah Hort, 15th May 1751; JRL, B 3/20/407, draft of Sir J. Caldwell to unknown [1755].

[12] PRONI, D 1634/1, item 6.

[13] JRL, B 3/30/74, Bishop A. Smyth to Lady Arbella Denny, 21st April 1759.

[14] JRL, B 3/29/58, Lady Caldwell to Sir J. Caldwell, 2nd February 1773; B 3/29/59, Sir J. Caldwell to Lady Caldwell, 6th February 1773.

[15] JRL, B 3/30/8, Lady Elizabeth Aylmer to Lady Caldwell, 8th May 1773; B 3/20/345-347, F. Sandys to Sir J. Caldwell, 10th April 1775, 13th December 1781, 4th June 1783; Irish Architectural Archive, *Biographical Index of Irish Architects*, *s.v.* Sandys, Francis. I am grateful to Ann Martha Rowan and Eddie McParland for the last reference.

[16] JRL, B 3/24/52, Calculations about letting house in Dawson Street, Dublin; B 3/21/3, inventory of leases and other legal documents at Castle Caldwell.

[17] JRL B 3/30/7-9, Lady Elizabeth Aylmer to Lady Caldwell, Dublin, 8th May 1773, 8th October 1773.

[18] JRL, B 3/30/145, Lady Shelburne to Elizabeth Hort, 14th July 1752. See A. Crookshank and D. Fitzgerald, Knight of Glin, *The Painters of Ireland, c.1660-1920* (London 1978) 86; A.

Crookshank and D. Fitzgerald, Knight of Glin, *Ireland's Painters, 1600-1940* (New Haven and London 2002) 99-101; W.G. Strickland, *A Dictionary of Irish Artists*, 2 vols (Dublin 1913) I, 515-23.

19 JRL, B 3/32/3 and 4, William Brennan to Lady Caldwell, 4th September 1756, 31st October 1756; B 3/20/260, 262, 263, 264, 267, 268, 270, James Maguire to Sir J. Caldwell, 20th October 1753, 20th August 1756, 3rd and 10th September 1756, 1st, 7th and 15th October 1756; B 3/32/43, Edward O'Neill to Lady Caldwell, 13th October 1756.

20 PRONI, D 1634/2/22, J. Hort to Lady Caldwell, 17th August 1758.

21 JRL, B 3/27/7, items 6, 7, 11, 26, 42, folio paper book in which are listed leases, letters and other papers.

22 JRL, B 3/27/7, items 9, 12, 24, 35, 37.

23 JRL, B 3/27/7, items 9, 24.

24 Brian Wragg, *The Life and Works of John Carr of York* (York 2000) 103-04.

25 JRL, B 3/29/20, Lady Caldwell to Sir J. Caldwell, undated [1763].

26 JRL, B 3/24/13, agreement of Whitmore Davis and Sir J. Caldwell, 3rd August 1762. No Davis is recorded in T. McMahon and B. O'Neill, 'The Ker estate, Newbliss, Co. Monaghan, 1790-c.1830', *Clogher Record*, XII, 1985, 110-26.

27 JRL, B 3/20/77, Whitmore Davis to Sir J. Caldwell, 26th May 1762.

28 JRL, B 3/24/17 and 18, Whitmore Davis to Sir J. Caldwell, 24th November 1762, 12th June 1763; B 3/32/6, same to Lady Caldwell, 4th December 1762.

29 JRL, B 3/32/7, Whitmore Davis to Lady Caldwell, 17th December 1762.

30 JRL, B 3/20/77, Whitmore Davis to Sir J. Caldwell, 26th May 1762.

31 JRL, B 3/24/17, Sir J. Caldwell agreement with Whitmore Davis, 24th November 1762.

32 JRL, B 3/24/13, 17, 20-3, agreements with and proposals of Whitmore Davis, 3rd August 1762, 24th November 1762, 12th June 1763, 11th and 26th July 1763, and undated.

33 JRL, B 3/24/16, proposals by Robert Wallace and William Moore, 24th May 1763.

34 JRL, B 3/29/19, Lady Caldwell to Sir J. Caldwell, 12th July 1763.

35 JRL, B 3/24/15, draft articles of agreement between Sir J. Caldwell and Patrick Gernon, undated [1762?]; B 3/24/8, estimate of carpenter's work done by P. Gernon for Sir J. Caldwell, 27th March 1762.

36 JRL, B 3/29/20, Lady Caldwell to Sir J. Caldwell, undated [1764?]; B 3/24/26, agreement of Christopher West with Sir J. Caldwell, 27th March 1764.

37 JRL, B 3/16/2 and 3, Revd John Alcock to Sir J. Caldwell, 5th and 14th June 1776; B 3/20/5, same to same, 12th July 1776; B 3/32/40, James Maguire to Lady Caldwell, 15th March 1757; B 3/16/261, Alexander Montgomery to Sir J. Caldwell, 26th August 1781; B 3/27/11/27, articles with H. Ward and P. Dolan; B 3/24/28, articles of Sir J. Caldwell with B. Ward, H. Ward and P. Dolan, 25th April 1768.

38 JRL, B 3/17/54, Bishop H. Maxwell to Sir J. Caldwell, 2nd May 1776; A. Rowan, *North-West Ulster* (Harmondsworth 1979)143.

39 JRL, B 3/27/7, pp.1-2, items 14/6, Boggs' estimate for tenements in Belturbet; B 3/16/96, J. Fortescue to Sir J. Caldwell, 7th April 1769; B 3/20/367, R. Stanford to same, 8th September 1768.

40 JRL, B 3/17/53-55, Bishop H. Maxwell to Sir J. Caldwell, 21st April 1776, 2nd and 18th May 1776.

41 JRL, B 3/17/55, Bishop H. Maxwell to Sir J. Caldwell, 18th May 1776; B 3/17/57, Bishop W.

Newcome to same, 10th February 1774.

[42] JRL, B 3/30/117, Mary Hort to Lady Caldwell, 19th December 1757.

[43] Bowood House, Wiltshire, Shelburne Papers, 6/18, Lady Caldwell to Dowager Countess of Shelburne, 20th October 1777.

[44] National Library of Ireland, Talbot-Crosbie MSS, folder 56, Lady A. Denny to Lady A. Crosbie, 9th [Feb?] 1748[9].

[45] For the Bookers, Barnard, *Making the Grand Figure*, 307; D. Fitzgerald, Knight of Glin and J. Peill, *Irish Furniture* (New Haven and London 2007) 83-85, 140-47, 261-62, 291; N.M. Roche, 'Irish eighteenth-century looking glasses: makers, frames and glass' in B. Austen (ed.), *Irish Furniture, The Furniture History Society* (London 2000) 16-23.

[46] JRL, B 3/30/86, 87 and 89, Lady A. Denny to Lady Caldwell, Dublin, 5th July 1769, 28th March 1770, 27th September 1770.

[47] JRL, B 3/30/88, Lady A. Denny to Lady Caldwell, 4th May 1770. For the availability and choices of wallpaper, see Barnard, *Making the Grand Figure*, 92-94; D. Skinner, 'Flocks, flowers and follies: some recently discovered Irish wallpapers of the eighteenth century', *Irish Architectural and Decorative Studies*, VI, 2003, 11-19; D. Skinner, 'Irish period wallpapers', *Irish Arts Review Yearbook,* 13, 1997, 52-61.

[48] JRL, B 3/30/86, Lady A. Denny to Lady Caldwell, 5th July 1769.

[49] JRL, B 3/30/72 and 73, Lady A. Denny to Lady Caldwell, 25th November 1758, 27th January 1759.

[50] JRL, B3/28/22, bill of G. Faulkner, 1759-61; B 3/28/31, bill of Francis and John Booker, 17th September 1771; B 3/28/37, bill of T. Read, 3rd August 1776.

[51] JRL, B 3/29/32, Sir J. Caldwell to Lady Caldwell, 18th October 1772. On Trotter, see Barnard, *Making the Grand Figure*, 155; Crookshank and Glin, *Ireland's Painters*, 98-99; Crookshank and Glin, *The Painters of Ireland*, 86; Strickland, *Dictionary*, II, 459-60.

[52] JRL, B 3/28/21, Sir J. Caldwell, account with Thomas Frye, 9th October 1760; D. Alexander, 'The Dublin group: Irish mezzotint engravers in London, 1750-1775', *Quarterly Bulletin of the Irish Georgian Society*, XVI, 1973, 73-87; T. Clayton, *The English Print, 1688-1802* (New Haven and London 1997) 200-01; Crookshank and Glin, *Ireland's Painters*, 49-50; Strickland, *Dictionary*, I, 385-90.

[53] JRL, B 3/29/109, J. Caldwell to Lady Caldwell, 8th June 1773; B 3/10, letter 509, Owen Wynne to Sir J. Caldwell, 22nd October 1777; B 3/14/156, same to same, undated [September or October 1777]; B 3/30/153, Mrs Wynne to Lady Caldwell, 30th September 1777; B 3/13/97, Lady A. Denny to Arbella Caldwell, 8th November 1783; B.B. Butler, 'Lady Arbella Denny, 1707-1792', *Dublin Historical Record*, IX, 1946-47, 19.

[54] JRL B 3/13/97, Lady A. Denny to Arbella Caldwell, 8th November 1783.

[55] JRL, B 3/29/69, postscript of A. Caldwell in Lady Caldwell to Sir J. Caldwell, Dublin, 24th March 1778.

[56] JRL, B 3/29/73, Lady Caldwell to Sir J. Caldwell, 2nd April 1778.

[57] JRL, B 3/10, letters 486, 493, A. Young to Sir J. Caldwell, 28th January 1777, 5th June 1777; A. Young, *A Tour in Ireland*, 2 vols (Dublin 1780) I, 263-68.

[58] T. Barnard, 'The cultures of eighteenth-century Irish towns' in P. Borsay and L. Proudfoot (eds), *Provincial Towns in Early Modern Britain and Ireland: change, convergence and divergence, Proceedings of the British Academy*, 108, 2002, 195-222.

[59] Barnard, *Making the Grand Figure*, 359.

60 JRL, B 3/16/43, R. Charleton to Sir J. Caldwell, 16th September 1774; B 3/16/137, J. Hawkesworth to same, 21st December 1770; B 3/16/303, G. Riddlesdale to same, 17th September 1774; B 3/16/320, R. Simpson to same, 2nd September 1776; B 3/16/381, B. Victory to same, 24th February 1773; B 3/16/382, Sir J. Caldwell to unknown, 13th April 1773; B 3/10, letter 402, Bishop F. Hervey to Sir J. Caldwell, 12th February 1775; B 3/20/259, H. Maguire to same, undated [October 1776]; B 3/27/7, pp 67, 68, lists of Sir J. Caldwell's music and musical instruments; B 3/28/4, lists of music and instruments, 29th October 1774.

61 JRL, B 3/29/55, Sir J. Caldwell to Lady Caldwell, 8th or 18th or 28th January 1773.

62 JRL, B 3/10, letter 509, O. Wynne to Sir J. Caldwell, 22nd October 1777.

63 JRL, B 3/16/114, David Garrick to Sir J. Caldwell, 14th May 1776; B 3/16/115, Sir J. Caldwell to D. Garrick, 3rd June 1776. The second letter is printed in *Notes and Queries*, 8th series, I, 1892, 1-3. It includes an uncollected verse by Jonathan Swift.

64 JRL, B 3/29/30, 32 and 34, Sir J. Caldwell to Lady Caldwell, 4th and 18th October 1772, 3rd November 1772. Substantial extracts from these letters are printed in Bagshawe, *The Bagshawes of Ford*, 323-35.

65 JRL, B 3/27/7, no 1, folio paper book of leases, letters and other papers; B 3/29/21 and 22, Lady Caldwell to Sir J. Caldwell, 5th and 6th April 1764; B 3/29/27, Sir J. Caldwell to Lady Caldwell, 28th September 1772; cf. Ward (ed.), *Prince of Dublin Printers*, 71-72.

66 For Ravensdale, see Young, *Tour*, I, 154.

67 JRL, B 3/29/38, 39, 57, 58, 61, Lady Caldwell to Sir J. Caldwell, 13th and 15th November 1772, 2nd and 10th February 1773, undated [1773].

68 JRL, B 3/29/61, 64 and 68, Lady Caldwell to Sir J. Caldwell, 10th and 23rd February 1778, 17th March 1778.

69 JRL, B 3/14/129, Sir J. Caldwell to Dowager Countess of Shelburne, 23rd February 1779.

70 Cunningham, *Castle Caldwell and its Families*, 146, 148.

1 – Hugh Howard, RALPH HOWARD MD (1638-1710),
PRESIDENT OF THE ROYAL COLLEGE OF PHYSICIANS IN IRELAND (1710)
(courtesy Board of Trinity College Dublin)

Hugh Howard (1675-1738), eclectic artist and connoisseur

NICOLA FIGGIS

HE LIFE AND CAREER OF THE ARTIST HUGH HOWARD WERE WELL DOCUMENTED by the late Michael Wynne, former Curator of Paintings at the National Gallery of Ireland.[1] The intention of this article is to revisit Howard's career based on subsequent research and to examine his own work, including his drawings in the collection of the British Museum.

Born on 7th February 1675,[2] Hugh Howard was the eldest son of Ralph Howard MD (1638-1710), President of the Royal College of Physicians in Ireland,[3] (Plate 1) and Katherine (fl.c.1655-1714), daughter of Roger Sotheby, MP for county Wicklow. His siblings were Robert (1685-1740), later Bishop of Elphin,[4] William (1680-1727), later barrister and MP, Frances, Katherine and Dorothea.[5] On the death of his father in 1710, Hugh Howard inherited the family estate at Shelton, county Wicklow, and in turn bequeathed it to his brother Robert. The Bishop subsequently left this property to his son Ralph Howard (1726-1789), created 1st Viscount Wicklow in 1785,[6] who was responsible for the building of Shelton Abbey (1770).[7]

In 1688, at the outset of war, Ralph Howard Senior left for England with his family. In 1689 he was attainted by the parliament of James II, and dispossessed of his estates in Ireland. After William of Orange's victory at the Battle of the Boyne, he recovered his property and acquired further land from the Duke of Ormond in Arklow, the revenue from which was to provide a generous source of income for his family after he died.[8] Most members of the succeeding generation were either art or book collectors, and, following them, Ralph Howard commissioned works of art while on his Grand Tour in 1751.[9] However, Hugh Howard stands pre-eminently amongst them as a connoisseur, since he became an advisor on the acquisition of art both in England and Ireland.

According to Horace Walpole, 'discovering a disposition to the arts and belles lettres', Hugh Howard, at the age of twenty-two, was sent to travel on the Continent.[10] A letter written from Whitehall on 17th April 1697 by John Ellis,

Under-Secretary of State to Matthew Prior (1664-1721), an English diplomat then serving in The Hague, introduced the young man:

> Mr. Howard, the person who will deliver you this, is son to a worthy gentle-man of my acquaintance, a doctor of physic; and his genius inclining him to painting, his father, though a wealthy man, will not oppose his inclinations, but rather seconds them by allowing him to travel, to make what improve-ment he can in an art he so much affects; and who knows whether he may not help to revive that noble science much fallen of late from its ancient splen-dour and perfection?[11]

In the same letter, Ellis gave indication of Howard's character and intention to receive instruction in Holland:

> I desire you will please to give the young man, who is so modest he will not be troublesome, such countenance and protection as he shall stand in need of for the better prosecution of his design at The Hague; and when he shall have a mind to go to Amsterdam or Leydon to see what those places afford for his instruction, that you will please to recommend him to some person there who may assist him in his laudable design.[12]

Later that year, Howard joined the entourage of Thomas Herbert (1656-1733), 8th Earl of Pembroke, on his mission as England's Ambassador at the Treaty of Ryswyck, which was signed on 20th September 1697, two miles south of The Hague. There, Howard would have met Prior, who was secretary to the negotiations. They remained on friendly terms. Howard was later to paint a portrait of Prior's mistress Anne Durham in the guise of Flora (untraced), and in 1709 Prior dedicated an 'Ode to Howard' in his *Poems on several occasions*.

Howard's route ultimately took him across Europe, from Holland to Italy. On 22nd November 1697 he was enrolled at the University of Padua,[13] from where he undoubtedly visited Venice. However, the climax of the aspiring young artist's visit abroad must have been his stay in Rome where, according to Lord Egmont, he acquired 'what Italians call la virtu and we a taste and insight in building statuary, music, medals and ancient history'.[14] There he received professional instruction with the leading painter of the day, the late Baroque artist, Carlo Maratti (1625-1713). According to Lord Egmont, the Master showed a fondness for the young artist, and directed what pieces he should copy and corrected his work with his own pencil.[15] At this time, Howard would have made his chalk drawing[16] after Maratti's self-por-trait, very likely copied from a preparatory study by Maratti for his oil painting now in the Musée des Beaux-Arts, Brussels.[17] The Brussels painting is itself likely to have been a study for the large canvas by Maratti entitled *Apollo leading the Marchese Niccolo Maria Palaviccini to the Temple of Virtu with the artist*.[18]

Howard returned to Ireland via France in October 1700, before settling the following year in London and establishing himself as a portrait painter. However, in this pursuit he was not entirely successful as, according to George Vertue, 'at that time he could not get reputation enough to make his way by Art'.[19]

In 1714, aged thirty-nine, Howard married Thomasine Langston (d.1728), daughter and wealthy heiress of General Thomas Langston, and later took up residence in fashionable Pall Mall. They sat for their portraits (Plates 2, 3) to the Swedish-born artist Michael Dahl (1656-1743), which in 1720 hung in their dining room.[20] Both Howard and Dahl were members of the Society of Virtuosi of St Luke in London,[21] and appear to have been on close terms.[22]

On 9th November 1714, through the influence of William Cavendish, 2nd Duke of Devonshire (1673-1729), Howard was appointed Keeper of the Papers and Records of State at Whitehall, which Vertue described as a 'Siné cure to him worth certainly 200 p Anm'.[23] Twelve years later, in 1726, Howard succeeded Charles Dartiquenave as Paymaster of the Royal Palaces.[24] In 1714, with his increased wealth added to the annual rents which he received from Shelton after the death of his father, Howard could afford to abandon his career as a portrait painter.[25]

When not absorbed with his official duties, Howard played an advisory role in the acquisition of works for collectors, including the amateur architect Henry Herbert, 9th Earl of Pembroke (c.1689-1750), William Cavendish, 2nd Duke of Devonshire, and Dr Richard Mead (1673-1754).[26] Whilst Howard had his detractors, like Jonathan Richardson the Younger, who considered him an upstart with pretensions to family connections with the Norfolk Howards,[27] his eye and knowledge of art were trusted by many collectors. With astute business acumen, he acquired works which had descended from Thomas Howard, 2nd Earl of Arundel (1586-1646), and the painter Sir Peter Lely (1618-80), which he subsequently resold, such as van Dyck's Italian sketchbook (containing 121 leaves, mainly with sketches after Titian), originally from Lely's collection.[28] Howard later sold this to the 2nd Duke of Devonshire, and afterwards made copies of some of the pages as a record for himself (Plate 4).[29]

Letters to Hugh Howard of 1723 and 1724 from Antonio Zanetti (1680-1767), a caricaturist, printmaker and collector, who acted as a middleman in Venice, show that Howard was using him as a source of prints, copies and original paintings, including works by Titian and Veronese, for the Duke of Devonshire.[30] Howard would most likely have met Zanetti while in London, when he purchased a group of drawings by Parmigianino from the Arundel collection.[31] Another supplier in Venice used by Howard was Joseph Smith (c.1674-1770), merchant, and later British Consul, evidenced by an account dated 22nd August 1730 for two pictures by Canelletto to the value of thirty-five Venetian *zecchins* (£18 7s 11d).[32]

Naples was also explored by Howard as a source, through the Irish artist

*2, 3 – Michael Dahl (1656-
1743), portraits of the artist
Hugh Howard and his wife,
Thomasine, painted 1714-20*
(private collection; photos courtesy
Pyms Gallery, London)

opposite

*4 – Hugh Howard
(after Anthony van Dyck,
after Titian)*
STUDIES FROM MALE PORTRAITS
inscribed 'Pensieri d'Titiano' with
transcriptions of van Dyck's notes,
pen and brown ink, 32.5 x 21 cm
(British Museum, Dept of Prints
and Drawings, Inv. 1874.0808.23)

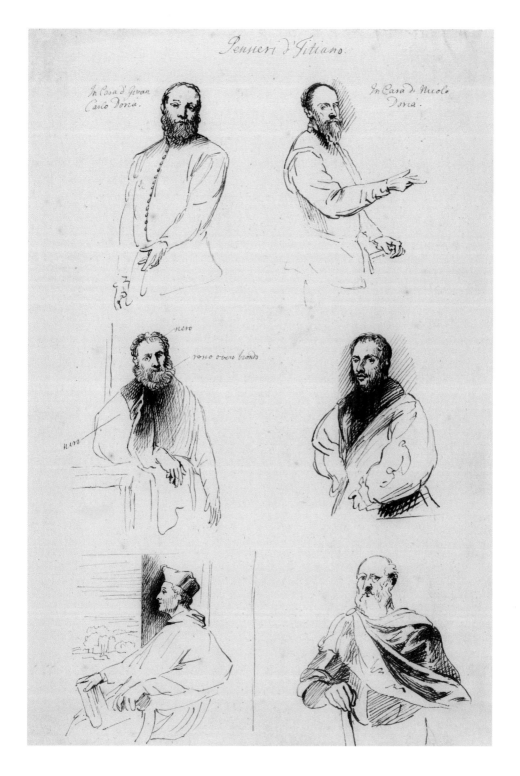

Henry Trench (*c*.1685-1726), who, while on his second sojurn in Italy from 1723 to 1725, studied under Francesco Solimena (1657-1747). In response to a letter of 15th March from Howard, Trench replied from Naples on 26th May 1724 concerning prints which he had sent to Leghorn – a Caracci for James Cavendish,[33] tables of Calabrian marble and pictures by Carlo Maratti and Francesco Solimena.[34]

The Wicklow Papers deposited with the National Library of Ireland reveal that Howard supplied his family and associates in Ireland with paintings, medals and books from London. Together with his brother Robert, Bishop of Elphin, he supplied paintings for Marmaduke Coghill for his new house in Drumcondra, who, in return, seems to have provided Hugh Howard with an original painting by van Dyck.[35] According to Toby Barnard, the Howard brothers were so successful that he compares, with a certain degree of irony, the niche market which they occupied to that of Cardinal Albani in Rome.[36] Whilst high-quality works were a rarity in the first decades of eighteenth-century Ireland, Hugh Howard would naturally have been on the lookout for any items of particular value to supply for his élite British clientele or to add to his own expanding collection. Letters between the two brothers mainly refer to works being sent from London to Dublin, with most of them being identified only as 'pictures'. Occasional elaborations were given by Hugh Howard, such as 'I have got You a good Copy of a famous picture of Guido for Yr Chimney piece, & send you a Magdelain [sic] after Luca Jordano [sic]',[37] and a list is given itemising paintings after Luca Giordano, Andrea del Sarto, Pellegrini hunting scenes by Wooton, and a version of a landscape by Gaspar Poussin.[38] These works were sent to Ireland more for the purpose of completing the decoration of rooms than for their aesthetic merit. In January 1731 the Bishop wrote requesting more paintings: 'I shall be glad of such pictures as you choose but you know I have an eye to furniture in them, not that that is my taste, but there are no Judges here'.[39]

HUGH HOWARD'S COLLECTION

Hugh Howard's own collection was extensive: the inventory of 1720[40] itemises his paintings as well as antiquities, but he was also an avid collector of rare prints and drawings, books and medals. In 1728 he inherited part of the library of James West from his brother William, which included prints after early German and Italian artists. By the time of Howard's death on 17th March 1738,[41] he had accumulated over 20,000 items, all of which were left to his brother Robert. Sketchcards (undated) (Plate 5), showing locations of paintings which later hung in Shelton Abbey, attest to the wealth of the collection, which by then had been added to by his nephew Ralph Howard, who, in 1752, commissioned the paintings by contemporary artists such as Vernet and Wilson while in Rome.[42]

In advance of two auctions at Sotheby's held in 1873 and 1874,[43] the British Museum purchased almost 2,500 prints and drawings from Hugh Howard's collection, which had by then descended to Charles Francis Arnold Howard, 5th Earl of Wicklow. Works acquired by the museum with the provenance of Hugh Howard reveal his eclectic interests in drawings from most European schools of the sixteenth to the early eighteenth century.[44] Drawings by Italian artists include those by Baldassare Peruzzi, Giulio Romano, Jacopo Ligozzi, Paolo Farinati, Parmigianino and Carlo Maratti, as well as others after Leonardo da Vinci, Bernini, Perino del Vaga and Giovanni da Udine. Northern artists are also well represented, with a special interest taken by Howard in the drawings of van Dyck, such as his studies of a horse for the portrait of Charles I on horseback.[45] From the Netherlandish School there are drawings by Rogier van der Weyden, Jan Swart and Lambert Lombard; from the German, Albrecht Durer, Francis Cleyn, Godfrey Kneller; and from the Dutch school, Rembrandt, Hendrik Danckerts, Jan van der Vaart, Peter Lely and Willem van de Velde II. Work by the British artists Isaac Oliver, Francis Barlow, Henry Cooke, Isaac Fuller and James Seymour were also collected by Howard, as were eighteenth-century French drawings by Antoine Watteau and François Boitard.

According to Sotheby's sale catalogue of 12th December 1873 (and the seven following days), many of the items from 'The Choice Collection of Rare Engravings & Drawings' came from 'the Portfolios of the Earl of Arundel & Sir Peter Lely'. The cover of the catalogue (Plate 6) highlights 'Fine drawings by Michael Angelo, Correggio, Guercino, Barocci, C. Maratti, an important life-sized head by A. Durer', along with other drawings by Rubens, van Dyck, Willem van der Velde, J.A. Callot, Hugh Howard and Sir James Thornhill. Included in the catalogue were studies by Alberti[46] and Michelangelo,[47] and a self-portrait in red chalk of Annibale Caracci as a youth.[48]

HOWARD'S WORK AS AN ARTIST

Of the existing early portraits by Howard, Maratti's influence can be seen in those of the Italian composer Arcangelo Corelli. Howard painted at least four versions of this sitter[49] (one presumably that's listed in the inventory of 1720 as 'Corelli's picture done at Rome'),[50] which include trappings of the Baroque style, such as an ornate decorative border within the painting (NGI version).[51] Since the figure of Corelli appears somewhat wooden, the portraits were almost certainly painted after originals by Maratti rather than from the life. The version at the Royal Society of Musicians in London appears to be a copy of the portrait of Corelli, formerly at Mount Edgecumbe, catalogued as by Maratti in the Royal Academy exhibition of 1938.[52] The influence of Kneller[53] is more apparent in Howard's later portraits, such

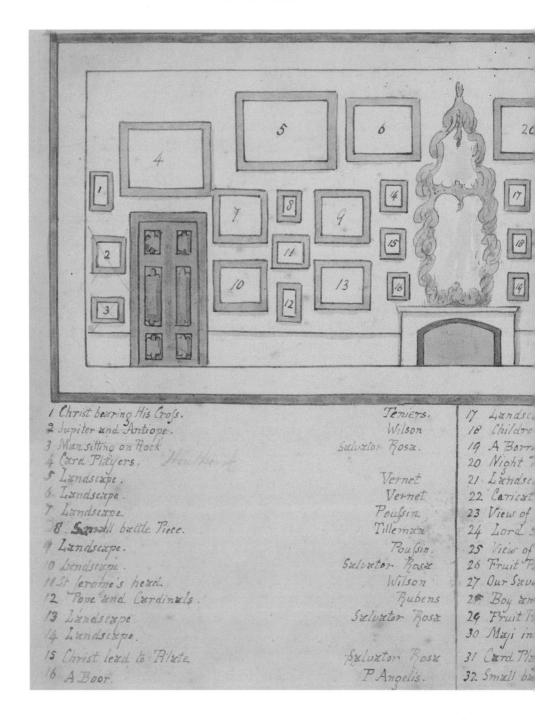

5 – Sketchcard showing the locations of paintings hung in Shelton Abbey
(courtesy NLI, Wicklow Papers, MS 38, 628/12).

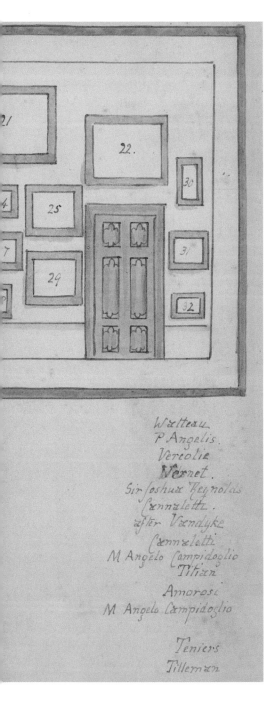

Watteau
P. Angelis
Vercolie
Vernet.
Sir Joshua Reynolds
Cannaletti.
after Vandyke
Cannaletti
M Angelo Campidoglio
Titian
Amorosi
M Angelo Campidoglio

Teniers
Tilleman

as those of Justinian Isham (1710; no longer extant, photograph Witt Library) and Anne Sotheby. His second portrait of Justinian Isham (1711; Lamport Hall, Northampton) resembles more the work of his contemporary, Charles Jervas. His sketches after van Dyck (in turn after Titian), serve as prime evidence for the connections and influences which descended from one artist to another (Plate 4).

Howard received certain high-ranking portrait commissions in Ireland, including one for Robert, 1st Viscount Jocelyn (1688-1756), Attorney General.[54] On 2nd December 1708, Howard was paid £10, on behalf of Archbishop William King (1650-1729), for 'your Graces [sic] picture'.[55] Works commissioned by Trinity College include those of the Provost Peter Brown (signed and dated 1710) and another of St George Ashe.[56] Another of Ralph Howard shown in his gown as President of the College of Physicians (Plate1), painted only months before his death on 8th August 1710, was presented by the artist to Trinity College. A letter of 8th March 1710, written by his mother to his brother William, stated 'he has done severall pickturs for the Colidg and is now about one of your dear fathers'.[57] Other family members who sat to him were his brother-in-law Sir Thomas Molyneux of Castledillon, county Armagh (Armagh County Council) and his brother William.[58]

Opinions varied as to the quality of Howard's own work as a portrait painter. His brother Robert, the least

6a, 6b – Sotheby, Wilkinson & Hodge, sale catalogue of 12th December 1873 (and seven following days)

37

HUGH HOWARD.

626 Studies of Portraiture, *in pen and red chalk;* a Cupid, *red chalk;* Virgin and Child, after Correggio, *in pen;* a Dog's Head, *in oil, &c.;* others from Ribera and Rubens   11

627 Studies from Pictures by Raphael, Domenchino, &c., *in pen and red and black chalk;* Portraits, one a sketch, *in oil* 11

628 Studies from Pictures by Titian, Guercino, &c., *in pen, red and black chalk and indian ink;* Portraits, *in pen*   11

629 Studies from Pictures by Raphael, Ribera, &c., *black and red chalk, in pen and bistre*   9

630 Studies from Pictures by Domenchino, Raphael, Guercino, &c., *black and red chalk and pen;* Portraits, *in pen*   10

631 Studies from Pictures by Raphael, Pordenone, &c., *black and red chalk and pen, washed with indian ink, one heightened with gold*   11

632 Studies for his own compositions, Jupiter and Semele; Judith with the head of St. John; others from the Antique; a Monogram in Italian Capitals, &c., *red and black chalk and indian ink*   12

633 Studies from Pictures by Annibale Caracci and Guercino, &c., *red and black chalk, pen and indian ink*   12

634 Studies from Titian, Correggio, &c., *red and black chalk and indian ink;* Portrait, *in indian ink;* Studies from the Antique   11

635 Studies from Pictures by Titian, Raphael, &c., *red chalk, pen and bistre, heightened with gold, on paper prepared with tempera;* a Portrait, *in red chalk on grey paper*   10

636 Studies from Pictures by Giulio Romano, Guercino, &c., *red chalk, pen and bistre, one heightened with gold;* Portraits; and a Study from the Antique

637 Liberality and Modesty, from Guido's Picture, *black and red chalk;* others of Portraits and Studies from Pictures; a Monogram, *in pen*   11

(*The Drawings continued at page 47.*)

objective, claimed that through him 'Ireland may in time produce a Raphael or Angelo'.[59] While Vertue mentioned 'a head 3/4 (I think his best done) of Mr Sothby ... painted by ... Howard. after his return from Rome. Very well done',[60] Justinian Isham only paid half the amount due for the portrait of his son, complaining it was not a good likeness.[61]

An early recorded portrait by Howard is of the dramatist William Congreve of about 1705, who mentioned in a letter to Joseph Keally [Kelly] on 9th December 1704, 'I thank you for [Howard's] acquaintance. I like him very well. I have sat to him and they say it will be a very good picture.'[62] Early in the following year, referring to a portrait of Kelly, Congreve wrote: 'I am glad you have received your picture ... Mine is not finished ... I have not had time to see Mr. Howard these six weeks.'[63] Four years later, dissatisfaction is implied over the portrait of Kelly: 'I was 6 or 7 times to look for Mr: Howard before I could find him. At last I saw him and your picture which is like you but too warmly painted as you hinted. I shall press him to make an end of it.'[64]

Howard's drawings in the British Museum remain the best single extant body of his work.[65] Some of these, according to Wynne, show the laboured effects of a copyist and would most likely have been carried out under the direction of Carlo

CATALOGUE
OF
THE CHOICE COLLECTION
OF
RARE ENGRAVINGS & DRAWINGS,
FORMED BY
HUGH HOWARD
AT THE COMMENCEMENT OF THE LAST CENTURY,
MANY OF THEM FROM THE PORTFOLIOS OF THE EARL OF ARUNDEL & SIR PETER LELY,
COMPRISING
OF THE ITALIAN SCHOOL,
Two Impressions of the rare and celebrated Print of the BATTLE OF THE GIANTS, by
A. POLLAJUOLO; other early specimens by BECCAFUMI, G. A. DA BRESCIA, ANDREA
MANTEGNA, R. BOLDRINI, DOMENICO and GIULIO CAMPAGNOLA, C. ROBETTA;
EIGHTY-FOUR EXAMPLES BY MARC ANTONIO,
THE MOST NOTEWORTHY BEING IN FINE CONDITION;
THE ADAM AND EVE; Proof of the PORTRAIT OF ARETINO, undescribed; LA VIERGE
AU BRAS NU; THE LAST SUPPER; MASSACRE OF THE INNOCENTS, both plates; the
set of the MEDALLION HEADS OF THE POPES, some undescribed; and several of his
rare early Works;
*Fine Specimens of his followers, Agostino Veneziano, M. da Ravenna,
and the Maitre au Dé;*
THE WORKS OF THE GHISI FAMILY;
A set of Proofs, in undescribed states, of the PROPHETS AND SIBYLS; nearly a complete
set of the PRINTS IN CHIARO-SCURO, by A. ANDREANI, UGO DA CARPI N. DA
VICENZI, &c.; ETCHINGS described in the XVII-XXI volumes of BARTSCH.
GERMAN SCHOOL,
Brilliant Impressions of MARTIN SCHONGAUER; ALBRECHT DÜRER (the Adam and Eve,
Melancholy, &c.); LUCAS CRANACH; Combat of Gladiators, by BARTHEL. BEHAM.
DUTCH AND FLEMISH SCHOOL,
Brilliant Impressions of the Works of LUCAS VAN LEYDEN; The Three Trees, by
REMBRANDT; others, by A. OSTADE, &c.
FRENCH,
A nearly complete series of the productions of J. CALLOT and C. MELLAN.
ENGLISH,
Fine early and rare Specimens in mezzotinto of the productions of I. BECKET,
A. BROWNE, J. FABER, W. FAITHORNE Jun., J. SIMON, G. and R. WHITE, and R.
WILLIAMS; nearly a perfect set of the Works of JOHN SMITH;
A few of the rare Productions of W. Hogarth, and other curious Satires.
FINE DRAWINGS,
By MICHAEL ANGELO, CORREGGIO, GUERCINO, BAROCCI, C. MARATTI,
AN IMPORTANT LIFE-SIZE HEAD, BY A. DÜRER,
RUBENS, VAN DYCK, W. VANDER VELDE, J. A. CALLOT, HUGH HOWARD and
Sir JAMES THORNHILL,
BOOKS OF PRINTS, &c. &c.
WHICH WILL BE SOLD BY AUCT
BY MESSRS.
SOTHEBY, WILKINSON & HODGE,
Auctioneers of Literary Property and Works illustrative of the Fine Arts,
AT THEIR HOUSE, No. 13, WELLINGTON STREET, STRAND, W.C.
On FRIDAY, 12th DECEMBER, 1873, and Seven following Days,
AT ONE O'CLOCK PRECISELY.

MAY BE VIEWED TWO DAYS PRIOR, AND CATALOGUES HAD.

DRYDEN PRESS: J. Davy and Sons, 137, Long Acre.

7 – Hugh Howard, CARDINAL GIANFRANCESCO ALBANI
red chalk, 31 x 23 cm

Hugh Howard

*8, 9 – pair of drawings after
Guercino's MADONNA OF THE
ROSARY WITH SAINTS DOMINIC
AND CATHERINE OF SIENA*
red chalk, 36 x 24 cm
*The paler one is a mirror-image
off-set which would have been used
in the engraving process to help
provide a print the same way
around as the original.*

10 – GRAPES
red chalk, 22 x 20 cm
*(BM, Dept of Prints and Drawings,
Inv. 1874.0808.115 and
1874.0808.111)*

11 – Hugh Howard, ITALIANATE LANDSCAPE WITH A FERRY, *pen and brown ink over graphite, 25 x 40.5 cm
(BM, Dept of Prints and Drawings, Inv. 1874.0808.125)*

Maratti. Howard's red chalk drawing of Cardinal Gianfrancesco Albani (Plate 7)[66] is
a case in point, which would appear to be a study after a portrait rather than a drawing *ad vivum*. However, others stand out for their freshness, such as a skilfully
drawn study of grapes (Plate 10)[67] which captures with great realism the differing
effects of light on the bunches attached to a vine stalk.

A number of caricatures in red chalk appear to be studies after Pier Leone
Ghezzi (1674-1755), as given by Binyon and Wynne, rather than after Maratti.[68]
Referring to a caricature, which may also have been by P.L. Ghezzi, in the collection of General Fred Hamilton, and hoping to acquire it for his collection, he gave a
description of it to Robert Howard:

> tis on paper of a little croked [sic] Painter ... & is one of those ridiculous
> drawings which the Italians cal [sic] Caricatura posibly [sic] it may have faln
> [sic] into the hands of sombody [sic] that neither values nor understands it. I
> wish you coud [sic] get it for me. It was formerly in a frame & glass & in the
> corner of the paper it is marked PL.[69]

Another pair of drawings points to the effective technical skills which Howard had
acquired in providing preparatory drawings after work of the Italian masters for subsequent engraving. Of the pair of drawings after Guercino's *Madonna of the Rosary
with Saints Dominic and Catherine of Siena* (Plates 8, 9),[70] the paler one is a mirror

image off-set, which would have been used in the engraving process to help provide a print with the image in the same direction as the original.[71]

An oval half-length portrait, *Girl with a Dove* (Plate12),[72] in chalks on blue paper, is the only drawing by Howard in the British Museum in which colour was used. This may point to its execution outside Rome (where red chalk was the norm for drawing at this period), possibly in Venice, leaving one to surmise that it might be after a pastel by Rosalba Carriera.

Landscapes by Hugh Howard include Italianate views (Plate 11) in graphite and brown ink in the manner of the seventeenth-century Bolognese artist G.F. Grimaldi.[73] A view of Hampton Court from below Hampton (Plate 13)[74] is dated 1722, showing that

12 – A Girl with a Dove

coloured chalks, 22.5 x 18 cm (BM, Dept of Prints and Drawings, Inv. 1874.0808.109/110 and 1874.0808.112)

whilst he may have abandoned his career as a portrait painter in 1714, he still sketched the occasional landscape.

One's main impression upon looking at these drawings and considering the extent of Howard's collection is the eclectic nature of his talent and interests. Certainly, he could be accused of having been a laborious copyist. However, his studies of the work after a great variety of masters would have informed his much more successful career as a connoisseur and advisor on works of art.

———

ACKNOWLEDGEMENTS

This article owes a debt to the late Michael Wynne, whose original research on Hugh Howard at the Centre for the Study of Irish Art at the National Gallery of Ireland was invaluable in the preparation of this article. Special thanks are also due to Eddie McParland for allowing me to use his transcripts of the Wicklow Papers, and to David White, William Laffan and Brendan Rooney for most generously sharing their knowledge and expertise.

———

ENDNOTES

The following abbreviations are used:

BM   British Museum
NGI   National Gallery of Ireland
NLI   National Library of Ireland
Vertue   George Vertue, 'The Note Books of George Vertue Relating to Artists and
                Collections in England', 6 notebooks, *Walpole Society*, vols 18, 20, 22, 24, 26, 30
                (1930-55)
Wynne, 1969   Michael Wynne, 'Hugh Howard, Irish Portrait Painter', *Apollo*, XC, 92, October
                1969, 314-17

A NOTE ON THE WICKLOW PAPERS (NLI) – The manuscript numbers used here for the
Wicklow Papers are given according to the newly sorted collection numbering in the NLI
Collection List No. 69, Wicklow Papers, compiled by Dr Niall E. Keogh, 2002-03 (on open
access in the NLI Manuscript Reading Room).

[1] Wynne, 1969, 314-17. More recently, see Anne Crookshank and Desmond FitzGerald,
     Ireland's Painters 1600-1940 (New Haven and London 2002) 28-30
[2] Walter G. Strickland, *A Dictionary of Irish Artists*, 2 vols (Dublin 1913) I, 529.
[3] First elected in 1695 and re-elected in 1701 and 1707.
[4] In 1724 Robert married Patience, daughter and heiress of Godfrey Boleyne of Fennor, county
     Meath.
[5] Frances, Katherine and Dorothea married respectively Sir Robert Kennedy, Baronet of Mount

13 – Hugh Howard, A VIEW OF HAMPTON COURT FROM BELOW HAMPTON
1722, pen and brown ink and grey wash, 20.5 x 32.5 cm, dated on verso in the artist's hand (detail)
(BM, Dept of Prints and Drawings, Inv. 1874.0808.105)

Kennedy, county Wicklow; Sir Thomas Molyneux, 1st Baronet of Castle Dillon, county Armagh; and the Rt Rev Anthony Dopping, Bishop of Ossory, Vice-Chancellor of Trinity College (1682-97).

[6] Ralph Howard married Alice, only daughter and heiress of William Forward of Castle Forward, county Donegal.

[7] See Mark Bence-Jones, *A Guide to Irish Country Houses* (London, 1978; reprinted 1996) 259.

[8] His heir, Hugh Howard, received rents from the properties. Annually, from leases, his widow received £100 and his sons Robert and William £750 and £550 respectively. (William, while training for the Bar at the Inns of Court in London, also received an annuity of £80.) For references to rental payments to Howard from his property in Ireland, see Wicklow Papers, MS 38,598(1-11), letters from Robert Howard to Hugh Howard. See also Toby Barnard, *A New Anatomy of Ireland: the Irish Protestants, 1649-1770* (New Haven and London 2003) 135.

[9] Cynthia O'Connor, 'Ralph Howard' in John Ingamells (ed.), *A Dictionary of British and Irish Travellers in Italy 1701-1800* (New Haven and London 1997) 528-30.

[10] Horace Walpole, *Anecdotes of Painting* (London 1872) 305.

[11] Historical Manuscripts Commission, Prior Papers, *Calendar of the Manuscripts of the Marquis of Bath preserved at Longleat, Wiltshire*, III, 1908, 110.

[12] *ibid.*, 110-11.

[13] NLI, Wicklow Papers, MS 38,599/19(3). A certificate dated by hand, 22 '9bris' 1697, attests that Hugh Howard was enrolled at Padua University.

[14] Historical Manuscripts Commission, Manuscripts of the Earl of Egmont, 23rd February 1731/2, *Diary of Viscount Percival afterwards First Earl of Egmont, 1730-33* (London 1920) 225.

[15] *ibid.*

[16] Courtauld Institute, London, Witt Collection, drawing Acc. No. D.1952.RW.2826, black and white chalks on blue paper, 22.6 x 22.5 cm. For illustration, see Wynne, 1969, 314.

[17] Musée Royaux de Beaux-Arts de Belgique, Bruxelles, *Catalogue de la peinture ancienne* (Brussels, 1957) 68, cat. 806.

[18] On display in the picture gallery at Stourhead House, Warminster (National Trust), Acc. No. STO/P/16, oil on canvas, 300 x 212 cm.

[19] Vertue, III, *Walpole Society*, XXII, 83.

[20] NLI, Wicklow Papers, MS 38,628/9, manuscript copy of a document entitled 'A Catalogue of my Pictures &c 1720'. The portraits were listed as 'my own & wifes [sic] pictures by Dahl'. The date of 1723 given on the lining of Howard's portrait is therefore incorrect. See Christie's, London, Irish Sale, 12th May 2005, lot 46. Howard's portrait by Dahl was reproduced in mezzotint by John Faber II in 1737.

[21] Howard also became a member of the Rose and Crown Club (*c*.1724) and Kneller's Academy in Great Queen Street. I. Bignamini, 'Art Institutions in London, 1689-1768, A Study of Clubs and Academies', *Walpole Society*, 1988, 42, fn.30.

[22] Howard left a ring to 'Mr Dahl'. NLI, Wicklow Papers, Extracts of Hugh Howard's Will, MS 38,617/3(2) f.1 and 1v, 10th March 1737/8.

[23] Vertue, III, *Walpole Society*, XXII, 83.

[24] Ellis Waterhouse, *Painting in Britain, 1530-1790* (Melbourne, London and Baltimore 1953) 96.

[25] Vertue, III, *Walpole Society*, XXII, 83.

[26] Barnard, *A New Anatomy of Ireland*, 136. Mead was the medical doctor of Howard and his wife. NLI, Wicklow Papers, MS 38,597/1(1 & 2), Hugh Howard to William Howard, 10th July 1716.

[27] Nicola Figgis and Brendan Rooney, *Irish Paintings in the National Gallery of Ireland*, I (Dublin 2001) 238.

[28] BM, Prints and Drawings Department, BM 1957-12-14-207.1.

[29] BM, Prints and Drawings Department, BM 1874,0808.23, nine sheets of copies in pen and brown ink by Howard after van Dyck . Howard's copy of van Dyck's sketch of Sofonisba Anguissola, aged 96, is inscribed 'This with four leafs of Pensieri d'Titiano are from Van Dykes [sic] pocket book now belonging to the Duke of Devonshire'.

[30] Paul Mellon Centre, London, Brinsley Ford Archive, Howard file, letters from Howard to Zanetti dated 16th April 1723, 21st January and 14th April 1724. These letters were included at the Sale of Shelton Abbey in 1950 by Allen and Townsend. See also NLI, MS 38,628/15, letter dated 14th March 1973, Alessandro Bettagno to Lord Wicklow.

[31] Franco Bernabei, 'Conte Anton Maria Zanetti' in Jane Turner (ed.), *The Dictionary of Art*, 33 vols (London 1996) vol. 33, 612.

[32] NLI, Wicklow Papers, MS 38,628/9, note of expenses connected with the paintings.

[33] Second son of 2nd Duke of Devonshire.

[34] NLI, Wicklow Papers, MS 38,628/9, Henry Trench to Hugh Howard, 26th May 1724.

[35] See Toby Barnard, *Making the Grand Figure: lives and possessions in Ireland, 1641-1770* (New Haven and London 2004) 174.

[36] *ibid.*

[37] NLI, Wicklow Papers, MS 38,598/3, Hugh Howard to Ralph Howard, 6th September 1726.

[38] NLI, Wicklow Papers, MS 38,598/5, Hugh Howard to Robert Howard, 1st[?] April 1729. See also Barnard, *Making the Grand Figure*, 174.

[39] NLI, Wicklow Papers, MS 38,598/11, Robert Howard to Hugh Howard, 6th January 1731.

[40] NLI, Wicklow Papers, MS 38,628/9.

[41] Hugh Howard was buried in Richmond, Surrey.

[42] NLI, Wicklow Papers MS 38,628/12. R.B. Ford, 'The Wicklow Wilsons', *Burlington Magazine*, 93, 1951, 157-66.

[43] Sotheby's 12th-20th December 1873 (1,710 lots; £4,606 6s realised) and 27th-28th November 1874 (406 lots; £3,030 5s 6d realised). V&A Art Library, ref. 23.XX. See Wynne, 1969, 317, fn.6.

[44] BM, Prints and Drawings Department, Merlin Collections Database.

[45] BM 1874.0808.22.

[46] Sotheby's, 12th-20th December 1873, lot 368. Giovanni Alberti, 'Study for a Cornice, enriched with landscape subjects and shields, one of the Papal arms'.

[47] Sotheby's, 12th-20th December 1873, lot 410. 'Michael Angelo Buonarroti: sheet of Studies. A highly wrought anatomical drawing of a Man's shoulder and arm'.

[48] Sotheby's, 27th-28th November 1874, lot 32: the drawing was inscribed *Ritratto d'Annibal'Caracci fatto da se medisimo nella sua pueritia*.

[49] In the collections of the NGI, the Faculty of Music, Oxford and the Royal Society of Musicians of Great Britain, London. A fourth appeared at Christie's, London, on 24th April 1987, lot 85.

[50] NLI, Wicklow Papers, MS 38,628/9.

[51] Figgis and Rooney, *Irish Paintings in the National Gallery of Ireland*, 239-42.

[52] *17th-Century Art in Europe*, Royal Academy of Arts, 1938, cat. 311; Wynne, 1969, 315. Although Wynne reattributed the Mount Edgecumbe portrait to Howard, a photographic comparison with Howard's known portrait of Corelli (RSM), engraved by Michael van der Gught, shows the Mount Edgecumbe portrait (now lost) to have been carried out by a more experienced artist, particularly in the detailing of Corelli's right hand and musical score.

[53] Howard was one of the first subscribers to Kneller's academy in Queen Street, Lincoln's Inn Fields. Vertue, VI, *Walpole Society*, XXX, 168.

[54] Sold Christie's, 14th November 1974, lot 9.

[55] Barnard, *Making the Grand Figure*, 157. TCD, Archbishop W. King Account Books, 1700-12, TCD MS 751/2, f.218; 1715-23, TCD MS 751/3, f.99. On 5th June 1719, £28 19s 7d was paid to Mr Hugh Howard (reason unspecified).

[56] Attributions to Howard have been given for the portrait of Narcissus Marsh and John Stearne. The latter, if by Howard, was painted posthumously. See Anne Crookshank and David Webb, *Paintings and Sculpture in Trinity College Dublin* (Dublin 1990); Wynne, 1969, 316; Michael Wynne, 'Portraits by Hugh Howard (1675-1738) in the College Collection', *Hermathena: A Dublin University Review*, CXI, 1971, 58-60.

[57] NLI, Wicklow Papers, MS 38,632/2, Katherine Howard to William Howard, typescript of letter dated 8th March 1710. Howard's portraits in Trinity College were previously dated to after Ralph Howard's death. See Wynne, 1969, 316.

[58] NLI, Wicklow Papers, MS 38,632/2, Katherine Howard to William Howard, typescript of letter dated 21st September 1710.

[59] NLI, Wicklow Papers, MS 38,597/24 (1 & 2), Robert Howard to Hugh Howard, n.d.

[60] Vertue, V, *Walpole Society*, XXVI, 42.

[61] Wynne, 315.

[62] J.C. Hodges, *William Congreve: Letters and Documents* (London 1964) 34. Photocopy amongst Michael Wynne's files on Hugh Howard, NGI, Centre for the Study of Irish Art.

[63] *ibid.*

[64] *ibid.*, 54.

[65] See Laurence Binyon, *Catalogue of Drawings by British Artists and Artists of Foreign Origin working in Great Britain preserved in the Department of Prints and Drawings in the British Museum*, 4 vols (London 1898-1907) II, 362-64.

[66] BM, 1874.0808.115.

[67] BM, 1874.0808.111.

[68] Wynne, 1969, 314; Binyon, *Catalogue of Drawings by British Artists*, II, 363-64. The BM Merlin Collections Database gives them as after Carlo Maratti.

[69] NLI, Wicklow Papers, MS 38,598/11, Hugh Howard to Robert Howard, 14th April 1730.

[70] BM, 1874.0808.109 offset BM 1874.0808.110. Guercino's original painting (1637) is in the collection of the Church of St Dominic, Turin. Luigi Salerno, *I Dipinti del Guercino* (Rome 1988) 255, cat. 168.

[71] See Paul Goldman, *Looking at Prints, Drawings and Watercolours: a Guide to Technical Terms* (London and Malibu 1988) 45.

[72] BM, 1874.0808.112.

[73] Wynne, 1969, 314.

[74] BM, 1874.0808.105.

———

1 – William Francis Dixon for Mayer & Co
Detail from east window at Clontuskert church, near Ballinasloe, county Galway

Nineteenth-century stained glass in the Church of Ireland diocese of Limerick & Killaloe

DAVID LAWRENCE

THE DIOCESE OF LIMERICK & KILLALOE EXTENDS OVER A HUGE GEOGRAPHIC area, embracing Valentia Island in the south and the town of Ballinasloe, county Galway, in the north, and taking in counties Clare, Kerry and Limerick, and parts of Offaly and Tipperary (Plate 2). The present-day diocese is a union of the eight historical dioceses of Limerick, Ardfert, Aghadoe, Killaloe, Kilfenora, Clonfert, Kilmacduagh and Emly. Four of the cathedrals are still in use for worship – Limerick, Killaloe, Clonfert and Aghadoe – and, of these, all except the latter have stained glass. In addition to these cathedrals, seventy-three churches are open and thirty-eight of these have stained-glass windows. With one exception, there is no discussion in this article on windows in closed churches: access to these can be difficult and the windows are often damaged or obstructed. The exception is Kilfergus church, county Limerick, where the quality, both of its architecture, by an Irish architect, and its stained glass, by an Irish artist, makes its inclusion impossible to resist.

The period under review does not stop strictly at the turn of the century. Windows will be considered dating from the early years of the twentieth century, but made by studios which were continuing to work in, what broadly might be called, the Gothic tradition. A fundamentally new direction in stained glass in Ireland was taken in 1903 with the founding of the Dublin studio An Túr Gloine (The Tower of Glass), and it is that event which defines the limits of the present study. There are several windows from that studio in this diocese, including outstanding work by Michael Healy at Lorrha, county Galway, and by Ethel Rhind at Kinnitty, county Offaly, but to comment on these would not cover new ground. However, examples of stained glass from the English Arts & Crafts movement, in which An Túr Gloine had its origins, are rare in Ireland, and this is a topic which

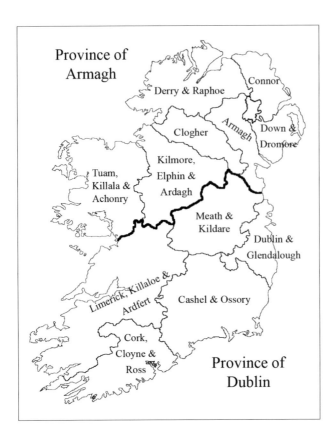

2 – Present-day dioceses of the Church of Ireland

will be considered. It is inappropriate to assess a stained-glass window in isolation from its context, and so there are brief descriptions of most of the buildings. Where possible, the patronage and dates of the buildings and the names of the architects are also mentioned, and there are some comments on furnishings and on other works of art.

Although there are nineteenth-century Irish windows in Church of Ireland churches, the majority were commissioned from the major English studios and from Mayer & Co of Munich. Several of these English firms are represented in this diocese, including Clayton & Bell; Heaton, Butler & Bayne; Hardman & Co; Kempe & Co; Lavers, Barraud & Westlake; James Powell & Sons; Shrigley & Hunt; William Wailes and William Warrington. Windows prior to 1860 are relatively rare in Ireland, but there are surprisingly many here: one by Warrington; a scheme of four windows, possibly based on designs by A.W.N. Pugin; and a rare example of a window by Thomas Wilmshurst. The span of forty years from 1860 until the end of the century was a highly productive period for English stained glass, and the outstanding windows from this era are those by Clayton & Bell at St Mary's Cathedral, Limerick. Complete schemes of windows throughout a church from a single studio are greatly to be valued, and here there are two, both by William Wailes of Newcastle.

What of the churches themselves? First the cathedrals: both Limerick and Killaloe are large and intact medieval buildings. Killaloe, which dates from the early thirteenth century, remains extraordinarily unaltered. Clonfert is tiny and bravely bears the scars of a troubled history. All three cathedrals have Romanesque doorways and that at Clonfert is magnificent. A fourth Romanesque doorway, comparable with Clonfert, forms part of the surviving west wall of the twelfth-century church at Roscrea, and a round tower stands nearby. Of the other churches, Tuamgraney is early, possibly dating from the tenth century, and both Adare and Lorrha are the churches of medieval monastic foundations. In Acheson's history of the Church of Ireland,[1] it is claimed that 633 Board of First Fruits churches were built between 1800 and 1829, so it comes as no surprise that several of the churches visited were in the characteristic First Fruits Gothic style.

The second wave of nineteenth-century church-building came in the years leading up to, and immediately following the disestablishment, in 1870, of the Church of Ireland. The principal architects at the time were Joseph Welland (1798-1860) and his son's partnership Welland & Gillespie. A large number of the churches in this diocese are by the Wellands, amongst them Valentia, Kinnitty and Ballingarry.

Joseph Welland was first appointed as one of the architects to the Board of First Fruits in 1826 and continued in that role when, in 1839, the Irish Ecclesiastical Commission replaced the Board of First Fruits. At first, there were four architects, each having responsibility for an ecclesiastical province: William Farrell for Armagh, John Semple for Dublin, James Pain for Cashel, and Joseph Welland for Tuam, but in 1843 Welland was given sole responsibility for architecture by the Commission.[2] Alistair Rowan has pointed out that this gave Welland 'a virtual monopoly of the Established Church's building programme for the next seventeen years'.[3] When Welland died in 1860, his son William John Welland (d.1895) was appointed joint architect in partnership with William Gillespie (d.1896). Rowan has a high opinion of the Wellands: 'Fortunately both Wellands were gifted men. As architects, they showed a happy sense of massing and a knack of economic detail and design that make their smaller rural churches delightful and eminently right for their setting.'[4]

The quest for stained glass took this writer to more than a dozen newly built mid-nineteenth-century churches in this diocese. In addition to those built by the Wellands, there are fine buildings by William Atkins, James Rawson Carroll, James Rogers and James Pain. Some of these, such as Killarney and Abington, have elaborately decorated interiors in the manner of the Tractarian churches being built in England at the time. Some of the most handsome Church of Ireland churches are those which had been, or still are, associated with country houses. Examples in this diocese are Birr, Ballyseedy, Kilfergus and Donanaughta.

THE APPRECIATION OF GOTHIC-REVIVAL STAINED GLASS

MOST PEOPLE FEEL COMFORTABLE WITH (INDEED, ENTHUSIASTIC ABOUT) medieval stained glass and about the work of the well-known Dublin artists and studios working in the early years of the twentieth century. But there has been a tendency for the immense body of nineteenth-century stained glass, about which so little was known or understood, to be dismissed, using blanket terms such as 'sentimental' or 'only Victorian', implying that it was worthless. To describe a stained-glass window as Victorian contributes little to serious discussion. No single adjective can usefully embrace the hundreds of artists who worked during the sixty-three years of that era. It was one of the most prolific, creative and diverse in church-building history. Those working in architecture and the applied arts drew upon sources from a wide variety of periods and cultures; there were several identifiable mainstream movements as well as numerous highly individual and idiosyncratic directions of development. In England, the earlier books in the Pevsner *Buildings of England* series were not helpful in this regard. Rather than identifying the artist, which should have been the prime objective, the authors would write off windows with quick, derogatory opinions.[5] It is significant, though, that where a provenance was easily identifiable (the best example being the work of Kempe & Co), that fact would be recorded and the subjective phrases avoided.

A good example of the lack of understanding of nineteenth-century stained glass can be quoted in the case of St Mary's church, Kington, Herefordshire, which has a remarkable series of early Clayton & Bell windows, similar in character and period to those at Limerick cathedral and at Ardamine, county Wexford.[6] For Fenn & Sinclair, the significance of Clayton & Bell's ten Kington windows could be summed up by naming one of the colours of glass used: 'The chancel windows were filled with their blue glass in 1862.'[7] As well as falling short of being a useful critical analysis, any study of the ten windows would quickly show that blue is not even a predominant colour, and that greens, ambers, blues and rubies all occur in similar proportions. Even as organ voluntaries are often heard but not listened to, so stained glass particularly suffers from being looked at but seldom seen. In the *Shell Guide*, we have Verey's inexcusable remark that the chancel at Kington 'is lit by lancets with execrable glass'.[8] Although Pevsner clearly likes the windows, he sadly misses the point by his use of the word 'imitation' in describing the windows as 'good imitation thirteenth-century glass'.[9] These three comments are in stark contrast to the opinion of the foremost authority on nineteenth-century English stained glass,

Martin Harrison, who has written that Kington possesses 'a series of most important windows representing the pinnacle of Clayton and Bell's High-Victorian idiom'.[10]

As the twentieth century drew to a close, there was, thanks to pioneering research work by Harrison[11] and a handful of other dedicated individuals, a far greater appreciation of the achievements of the nineteenth-century stained-glass studios. Apart from having been given the means for assessment and criticism by these researchers, the simple fact of their making the names of artists and studios available for common use assisted immeasurably in the reassessment of their work. Most stained-glass windows being unsigned, this vast body of work had been daunting in its anonymity, and this alone was sufficient to put appreciation beyond the grasp of many, but to recognise, say, the early work of Clayton & Bell was not only immensely rewarding, but it also provided the starting point for real understanding and awareness. Those who thought that only medieval stained glass or 'modern' stained glass was of importance were beginning to have the veils pulled from their eyes. As research continued, not only could a window be attributed to a particular studio, but also the names of some of the designers started to come to light. Many were on the studio payroll, and often their work conformed to a house style. Some studios also commissioned drawings from artists of the greatest stature and from lesser-known, but highly distinguished freelance designers.

THE EARLY YEARS OF THE GOTHIC REVIVAL

THE NINETEENTH-CENTURY GOTHIC REVIVAL WAS GIVEN IMPETUS BY THE OXFORD Movement and by the writings and work of the architect Augustus Welby Northmore Pugin (1812-1852), notably his book *The True Principles of Pointed or Christian Architecture*.[12] The intention of the exponents of the Oxford Movement – John Henry Newman, Edward Bouverie Pusey and John Keble – expounded in their *Tracts for the Times* (1835-41), was to reinstate the catholic tradition within the Church of England. The theories both of Pugin and of the Tractarians were embodied in the Cambridge Camden Society. It was formed in 1839, changing its name to the Ecclesiological Society in 1846. Passionately committed to the teachings both of the Oxford Movement and of Pugin, the Society's aim was to make these ideals manifest in ecclesiastical architecture. Through the medium of their journal, *The Ecclesiologist*, which ran from 1841 to 1868, the Ecclesiological Society promoted what Brooks has described as 'a compound of dogmatic theology gleaned from the Tractarians and dogmatic architectural theory gathered from Pugin'.[13]

The churches that were to be restored and the new churches that were to be built had to embody the catholic principles of the medieval church. They abhorred what they described as the 'preaching boxes' of the eighteenth and early nineteenth century, with their galleries, box pews and emphasis on the pulpit. The Ecclesiologists called for churches to be axially arranged, with the congregation sitting on east-facing benches focused on the altar, which was to be placed in a distinct and substantial chancel, reached if possible by a series of steps. The architectural style was to be thirteenth-century Gothic, and, central to the present discussion, the windows were to have stained glass, and other forms of decoration were to be encouraged. It might be imagined that these tenets did not cross the sea to the Church of Ireland. On the contrary, not only was there High Churchmanship here, but its revival preceded, and was independent of the Oxford Movement. Acheson has explored this thoroughly:

> In the early decades of the nineteenth century, the old High Church tradition of the Church of Ireland experienced a revival. Its continued progress during the 1830s was independent of (though initially linked with) the Tractarians, for it was an indigenous tradition with its roots in the seventeenth century ... Distinctive doctrines and practices, many of them anticipating the Tractarian movement, were recovered in the early nineteenth-century church.[14]

Although in a minority, the movement persisted, survived disestablishment, and was permitted to co-exist with the mainstream evangelical movement. In its wake came a surpliced choir and choral eucharist at St John's church, Limerick, and the choral tradition of St Patrick's Cathedral, Dublin, and High Church ritualism in some well-known Dublin churches, as well as in other unsung churches in various parts of the country. The best-known of these Dublin churches are All Saints' in Grangegorman, St John's in Sandymount, and St Bartholomew's on Clyde Road, and at the latter two the traditions have remained to this day. Sadly St John's, Limerick, a rare exercise in Romanesque by Joseph Welland, now has an alternative use and all the furnishings and decorations have been stripped out. Only the blue and gold starred ceiling of the apse remains to speak of the rich traditions of its past.

The Catholic revival, however, was to have an influence much more widespread than the promotion of High Church traditions in certain churches. There were to be lasting consequences on the approach to church buildings and their furnishings and decorations in the second wave of nineteenth-century church-building. And this was not just within the High Church wing. In the diocese of Limerick & Killaloe, many of the churches date from this era – for example, those built or added-to by the Wellands. Their churches broadly embody the 'true principles' of the Ecclesiologists. They are very unlike the modest First Fruits churches of the previous generation. Acheson has described the radical changes which took place:

> A new style replaced both the concept of the auditory church and the austere simplicity of the tower-and-hall church. Its inspiration was medieval, with a

long chancel separated from the nave by steps as its characteristic feature. Box-pews were discarded, three-decker pulpits were replaced by a simple pulpit, a nave lectern and a litany desk ... and the 'lightsome' Georgian windows [replaced] by stained glass. The font was moved to the west end, and the choir from the western gallery to the chancel. Victorian churches were built in the new style ... and many older churches re-arranged to accommodate it.[15]

The diocese of Limerick & Killaloe contains many examples of churches which demonstrate the change of approach, and they fall into three categories: those, such as Listowel, county Kerry, to which chancels were added and internal arrangements re-ordered to conform to the new principles; new churches, such as Kinnitty, which modestly embodied the principles in an understated way; and new churches, such as Abington, county Limerick, and Donanaughta (Eyrecourt), county Galway, which were richly embellished and ecclesiological, and to which the term Tractarian could be applied. It is beyond the scope of the present article to establish what the traditions of churchmanship may have been in such buildings, although the writer has come across unlikely examples, such as the remote and tiny church of Kilronan, county Rosscommon, where there is anecdotal evidence that the liturgical traditions matched the architecture and decorations. This could be a fruitful area of research. Of those churches in this diocese which were altered, a chancel was added to the single-cell First Fruits nave at Croom; at Castleconnell a previous re-ordering was reversed and an east chancel recreated; the changes were achieved internally at Kilnasoolagh without any new building.

Two of the key figures in the revived tradition were John Jebb (1775-1833), Bishop of Limerick, Ardfert and Aghadoe, and his son Prebendary John Jebb. According to Acheson, this bishopric became 'a High Church centre for both clergy and laity', and, through publications and personal influence, 'High Churchmen stressed the primitive and catholic aspects of their church's heritage'.[16] Some extracts from Charles Forster's *The Life of John Jebb*, published in 1837, give a good idea of the unconventional ministry and of the popularity and influence of this remarkable man. Jebb had previously been Rector of Abington, and during that time established a unique dialogue with the Roman Catholics:

It was agreed that, upon the following Sunday the clergy of the two communions should meet, after morning service, in the chapel of Murroe; and the Protestant rector and the Roman catholic priest should successively address the people ... [Jebb] was heard with breathless attention: some were affected with tears. All eyes were rivetted upon him, as he told the men of Abington, that he lived among them without a fear; that his doors were unbolted, his windows unbarred.[17]

His reputation was widespread:

> An eminent English barrister happened to pass through the disturbed country at the time ... as the coach passed within sight of Abington Glebe, the coachman pointed towards the house ... 'That house is the residence of Archdeacon Jebb; the parish in which it stands is the only quiet district in the country; and its quiet is entirely owing to the character and exertions of the protestant rector.' [18]

On being elected Bishop, his home was greeted with extraordinary scenes:

> His return to Abington as Bishop-elect of Limerick, was hailed with universal joy by the Roman Catholic population, a joy damped only by the feeling that they were about to lose a friend and benefactor who had lived among them for more than twelve years in the constant exercise of kindness ... He was met on the border of the parish by a body of the peasantry who would not be withheld from taking off the horses, and drawing his carriage, preceded by a band of rustic music, for considerably more than a mile to Abington Glebe.[19]

Jebb's attitudes to doctrine were ahead of their time and pre-empted a degree of liberalisation that was not to be universally accepted within the Church of Ireland for another century:

> The Feast of St Michael and All Angels (a church festival which Bishop Jebb enjoyed in the spirit of a true catholic) falling this year upon Sunday, he was desirous to employ the day in reading suitable to it: accordingly, he requested to have brought him *A Discourse of Angels, their Nature and Office*. And thus, in the spirit of Hooker, employed the day, in meditating the number and nature of angels, and their blessed obedience and order, without which, peace could not be in heaven.[20]

Central to the present discussion is the fact that, with the new approach to church-building, restoration and adornment during these years, there came in parts of the country a more liberal doctrine which opened the door for the introduction of stained-glass windows into the Church of Ireland. Attitudes to anything other than simple coloured-glass glazing are epitomised by the battles which were fought in Cork over the plan to introduce stained glass into the new cathedral. When the designs were presented to the building committee, objections such as the following were handed in:[21]

———

3 – Detail from east window by Thomas Jervais at Agher church, county Meath, in the diocese of Meath & Kildare

I beg leave to protest against the introduction of any likeness of any object of the worship of the reformed church into the windows for the new cathedral.

We beg leave to object to any figures being introduced into the windows of the cathedral.

There were particular objections to images of Christ:

I beg leave to protest against the introduction of the likeness of the Lord Jesus Christ into any windows to be erected in the cathedral.

These notions were based on principles established at the Reformation and probably first seen in Ireland in 1636 under Archbishop George Browne, who, according to Kenneth Milne, was

A "reformer" and enthusiastic in his efforts to banish images from churches and to emphasise the authority of the Bible.[22]

However, from the 1850s onwards, stained glass containing religious images was gradually introduced into Church of Ireland churches. For most of the new windows, the patrons went to the reputable English studios. With the new ecclesiology, the stained glass, like the buildings themselves, was to be very different from that which had gone before. If the windows were to be equal to the demands of the Gothic Revival, there would have to be a radical change in design, technique and materials.

The approach in the eighteenth century had been for the picture to be painted in coloured enamels onto large pieces of clear glass. Stained-glass artists of this period would often make use of figures from well-known oil paintings or would commission original paintings from which to work. A good example of this is *St Paul Preaching to the Athenians*, a window by Thomas Jervais (d.1799) at Agher, county Meath, based on the painting by Raphael (Plate 3).[23] In complete contrast, the medieval artists painted details of line and shadow in brown and black oxides onto small pieces of coloured glass, joined by a network of lead strips. Along with these two opposing techniques, there were two entirely different approaches to design, one being pictorial and the other mosaic-like and devoid of perspective. Spurred on by the ideals of the Ecclesiologists, various attempts were made to rediscover the method of making coloured glass. The breakthrough came in 1847 when Charles Winston (1814-1864) published his researches – made at the glassworks and studios of James Powell & Sons in London – on the chemical analysis of coloured glass used during the medieval period, and Powell's went on to manufacture coloured glass according to Winston's principles.[24] Although Winston's research in London is well documented and much quoted, it seems that similar goals had previously been sought and apparently achieved to a greater or lesser extent in Dublin, Munich and Paris.

William Warrington of London

The earliest window in the diocese is one made before 1850 by William Warrington (1786-1869) for Kirwan House Orphanage, Dublin, and moved to Kilnasoolagh Church, Newmarket-on-Fergus, county Clare, in 1959.[25] Warrington was a pupil of the pioneering stained-glass artist Thomas Willement (1786-1871), and was active in stained glass when the revival was in its infancy: he made Pugin's windows from as early as 1838. Three angels with scrolls occupy only a small proportion of the window; the remainder consists of medallions of roses and scrolls set against vine-based ornamental work. The vine leaves are in bright amber and the diapered backgrounds are in deep rubies and hot blues. The window is similar in character to the east window at Lissadell, county Sligo, which also has small figure-medallions and large areas of ornamental vine-work and canopies.[26] A characteristic feature of Warrington windows of this period is the quirky figure-drawing in a thirteenth-century manner, and with what was described by one critic in his day as 'hair somewhat uglier than a rope mat'.[27]

Kilnasoolagh church, a simple single cell with late pointed fenestration, was built in its present form in 1815 by James Pain (1779-1877), and re-ordered by Welland & Gillespie in 1864.[28] The English-born James Pain and his younger brother George were pupils of John Nash, and both set up practices in Ireland – James in Limerick and George in Cork. In 1823 James Pain was appointed architect to the Board of First Fruits for Munster. The church stands near the gates of the FitzGeralds' Carrigoran House, and is about one mile distant from Dromoland, seat of the O'Brien family. Elaborate monuments to both families and several armorial stained-glass windows give the interior the dignity which was required, but the real delights of the interior are the furnishings, great and small, and primarily the great oak screen which creates a token chancel. It is pierced with lancets and quatrefoils and has a grand central arch – analogous to a chancel arch, but also having echoes of a rood-screen. The church is lit by eight single standard oil lamps in the nave and two doubles in the chancel. Welland & Gillespie's re-ordering of 1864 brought the prayer-book interior in line with the new ecclesiology. The box pews and the triple-decker pulpit were removed, and the baptismal font, adjacent to the pulpit, was placed at the west end. A series of four steps up to the sanctuary was created.

Amongst the other excellent examples of Warrington's work in Ireland are those at St Ann's Church, Dublin; Kilnamanagh, county Wexford; and Kells, county Kilkenny.[29] These last two both date from 1865, and it is interesting to see the way the style of drawing and painting had developed and become more polished by then although the palette remains similar. The faces are executed in a refined painting style with conspicuous whites-of-the-eyes, giving them the character of porcelain dolls. And it is in this same year, 1865, that two Warrington windows were put into

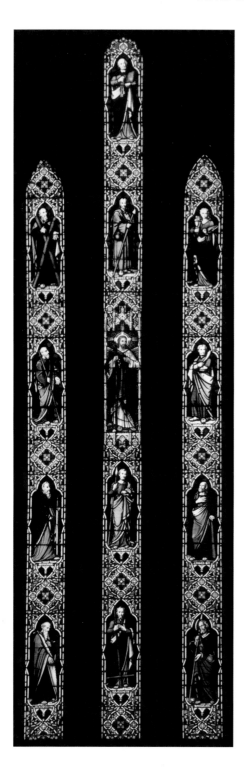

Killaloe cathedral.

Killaloe is a complete, and largely unaltered cruciform, transitional, early thirteenth-century cathedral church. The vast and dimly lit space of the nave, with its floor of flags, devoid of pews, preserves a pre-Reformation feeling. The lofty south transept could do the same were it not for the south-facing altar table, diagonally set pews, and the presence of secular utensils. Sadly (but understandably) the cruciform character has been lost: part of the 1887 restoration[30] by James Franklin Fuller (1835-1925) was the introduction of a glazed oak screen at the crossing, clearly inspired in design by the west façade of a French cathedral and incorporating a sixteen-sector wheel-tracery opening; this cuts off the nave. The organ and a simple glazed partition cut off the south transept, and the north transept is walled-up to provide essential function rooms. Fuller's other work in this diocese includes the restorations of Killarney (1888-89) and Clonfert (1896-1900).

The east window, of 1865, which is more than ten metres high, consists of three narrow lancets, and the arches are elaborately carved. Warrington's *Apostles* could not be more suitable for this building (Plate 4). Each apostle is set in a medallion, in the thirteenth-century manner. The removal, sometime in the last century, of the central figure of St Paul and its replacement with a figure of Christ in an entirely unrelated style was badly misjudged. The window is matched in

5 – The missing St Paul from the east window at Killaloe

opposite

4 – East window by William Warrington at Killaloe cathedral, county Clare

excellence and in character by the 1865 single-lancet Warrington west window, depicting Faith, Hope and Charity. The south transept is lit by three prodigiously tall, narrow lancets and by a twin-lancet window-opening of exceptional beauty and rare design. This was clearly the focus of a side chapel of some importance in the medieval religious life. Set high in the wall is a wide opening, framed by a Gothic arch, with mouldings and foliate capitals. Within this, and within the thickness of the wall, are doorways to internal passages; these flank a central twin-lancet window, again with mouldings, engaged columns and foliate capitals. And there, in one of the lancets, is the missing St Paul from the east window (Plate 5). It is to be hoped that it will, at some time, be put back and the integrity of the east window restored. In addition to the carvings to the east window opening, there are other contemporary stone-carvings, including the corbels from which the roof would originally have sprung; one has birds, one has a strange group of kilted figures, others have plant forms. The crossing, with its simple rib-vaulting, springs from four carved corbels set into the stone walls with no columns or mouldings. Built into the south wall of the nave is a twelfth-century doorway, possibly from an earlier church, richly carved with animals and plant-forms, and nearby is the thirteenth-century font.

Hardman & Co of Birmingham

In 1845, John Hardman (1811-1867) added a stained-glass department to his Birmingham firm of ecclesiastical metalworkers at the instigation of Pugin. The foremost figure in stained glass of the time, Pugin remained as chief designer at Hardman & Co until his death in 1852, when the work was taken over by Hardman's nephew, John Hardman Powell (1832-1895). Pugin described Powell as his 'only pupil'.[31] In the diocese of Limerick & Killaloe there are four windows from Hardman & Co, dating from the 1850s, at Adare, and two late windows – from the end of the century – at Clonfert cathedral. At first sight, the Adare windows seem to be the work of Pugin, although closer investigation into dates, in the Hardman archive, make it more likely that they are the work of Powell, since they appear in the records a couple of years after the death of Pugin in 1852.

However, stained-glass windows are not conceived and made at a single stroke by a single hand, and there is a strong possibility, supported by some evidence, that Pugin himself was in fact involved in the design of some of these windows. His influence was to be seen in Hardman's output for many years following his death, especially in the style of figure-drawing, drapery and glass-painting, and in the details of background decoration, canopies and borders. As Dr Stanley Shepherd has commented, there were still good reasons to continue to produce works in the Pugin mode: 'one was continuity ... another was client-pressure'.[32]

Although the decorative details persisted and the overall character continued broadly in the Pugin mould, Powell gradually developed his own more aesthetic style of figure-drawing with refined and moulded glass-painting.

Of the four Adare windows, possibly all were sketched by Pugin, and the east window (Plate 6), a memorial to the Earl of Dunraven who died in 1850, could well have been worked up into a full cartoon under his supervision. The other three seem more likely to have been cartooned by Powell, either under Pugin's influence or making use of his sketches. The dates given in the Hardman archives for the windows are 1854 and 1855, but delays between conceiving and installing stained glass can amount to several years. Writing in 1865, Caroline, Countess of Dunraven, has provided firm evidence that other work at Adare Manor, designed by Pugin, was still not executed some thirteen years after his death:

> The dining room is not yet decorated according to the beautiful plans of the late Mr. Pugin; they consist of panelled walls and ceiling, a lofty and highly ornamental mantelpiece and a carved oak screen of rich design supporting a minstrel's gallery. The billiard room and library are also still unfinished.[33]

Phoebe Stanton's research into the Dunraven archives gives us the firmest indication of Pugin's personal involvement in the Adare windows:

> Adare Manor. Built for and by the second Earl of Dunraven. Details in the hall, various fireplaces, general design of the dining hall taken from the A.W.N. Pugin drawings which are in the collection at Adare Manor. Drawings dated 1846-1847. In addition Pugin added a new roof and stained-glass windows in the village church, which he probably also totally restored.[34]

There were three monastic foundations at Adare: the Trinitarian priory, founded in 1230, which was restored in the nineteenth century by the 1st Earl of Dunraven to become the Catholic church; the Franciscan friary, founded in 1464, the extensive and picturesque ruins of which stand in the demesne of Adare Manor; and the Augustinian priory, founded by John, Earl of Kildare in 1315, which was restored in 1806 to become the Church of Ireland church. The group of buildings forming what remained of the priory consisted of the church, the fifteenth-century cloisters, the refectory (or possibly dormitory) with rooms beneath, a gateway and a long building extending to the north. In 1814 the refectory was restored for use as a school, and further restoration of the church was carried out between 1850 and 1854 by Lady Dunraven. The immaculate restoration is completely in sympathy with the spirit of the priory church, and what we have today is an unusually complete and homogeneous early fourteenth-century abbey church with a somewhat later (c.1350) south aisle. One of the most remarkable architectural features is the ribbed-vaulted

148

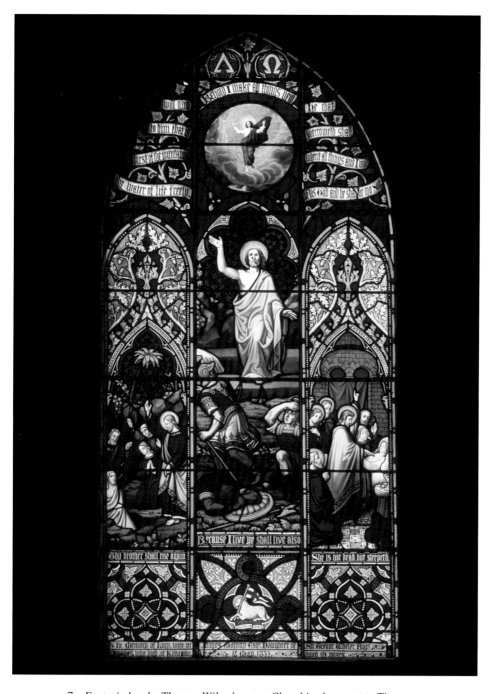

7 – East window by Thomas Wilmshurst at Cloughjordan, county Tipperary

opposite 6 – *East window by Hardman & Co at Adare, county Limerick*

volume beneath the central tower with its tall, narrow, simple arches. This would be the crossing if the church were cruciform, and it serves to add greater distance from the nave to the sanctuary at the far end of the already lengthy chancel. The nave is immensely tall and narrow, and must have looked even more so before the addition of the south aisle. The north wall is an uninterrupted cliff of masonry, with the cloisters beyond. The south wall has been crudely pierced with three simple pointed arches. The other windows at Adare are by Mayer (1886) and Heaton, Butler & Bayne (1891), and, however good in themselves, their introduction was a misjudgement in this context and in juxtaposition with the Hardman windows.

Even as Pugin's influence was to be seen at Hardman's long after his death, notably in the work of Powell, so the influence of both of them was to persist after Powell's death in 1895, as can be seen in two late Hardman windows put into Clonfert cathedral under the supervision of J.F. Fuller. We will divert briefly from the chronology to consider these. They occupy two narrow round-headed thirteenth-century lancets set in deep reveals, with engaged shafts and blind lancets on each side. This unique design was described in Brash's *Ecclesiastical Architecture of Ireland* as being 'exceedingly chaste and beautiful and the mouldings superior to anything I have seen either of ancient or modern times'.[35]

The Hardman glass is of great strength. The figures are robustly drawn and set against chunks of unpainted and strongly coloured glass within the niches, decorated, somewhat surprisingly to our eyes, with the early Christian symbols known as fylfots. *St Peter* has drapery of a cobalt blue against a deep vermilion background. *St Paul* has a verdant green against a cobalt background. The strength of colour, especially within the blue, varies delightfully. Above and below the figures are exceptionally successful panels of Celtic decorative work in brilliant, kaleidoscopic colours, inspired by illuminated manuscripts. Fuller was a major figure in reviving the Hiberno-Romanesque school of architecture, and doubtless insisted on Hardman's coming up with these decorations. He also seems to have leaned on Watson & Co, another studio represented here. Their windows, of similar date to the Hardman windows, also include Celtic devices.

Two rare discoveries were made of pre-1860 glass. The first is a group of five windows at Limerick cathedral which the writer attributes to Josef Gabriel Mayer (1808-1893), the founder of the well-known studio Mayer & Co, but predating by about twenty years the earliest Mayer windows previously recorded in Church of Ireland churches. The second is a window at Cloughjordan of considerable interest (Plate 7). It is one of a very few windows designed by Thomas Wilmshurst (1806-1880) who first achieved recognition as early as 1830.[36] The Cloughjordan window, although dating from around 1855, is in the pictorial style of the 1830s and 1840s, and it was for the tendency to look back to this era that his work was not favoured by the ecclesiologists: 'He has adopted the worst landscape style of thirty years back.'[37] According to Martin Harrison, Wilmshurst was, for a while, in partnership with Oliphant. He was never prolific, and little seems to have been heard of him after 1861, 'by which time, in the heyday of the Gothic Revivalists such as Clayton & Bell, the demand for his pictorial style no longer existed'.[38] The window is similar in character to his *Crucifixion* window at Leigh Delamere, Wiltshire, dating from around 1848, the inspiration for which draws heavily on the sixteenth-century glass in St Margaret's, Westminster, London.

Cloughjordan church, prettily sited on the village green, was originally a simple single-cell First Fruits church, built about 1810, with a small sanctuary to the east and entrance lobby to the west. In 1837 it was reorientated and a tower with spire added on the north elevation, opposite a sanctuary added on the south. The resulting church is of unconventional and uncomfortable proportions, with a nave of extreme width and shortness. The former sanctuary and lobby have become miniature 'transepts'. The interior was drastically re-ordered in 1992 when all the Georgian furnishings and fittings were swept away and replaced by commercially made church furnishings and pews.

THE HIGH VICTORIAN ERA

DESPITE THE INDEPENDENCE IN ORIGIN OF THE REVIVAL MOVEMENTS IN IRELAND and in England, those with the inclination (and the money) were permitted, within the terms of Joseph Welland's appointment, to bring in their own architects, and they frequently turned to the English architects of the Gothic Revival. Such buildings, great and small, can be seen throughout the country, including some by the best-known English and Irish architects of the day. As well as the importance of their buildings, these architects made a significant contribution to the decoration of churches and to the design and role of stained glass. Harrison observed that they were all in varying degrees committed to improving the standards of church decorations:

> They all, too, showed a particular concern with the stained glass made for their churches. The close supervision of interior, as well as external, colour and design which these leading architects would demand was the single most significant factor for the development of stained glass during the High Victorian period, added to which was the intense involvement in church decorations of a vast body of wealthy patrons, clergymen and ecclesiologists of all kinds.[39]

It was in 1970 that Martin Harrison first borrowed the term High Victorian to describe a particular era and style of English stained glass. In two recent lectures he has developed this concept. He defines the period concerned as 1858 to 1868 and characterises the windows as 'vividly coloured', 'two-dimensional', 'having no perspective or possibly being planar', 'employing mosaic-like small piece of glass', 'intense' in mood, and influenced by French stained glass of the thirteenth century, for example those in the Sainte-Chapelle in Paris.[40] There are twenty or so windows in the diocese which date from the High Victorian era of English stained glass, and two Mayer & Co windows of similar date will also be discussed in this section.

Clayton & Bell of London

Maurice Craig, commenting on the astounding cathedral-building enterprise by the Church of Ireland in the years leading up to disestablishment in 1869, believes that 'the universally accepted imperative of the time to "Build churches!" was felt to be valid, and especially so where the cathedral bequeathed by the chequered past was felt to be inadequate or unworthy'.[41] No less than five Church of Ireland cathedrals were either built from scratch or comprehensively rebuilt within a few years, starting with William Slater's Kilmore, county Cavan (completed 1860). There followed in rapid succession Tuam, Cork, Kildare and Christ Church, Dublin. As far as the Cathedral of St Mary, Limerick, was concerned, no rebuilding was required but major works were undertaken by William Slater. These included essential structural work and re-ordering to bring the interior into line with the principles of ecclesiology, in a manner worthy of the Jebb legacy. Slater was also behind the commissioning of a set of stained-glass windows by Clayton & Bell, some of which are of exceptional beauty and significance. Some of the earliest of the collection were cartooned by John Richard Clayton (1827-1913), and one could possibly be the work of Alfred Bell (1832-1895). They had set up in partnership in 1855, and although they were soon to employ other artists and cartoonists in the studio, both were artists of considerable stature in their own right. There are a few other excellent examples of early Clayton & Bell work in Ireland designed by Clayton, notably at Ardamine (under George Edmund Street) and at Kilmore (under William Slater).[42]

The partners were greatly encouraged in their early work by Street, and the resulting windows were a brilliant interpretation and development of thirteenth-century Gothic, making full use of the wide range of richly coloured glass now being produced. In the same year, 1859, that Slater commissioned the great east window – the first of the Limerick windows – Street, having previously contracted William Wailes for his stained glass, turned to Clayton & Bell for his first London church, St

---

8 – Detail from the south transept window at Limerick

James the Less in Pimlico.[46] The results were a resounding success, and this collaboration between Street and Clayton & Bell was to be the first of many. The next year, 1860, Street began work on Ardamine, with its archetypal examples of Clayton & Bell's thirteenth-century-inspired-style stained glass, and in 1861 Slater designed the new south transept window for Limerick and ordered its breathtaking stained glass.

At Kildare and at Tuam, the restoring architects were faced with ruins, but here at Limerick Slater took on a magnificent and remarkably intact early thirteenth-century cathedral church. The main cruciform structure dates from the very beginning of the century and incorporates an earlier Romanesque west doorway. The nave has north and south arcades, each consisting of four massive square piers with simple, unmoulded transitional arches. High above these there is an architectural amalgam of triforium and clerestory, with lintelled passages running through the walls, lit by lancets. This is an uncommon, but not unprecedented concept, with other examples at Laon cathedral in France and León cathedral in Spain. Sometime in the fifteenth century, chapels were added to the north and south aisles, running the full length of the aisles and extending beyond the full depth of the transepts.

Slater's task consisted of building a new roof over the nave, major works to the chancel and south transept, and internal re-ordering and furnishing; this was carried out between 1858 and 1863. *The Dublin Builder* reported that part of the work to the chancel included the removal of the 'modern perpendicular window', which was 'out of character', and replacing it with a new stone window-opening and stained glass.[43] The south transept was also to have a new rood and a 'new roof, new stone window with stained glass and complete fitting up'. The summary of other works is particularly useful:

> Seats for the choristers; canopies over the stalls; new floors to the chancel and choir; open up the clerestory windows to the choir; remove the organ gallery and open up the arches; new organ gallery; remove monumental tablets into the north chapel; floors of aisles – limestone flags removed and Minton tiles set; red marble steps at the entrance to the choir; open up circular window in chancel.[44]

Sadly, most of Slater's inspired plan for internal arrangements of this cathedral, together with his furnishings and floors, were removed during the 1990s, and we have only contemporary photographs[45] to show us how brilliantly Slater had married his work with existing historic furnishings and how he had successfully created the feeling of one of the great cathedral chancels, such as Canterbury, with collegiate stalls. He had some wonderful medieval material with which to start – sedillia, piscina, credence table – and, above all, more than twenty fifteenth-century misericords in carved oak, unique in Ireland and now relegated to the peripheries.

The decision, in 1858 to remove the late pointed east window-opening on purely aesthetic grounds was bold. It had been put in by James Pain as recently as 1843. It was to be replaced by three simple lancets. Clearly, no expense would be spared to recreate the thirteenth-century character in accordance with Pugin's 'True Principles'. The Clayton & Bell stained glass precisely complements this aim, and the studio's mastery of the architectural role of stained glass and of colour is immediately apparent. A central vesica in the east window has the figure *Our Lord Enthroned*, and smaller circular medallions have *The Acts of Mercy* – the groups of figures drawn in Clayton's thirteenth-century style and set against backgrounds of chunks of unpainted blue glass. According to a contemporary report, James Pain's Perpendicular window-opening, having been removed from the cathedral, was 'reduced in dimensions and made suitable for the smaller church of St Michael'.[46] The present cathedral guidebook, drawing upon a secondary source,[47] records the intriguing fact that the stained glass to the east window was 'renovated, releaded and cleaned in the year 1923 by the Dublin Co-operative Stained Glass Works under the supervision of Miss Sarah Purser.' Evidently, Sarah Purser's stained-glass studio, An Túr Gloine, also undertook restoration work, trading under a different name.

It is difficult to find adequate superlatives to describe Slater's and Clayton & Bell's great five-light south transept window. It is a tour de force of creativity, with over fifty Old Testament medallions, each packed with activity and inventiveness (Plates 8-10).[48] They are set against blue quarries with narrow red borders, as at Chartres. Martin Harrison has identified some sources of inspiration: 'That wonderful window at Limerick, with it French early thirteenth-century arrangement, quotes from three specific sources – Bourges, Beauvais and Laon.' As to the designer, 'I would have been inclined to say Clayton designed it, but Bell looms ever larger ... I am most excited by his figure designs, his continual fighting against Gothic – or at least his fractious dialogue with it.'[49]

In the adjoining south chapel there is another Clayton & Bell window, *Three Parables*, of the early 1860s. The window-opening is a most remarkable structure consisting of five lancets with a filigree of thirty-five reticulated tracery lights in the early fourteenth-century manner, and Clayton & Bell have responded to this later Gothic tradition. The scenes occupy rectangular panels with decorated diamond quarries above and below. There are eight Clayton & Bell windows at Limerick; others from this early period include Clayton's monumental west window of 1863 and, high up in the west end of the north aisle, his single-light *Angel of Hope*.

It is greatly to be regretted that the rubble walls, which were stripped of their plaster in recent years, have not yet been replastered and limewashed. The visual consequences for this historic interior are grave as a whole, and particularly so for the stained glass. The vast rubble-walled chambers, with their upper galleries and passageways, are as grim as Piranesi's imaginary Roman prisons. The great nineteenth-century studios were essentially architectural artists and would always see

9 – South transept window by Clayton & Bell at Limerick cathedral

10 – Detail from the south transept window at Limerick

their windows as part of the architectural whole. Clayton & Bell were the supreme masters of relating art to architecture, both in overall concept and in the immediate interplay of architectural elements. They would see the treatment of the window reveals and adjacent walls as crucial to the success of the stained glass. In some cases they would even go one step further and conceive integrated designs for stained glass and wall decorations. It is greatly to be hoped that the programme for replastering can be completed in the near future.

William Wailes of Newcastle-Upon-Tyne

William Slater employed the Clayton & Bell studio with resounding success at Limerick, but he was not exclusively wedded to it. For the massive five-light *Parables* window at his newly built Kilmore cathedral, county Cavan, he turned to the old-established firm of William Wailes. The cathedral, together with this window, was completed by 1860, by which time Slater had already embarked upon Christ Church, Bray (1860-65), and there also he commissioned Wailes to make the huge *Last Supper and Ascension* east window.

William Wailes (1808-1881) established his stained-glass firm in Newcastle-upon-Tyne in 1838, and it rapidly became very large and successful, matched in size amongst provincial studios only by Hardman of Birmingham. Having fallen out with Warrington, Pugin took his work to Wailes from 1842 until 1845, when he became closely involved in the setting up of the stained-glass department at Hardman's. At that time, F.W. Oliphant (1818-1859), who had been in partnership with Wilmshurst, was chief designer for Wailes before moving on to work with Pugin at Hardman's. Wailes's style is strongly influenced by that of Pugin and Oliphant. Possibly Wailes's greatest achievements in Ireland are the huge west and south windows of 1865 at St Patrick's Cathedral, Dublin.

It is a fortunate circumstance when all the windows in a church are from the same studio and, even more so, when they are designed at a single stroke. This leads to the best in what is, after all, essentially an architectural artform. The superlative example in Ireland is the scheme of eighty windows at William Burges's Cathedral Church of St Fin Barre, Cork.[50] Whilst there is nothing approaching this scale in the Limerick & Killaloe diocese, there are two comprehensive schemes and both are by William Wailes – all thirteen windows at Ballyseedy and eleven out of twelve at Killarney.

Ballyseedy, the estate church for Ballyseedy Castle near Tralee, seat of the Blennerhassett family, stands on the edge of the demesne. It is an excellent polychromatic building, consisting of chancel and nave, built around 1865 in the Early French style. It is built in grey ashlar with deep voussoirs, long-and-short jamb-stones and quoins, and string-courses in red sandstone. The gables to the nave, to the chancel and to the elegantly contoured south porch are tall and sharply pointed. There are slender buttresses. Research to date has not come up with the identity of the architect, although it is reminiscent of the buildings of James Rogers, such as Kenure and Kilfergus. The complete glazing scheme is by Wailes and has a single iconographic programme based on the *Miraculous Healings of Christ*. Most of the windows were given by the Blenneshassett family. They are all contemporary, dating from the early 1860s, and the scheme was no doubt conceived by the architect. One must assume that the plaques, giving dates of donation and names of donors, were applied retrospectively to the scheme since some of the years pre-date and other post-date the windows themselves. The scheme is inspired by thirteenth-century French glass as an apposite response to the Early French architecture. Each scene occupies a cusped rectangular medallion set against grisaille backgrounds with acanthus-form decoration and foliate borders.

The other scheme of Wailes windows is at Killarney. It is much later than the Ballyseedy scheme, dating from the 1880s, and so does not conform to the period under discussion in this section, but it seems logical to deal with it next. The collection of drawings in the Representative Church Body Library includes three different schemes by Joseph Welland, dating from 1859/60, for a new church at Killarney, but apparently none was implemented. Instead, the church, as standing today, is essentially that designed in 1868 by the Cork architect William Atkins (1812-1887), for which the drawings are also extant:[51] it is cruciform, with a three-bay nave, a tower standing beyond the south-west corner, and a chancel and semi-circular apse. In 1869, R.W. Edis, an English journalist visiting Killarney, wrote that:

> Mr. Atkins of Cork has just completed the new church, a carefully thought-out design with some good detail but thoroughly French in general feeling and giving the idea that the architect had studied Mr. Burges's new cathedral rather than the ecclesiastical buildings of his own country.[52]

There is considerable confusion surrounding the extent to which a fire in 1888 damaged Atkins's church. In the popular view, it was disastrous. Jeremy Williams writes that the church was 'gutted by malicious fire in 1888'.[53] And, similarly, in reporting the restoration, the contract for which was awarded to J.F. Fuller and carried out during 1888-89, *The Irish Builder* writes that the church had been 'almost totally destroyed by fire, the work of an incendiary'.[54] Yet the stained glass, most of which pre-dates the fire, shows no sign of heat-damage, and the organ, built in 1876, also apparently survived. This is not consistent with the building's having been almost totally destroyed, or with the catalogue of repairs given in the same *Irish Builder* report, which refers only to work to the roof, heating system, encaustic tiles (by Maw & Co), interior decoration (by Mr Robert Mannix) and the supply of new

*12 – Detail from MIRACULOUS
FEEDING window by William
Wailes at Killarney*

opposite

*11 – LAST SUPPER window by
William Wailes at Killarney*

pews. Mannix had also been behind the commissioning of the Wailes windows, as reported in 1883, and we can safely assume that those pre-fire Wailes windows are those which are still in place in the church.[55] Just one window, the odd man out by Heaton, Butler & Bayne, dates from after the fire, sometime around 1900.

The received knowledge about the extent of damage to the building provides the opportunity for some light relief by dispelling two other myths fed to visitors to Killarney. The head of the infant Christ in the baptism window had at sometime been defaced by a prankster using a varnish-like material, clumsily applied, to draw a beard. This was swiftly removed by the present writer in 2005 to enable the photographic recording to take place. However visitors to the church had been treated to the colourful interpretation that 'The manger scene has a bearded baby Christ, the artist's way of conveying the idea of the Eternal and Ancient God being in the Baby.'[56] Visitors are also told that the architect committed suicide when he found that his design for blind arcading on the tower was incorrectly calculated, so that, when built, the arcading had to be asymmetrical. Not surprisingly, the drawings, preserved in the Representative Church Body Library, clearly show that the design, as built, is exactly as intended and drawn by Atkins, who, incidentally, lived on until 1887.

Each of the nave windows has plate-tracery consisting mainly of a cinquefoil so large as virtually to be a rose window in its own right. The north and south transepts have rose windows in the gables and lancets below. The west rose is incorporated into the plate-tracery above the large four-lancet window. The apsidal chancel, which is partly lined with green marble, has three pairs of lancets, each with rose plate-tracery, and linked by an inner arcade of lancets with engaged columns in red marble with annulets and elaborate foliate capitals, in the manner of Burges at Cork. The stencil-work, although not original, is in the correct spirit, and some is really very good. A photograph in the National Library, possible dating from the early twentieth century, shows stencilling in all the areas as at present, but to different patterns.

The Maw & Co floors throughout are liturgically symbolic. The tiles in the nave are simple and, in a way, secular. The crossing and transepts have encaustic tiles based on floral and geometric motifs. Two steps (in red Irish marble) lead up to the choir which is floored in marble mosaic with sacred symbols – alpha and omega, and iota, eta and sigma. One further step leads up to the sanctuary with richly decorated encaustic tiles. Sadly, the elaborate communion rails, probably dating from Fuller's restoration, have been moved from the sanctuary step and placed at the chancel steps, thereby minimising the significance of the chancel. Also, the choir has been obstructed by the forward placing of the altar. It is to be hoped that the rails and the table can be put back to their correct places and collegiate stalls reinstated in the choir.

Unlike the Ballyseedy windows, the eleven windows (plus some ornamental roses in the south transept) by Wailes have no obvious iconographic programme, but their uniformity of provenance, style and colour contribute immeasurably to the rare homogeneity and harmony of this rich interior. The various scenes from both Testaments within the west window are all dedicated to the Eucharist, including a thrilling and unusual *Last Supper* (Plate 11) which makes imaginative use of the large circular space of the west rose. *The Miraculous Feeding* (Plate 12) is cleverly depicted by as many as twenty figures jostling around Christ within the small space of a Puginesque tabernacle. Much of the iconography would have been unthinkable, on doctrinal grounds, in the Church of Ireland earlier in the century. There are no less than eighteen angels in the various rose tracery-lights, numerous images of the Virgin Mary, and the east window is devoted to the Crucifixion and Deposition (Plate 13). There are just one or two odd lapses of judgement, such as the commonplace use of the Holman Hunt *Light of the World* and the incongruous use of portraits of the dedicatee in the *Ruth and Naomi* and *Mary and Martha* window. Stylistically, the scheme of windows owes a debt to Pugin, despite its date, and shows his lasting legacy at Wailes's studio. Atkin's Early French architecture, including the deep chancel and the west baptistry near the door, Fuller's furnishings, Wailes's windows and the other decorative elements, such as the stencilled walls, all combine to give a Tractarian ambience to the interior. This is further enhanced by the two delicately painted and stencilled front ranks of pipes of the Conacher organ – the west-facing open diapason for the benefit of the congregation, and the south-facing stopped diapason for the benefit of the choir.

Two windows attributable to Wailes are to be found at Tralee, although the attribution is not supported by three confusing contemporary references.[57] The apse has a delicate, brilliantly coloured window of 1855 by Wailes, largely in grisaille with two *Miracles* medallions, and is quite similar in character to the Ballyseedy windows. It is flanked by two ornamental windows in a similar style. Elsewhere in the church is a much later Wailes window depicting the parable of the Good Samaritan.

The present large cruciform church occupies an ancient site on which a series of churches has stood. A church, dating from about 1700, was remodelled by Sir Richard Morrison (1767-1844) in 1819, and a 1623 stone font survives. The liturgical orientation was altered and a new apsidal chancel added to the south. The fenestration is also from this period. Despite the strange orientation and seating plan, the interior has an undeniable dignity. An immense space, especially at the crossing, has been created by building the new transverse nave and apsidal chancel. The spectacular arch-braced roof springs from low corbels, set no more than halfway up the walls; this structure is an especially ambitious means of supporting the roof of the crossing. The furnishings, such as the three elaborate electroliers in brass and enamel and the large three-manual organ with decorated front rank, contribute to the feel-

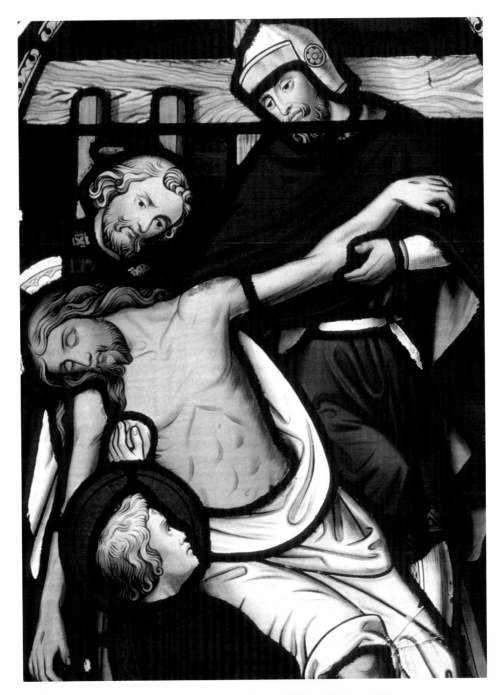

13 – Detail from DEPOSITION *window by Willaim Wailes at Killarney*

opposite 14 – Contract drawing by James Rogers for Kilfergus church, Glin, county Limerick

(photo courtesy RCB library)

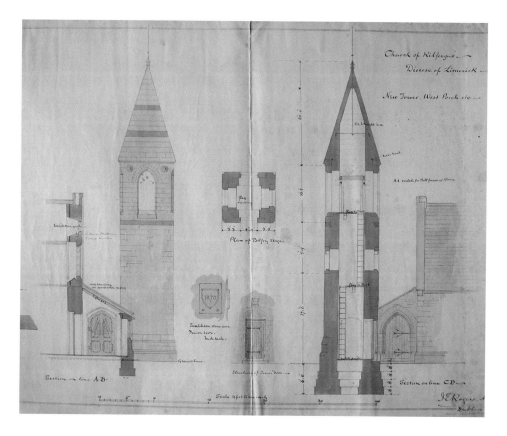

ing of grandeur, and all is well cared-for and highly polished. That there is some mystery surrounding the original orientation is apparent when one discovers that the tower is at the east end of the former nave, and so seems to have been built on the site of the former chancel. The space beneath the tower, which liturgically has become a 'north' transept, retains a sanctuary and is home to an interesting early coloured-glass window of unknown provenance, set in an opening with reveals, having panels of moulded plasterwork.

Earley & Powell of Dublin

The roles of both Pugin and J.H. Powell at the Hardman studio have already been discussed, and two other Hardman men are important in the Irish context. Born of Irish parents in Birmingham, two brothers, Thomas Earley (1819-1893) and John Farrington Earley (1831-1873), were both apprenticed at Hardman's under Pugin. Thomas worked for a while with Pugin at his house in Ramsgate, Kent, where some of his cartoons were prepared. By 1853 Thomas Earley had moved to Dublin to run an Irish branch of Hardman's. An advertisement of 1859 makes it clear that the range of products offered by Hardman at the time was wide:

> John Hardman & Co., 48 Grafton Street, Dublin. Metal Works, 166 Great Charles Street, Birmingham. Stained Glass Works, 43 New Hall Hill, Birmingham. Artists, Glass-Painters, Church Decorators & Embellishers. Workers in Gold, Silver, Brass & Iron. Makers of All kinds of Sacred Vessels, Chalices, Monstrances, &c. Altars in wood or stone, Tabernacles, Banners, &c. Designs and Estimates sent on application to Mr. T. Earl[e]y at the Depot, 48 Grafton Street, Dublin.[58]

It is apparent that both the stained glass and the metalwork for the Irish market was, at this time, being produced in Birmingham, but also that Thomas Earley was running a stone-carving department in Dublin. Earley's role was not just administrative; he was a designer of considerable stature, and it seems that some commissions, including wall paintings, were carried out in his own name. A report of the completion of St Saviour's Church, Dublin, in 1860 records that the stained glass was by O'Connor, the metalwork by Hardman, and the painted decoration by Thomas Earley.[59]

In 1864 the Dublin studio became independent when Thomas Earley, together with Henry Powell (d.1882), set up the partnership of Earley & Powell,[60] the name changing to Earley & Co towards the end of the century. By the time the partnership was set up, the Dublin works included a stained-glass studio, and the firm was also to produce elaborate stone and marble altars, sculpture and painted decorations. Recently a collection of drawings and other documents relating to Earley & Powell has been put into the public domain.[61] Some preliminary research into this collection has enabled the writer to start to put some shape to the development of this Dublin studio. Amongst the papers are drawings of stained glass, sculpture, painted wall decorations and altars. Several designs for stained glass dating from the period 1864 to 1869 are bound into a scrapbook. The designs are in the Pugin tradition, and at least one bears the initials 'TE'. So it could safely be assumed that these are the work of Thomas Earley, with just the possibility that some could be by his brother John. Although much of Earley's work was for the Roman Catholic Church, the writer has come across a few windows by various members of the studio in Church of Ireland churches, and Thomas Earley's scrapbook includes the designs for windows at two Dublin churches – St John's in Sandymount (1867) and St Ann's on Dawson Street (1864).

There is stained glass by Earley & Powell at Kilfergus, the estate church for Glin Castle, built by the Irish architect James Rogers (1838-1896) in 1865. The Representative Church Body Library holds an exquisite set of drawings (Plate 14), in which every detail is minutely specified, signed by Rogers, dated 1865, and countersigned by Welland & Gillespie.[62] The new chancel-and-nave church incorporated the west tower of the former church – a strategy favoured by Rogers (he did the same both at Howth and Holmpatrick) – but in 1870 he designed a new detached tower with square, pyramidal spire standing beyond the south-west corner and linked by a porch. The church, in a muscular Early French Gothic, is small and plain. The five-bay nave is lit by ten simple lancets and each has original and distinctive ornamental leaded lights, designed by Rogers. Sadly they are all badly smashed. The chancel arch springs out of the plastered walls, and consists, in effect, of a deep Burgesian voussoir. The stained-glass east window (Plate 17), *Christ Walking on the Water*, and the ornamental west rose are by Earley & Powell and clearly stem from the Pugin/Hardman stable. The watercolour design for the east window, by Thomas Earley himself, is in the recently discovered scrapbook mentioned above. The windows' donors, in 1867, were Richard and Sarah Georgina FitzGerald of the Glin family, and Isabella FitzGerald, wife of the 26th Knight of Glin, in memory of her brother Llewyllen Lloyd Apjohn who died in 1866. This is recorded on a brass plaque in the church and on one of the windows itself.

There has been some interest in Rogers in recent years, leading to two papers in the journals and a section in a monograph on Deane & Woodward.[63] His career was an intriguing one, in that, with minor exceptions, it spanned only seven years (from 1864 to 1870), but the work is mature and of high quality. His seven churches, all for the Church of Ireland, include Kenure, Howth, Holmpatrick and Kilfergus, and he built rectories at Kenure and at St Bartholomew's, Clyde Road in Dublin. His commissions also include a stained-glass window at All Saints', Grangegorman, Dublin (1863), and one at Christ Church Cathedral, Oxford (1864).

Two Earley & Powell windows are to be found at Drumcliffe church, Ennis, county Clare. The one dating from 1880, which includes the parable of the Good Samaritan (Plate 16), can be attributed to John Bishop Earley (1854-1935), son of John Farrington Earley. A page torn from a journal of 1901 and stuck into a Vestry minute book at Drumcondra church provides a vital piece of evidence and enables the nature of his work.[64] The page identifies the artist of a distinctive Ascension window there as being 'John Earley of 1 Upper Camden Street', and the only John Earley living at that date was John Bishop Earley. The most readily recognisable characteristics are his soft painting style and the overall orange/amber colour-cast, as if the glass were illuminated by the dawn light. Other examples of his work have been identified at Clontarf and Milltown churches.

Mayer & Co of Munich

The richness of church architecture, furnishings and decorations engendered by the principles of the Ecclesiologists can be seen at the remarkable churches at

15 – East window by Mayer & Co at Abington

*16 – GOOD SAMARITAN window by John Bishop
Earley at Drumcliffe church, Ennis*

*above 17 – East window by Thomas Earley at
Kilfergus*

18 – Contract drawing by
James Rawson Carroll for
Abington church, county
Limerick
(photo courtesy RCB library)

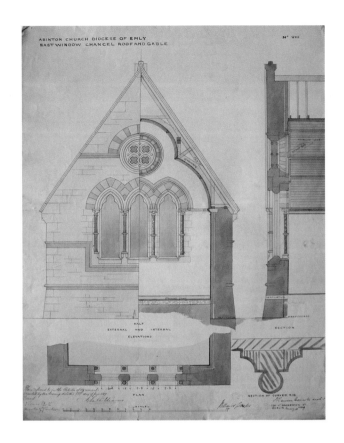

Abington, county Limerick, and Donanaughta church, Eyrecourt, county Galway. Both have early windows by Mayer & Co, thereby providing a rare opportunity to compare the developments in stained glass in the 1860s in a German studio with those in England. St John's, Abington, was designed in 1869 by James Rawson Carroll (1830-1911) and consecrated in 1870 by John Gregg, Bishop of Cork.[65] The principal patrons were Lord Cloncurry, and the Barrington family of nearby Glenstal Castle. Whereas this massive castle (by William Bardwell) is in a lumbering Norman Revival style, the church is delicately detailed and based on Early French Gothic models. The wonderful contract drawings, preserved in the Representative Church Body Library (Plate 18), are works of art in themselves, and show the internal and external polychromy in pen and ink and colour washes.[66] A lengthy description appeared in *The Irish Builder* in November 1870, of which the following is an extract:

> It is constructed of white, buff and red sandstone ... The style is geometric gothic and the ground-plan comprises a nave, chancel, robing room, porch and bell-tower with spire. The chancel is separated from the nave by a richly

moulded and pointed arch of cut stone, supported on four polished red marble shafts with carved capitals and is lighted by a three-light window having trefoils and moulded arches resting externally on red stone pillars also with carved capitals.[67]

This is the window which was very shortly to have the early Mayer & Co stained glass. The description continues:

The west gable has a circular window surrounded by eight quatrefoils within a pointed arch, supported on red stone shafts ... The tower is square at the base and octagonal above and the belfry stage has eight openings with moulded arches, resting on red stone pillars. All the internal finishings of doors and windows are of cut stone and the floors of aisle and chancel are laid with encaustic pavement. It is intended to fill the east and some other of the windows with stained glass.[68]

The choice of Bishop Gregg at that time was appropriate, since this was the year of the consecration of St Fin Barre's Cathedral in Cork, the building of which had come about largely through Gregg's efforts and enthusiasm. Cork is the most elaborately adorned church in Ireland, and in a small way the little church of Abington reflects this richness. Its qualities were certainly well appreciated by Gregg, as is clear from the sermon preached at the consecration, as reported by the *Limerick Chronicle*:

Every object of His creation is characteristic of magnificence ... why not the dwelling-house of God – where the service of God is performed, where souls are quickened and minds enlightened, and hearts are sanctified ... It was a most preposterous notion to say that such a building should not have the beauties of architecture. [Gregg] was glad that they had abandoned the barbarism of bye-gone days and had come to the conclusion that no building could be too magnificent, no edifice too lovely for the King of Kings to dwell in.[69]

Of the five windows by Mayer & Co, three, including the east window (Plate 15), date from around 1870 and compare in some ways to the windows of the High Victorian era in English stained glass, notably in the use of brilliant colours. However, some pictorial elements remain, and enamels are used in places to add colour. For example, the *Good Samaritan* window has enamelled flesh (and blood!) and a decidedly pictorial landscape. The decorative panels above and below are based on the vine and mystic rose. Those for the east window are based on thirteenth-century acanthus forms.

Another Mayer window from this era can be seen at a remarkable church which would not look out of place in the English Home Counties. At first sight,

Donanaughta church (Plate 19), at Eyrecourt, with its lofty nave and chancel, could be the work of Butterfield, but is in fact by William Edward Martin (1828-1900), and the date is 1867.[70] Martin was architect to the Corporation of Birmingham, and his only other known church is St John the Evangelist, Sparkhill, Birmingham. Donanaughta was built by the Eyre family of Eyrecourt Castle. The nave is of four bays with a steeply pitched roof of great height. A tower was planned but not built beyond the first storey. There are nominal 'transepts', of no depth and apparent in the gables only; nevertheless, they have real transept windows of three lancets with six-lobe roses over. To those approaching the church, the unique porch promises everything, and there are no disappointments to follow. It rests on truncated red marble columns with foliate capitals, and from there rises to a great height. The entrance is flanked by two panels of decorated tiles.

The interior of the nave is polychromatic, mainly of warm red brick with black and white string courses. And there is the grandest of chancels, in the Cambridge Camden Society manner, reached by four steps from the nave. In their ordained places are choir stalls and a two-manual organ, by Conagher of Huddersfield, and far away, at the west end, in its ordained place, is the font, as near to the south-west door as it possibly could be. The interior and its furnishings are unaltered. Stone-carving is plentiful, including the entertainingly oversized corbels supporting the chancel arch and carved as angels. A *Baptism of Christ*, probably contemporary with the church, occupies the east window (Plate 20). Like the early Mayer window at Abington, it is in bright lithographic colours, but the treatment could not be termed pictorial. The composition is unconventional and informal. Flesh colours have been achieved by back-painting and the eyes left as white. Very large pieces of glass are used, and the glass-painting is kept to a minimum, the drapery being virtually unpainted.

James Powell & Sons of London

There is another window from the 1860s at Donanaughta and this is by James Powell & Sons, a firm which had been founded in 1834 and which produced highly accomplished work for a period of a hundred years. During the Victorian and Edwardian eras, Powell's employed – both on the staff and in a freelance capacity – a large number of the most distinguished artists and cartoonists of the day. The studio was unique in also making its own extremely beautiful sheets of coloured glass, and, indeed, supplying these to other studios. As noted above, Powell's had been involved in the 1840s in pioneering researches into the manufacture of coloured glass according to medieval principles.

The Donanaughta window, dating from 1868, is the work of the freelance

*Donanaughta church,
Eyrecourt, county Galway*

*19 – Designed by William
Edward Martin*

*20 – Detail from east window
by Mayer & Co*

opposite

*21 – Detail from south
window by M. & R. Sillery at
Clonfert cathedral, county
Galway*

Maltese artist Henry Casolani, who provided several designs for Powell's during the 1860s. His work can also be seen at Stradbally, county Laois. The figurative work is restricted to one medallion, *Eli and Samuel*, in the centre of a three-light window; and a further scene, *Timothy with Eunice and Lois*, in the rose tracery above. The decorative quarries in this window and in three neighbouring windows are made of Powell's patented moulded glass, which provided a low-cost alternative to traditional stained glass for filling large areas. There was a wide range of available patterns for these quarries, and in these windows there are grapes, wheat, holly, ivy and acorns.

Just one more window from the 1860s remains to be discussed. It is by the Dublin firm M. & R. Sillery and is to be found at Clonfert cathedral, county Galway.

M. & R. Sillery of Dublin

These are early days in building up a picture of M. & R. Sillery and the extent of their work. It could be a useful subject for research. Some clues can be had from advertisements in *The Dublin Builder*. They seem to have been long-established, claiming 'upwards of half a century' in an advertisement in 1859. They possibly did not always set their sights high. The main message of the advertisement is the dubious recommendation of the lowness of their prices: 'M. & R. Sillery beg to inform that they can supply [windows] at much lower prices than other houses.'[71] Not all of their work was destined to serve in the worship of God: 'Enamelled flocked patterns for obscuring the view, suited for water-closets.'[72]

The Clonfert window (Plate 21) is signed 'Sillery 107 Abbey Street, Dublin', and has a memorial date of 1868. It consists of a somewhat sentimental figure of an angel set in a medallion, and the background of blue and red quarries takes its inspiration from thirteenth-century French glass. The glass was brought in from elsewhere and the opening built to accommodate it. There are Sillery windows at the Church of Ireland churches at Narraghmore, county Kildare, Bannow, county Wexford, and Banagher, county Offaly.[73]

The west front of Clonfert includes a remarkable Hiberno-Romanesque doorway of eight orders, with a pediment above, similar to, but more elaborately decorated than the doorway at Roscrea. The carvings are of animal heads, human heads and possibly sea creatures, as well as foliate forms. The famous mermaid carving on the chancel arch is later in date, a similar carving appearing at the fifteenth-century Clontuskert Abbey nearby providing a clue as to its date. The present building dates from around 1200 as a simple single-cell church to which a chancel was added in the thirteenth century and transepts and a tower added in the fifteenth century. A sobering summary of the woes which had befallen this historic church was given in *The Irish Builder* in 1896 at the start of a programme of restoration by J.F. Fuller:

> Clonfert Cathedral was founded by St Brendan AD 557 or AD 563. The cathedral appears to have been subjected to the usual disasters of all religious establishments in this country. It was burnt in 744, 842, 1015, 1045, 1164 and 1179 and plundered in 949, 1031, 1065. In 1541 came the destruction of the church and monastery.[74]

Fuller's restoration was completed by 1900. He removed the gallery and opened up original arches; there were new floors and stalls and pews.[75] Presumably, the encaustic tiles throughout the chancel are his, and also the oak pulpit – carved with the emblems of the Evangelists – the bishop's throne and altar table, all of the highest quality. The Hardman and Watson stained-glass windows also went in during the course of the Fuller restoration.

Another distinguished London firm which produced archetypal High Victorian work was Lavers, Barraud & Westlake, although their two windows in this diocese date from a later period. It is to this studio that we turn next.

THE LATER YEARS OF THE NINETEENTH CENTURY

Lavers, Barraud & Westlake of London

The partnership of Lavers & Barraud was founded in 1858 by Nathaniel Wood Lavers (1828-1911) and Francis Philip Barraud (1824-1900). Both men had worked at James Powell & Sons: Barraud was the artist and Lavers the craftsman. In 1860 they took on the services of the first-rate designer Nathaniel Hubert John Westlake (1833-1921). In 1868 Westlake became a partner, and the name of the firm changed to Lavers, Barraud & Westlake. There are some outstandingly beautiful windows by Lavers, Barraud & Westlake in Ireland: at Kilmalooda, county Cork, designed by John Milner Allen; at Ardcarne, county Rosscommon, designed by Barraud; and at St Canice's Cathedral, Kilkenny, designed by Westlake. An unusual commission by Westlake in Ireland is a set of oil paintings of the Stations of the Cross at Maynooth.

Kilgobbin, county Kerry, is a modest First Fruits church (Plate 23), built in 1824 in a remote pastoral setting on the shores of Tralee Bay, with the Slieve Mish mountains behind. The church, surrounded by an extraordinary number of large sepulchres, and the former rectory make a fine group. A fragment of a medieval font, kept in the church, indicates that, without doubt, this is an ancient site, and this comes as no surprise. The sanctuary furniture is in a splendid fairytale gothick style, with reredos, table and rails all as a single item, and there is a lectern to match. The small furnishings have all survived, such as the candle-snuffer and the pewter measure for holy water. The pews, pulpit and desks were designed by Welland & Gillespie in 1862,[76] but sadly the pulpit has been lost and replaced with a redbrick object of brutal design. The vestry has exceptionally finely detailed Regency joinery, including a seven-panel door with pointed upper panels and a unique window with moulded surround and shutters.

Two windows of c.1880 by Lavers, Barraud & Westlake, designed by Nathaniel Westlake for Kilshannig church, county Cork, were moved here. One is placed in the porch, the other in the sanctuary. Although the adaptation of the three-light east window (Plate 22) is not perfect, it is satisfactory and it greatly enriches this simple interior. The window has all the hallmarks of this studio's fine work – the richest of thirteenth-century-inspired grisaille to left and right, the central lancet having deep red quarries decorated with fleurs-de-lis, glazed with narrow borders between each quarry, which is the setting for brilliantly conceived groups of figures, full of interest and movement. The colours chosen are from Westlake's characteristic palette – olive greens, deep blues and sandy ambers.

Kempe & Co of London

Of the many artists who trained at the Clayton & Bell studio in the 1860s, the most successful were John Burlison (1843-1891), Thomas John Grylls (1845-1913) and Charles Eamer Kempe (1837-1907). Burlison and Grylls set up their own studio in 1868. Kempe was to become one of the best-known figures in nineteenth-century stained glass, and the large studio which he established in 1869 was to be one of the most prolific. Both Burlison & Grylls and Kempe & Co took their inspiration from

22 – East window by Lavers, Barraud & Westlake at Kilgobbin

23 – Kilgobbin church, Camp, county Kerry

opposite

24 – Detail from east window by Kempe & Co at Birr, county Offaly

Flemish art and English stained glass of the fifteenth century, such as that in the Beauchamp Chapel of St Mary's Church, Warwick. Both studios became particularly associated with High Anglicanism, and examples of their work are relatively rare in the Church of Ireland. A few Kempe & Co windows have come to light – for example, at Piltown, county Kilkenny, Killeskey, county Wicklow, and St Patrick's Cathedral, Dublin.

The galleried church of St Brendan, Birr, consecrated in 1816, was built by John Johnston,[77] who had also carried out work at the castle for the 2nd Earl of Rosse, including the creation of the Gothic saloon. The church stands at the eastern end of an avenue leading from the castle gates and lined with Georgian houses. Between 1877 and 1879 Sir Thomas Drew made alterations and additions to the church, principally the building of a lofty and deep chancel in late pointed Gothic.[78] In addition to this, Drew cleverly created a choir, with associated organ by Abbot & Smith of Leeds, within Johnston's nave. Three white marble steps lead up to the choir, and then, passing through the soaring chancel arch, more steps lead up to the chancel.

At the far end of Drew's chancel is the great east window in the Perpendicular style, with six lancets and extensive panel tracery. It has Kempe's suitably dignified and restrained stained glass (Plate 24), with a sequence of Passion scenes at the base, Old and New Testament figures above, and high-up in the centre of the tracery, overseeing the whole church, is the Archangel Michael triumphing over the dragon. Another Kempe window is to be found in the south gallery. The studio's early work was by far their best, and by the 1890s, when the two windows at Birr were executed, much of the work tended to have an overall heavy green cast and became overloaded with figures and canopies. Here at Birr, however, the fifteenth-century-inspired canopy work in both windows has a welcome brightness, and the colours of the figures and backgrounds are well chosen, if heavily painted. Nevertheless, the studio had become over-confident and unchanging, working to well-tried formulae, and made few concessions to the character or the needs of the building.

Johnstone's elegant galleried gothick nave has rib-vaulted ceilings with foliate bosses, and is supported by north and south arcades of slender shafts which pass through the galleries. The aisles thus formed are also separately and finely vaulted. The interior, almost unaltered since Drew, has a quiet and dignified grandeur and an air of refinement suited to its noble purpose as the estate church. Sadly, the word 'almost' is needed because the six modern stained-glass windows (by, at present, unidentified artists) provide a jarring note and disturb the harmony, bearing no relation to the building and serving only to give an uncalled-for feeling of enclosure and an unwelcome loss of light.

Reference was made earlier to fundamental difficulties with the introduction of images into Church of Ireland churches, and how, to some extent, these were overcome. That such doctrinal difficulties did not universally disappear is clear from two controversies which arose at Birr. One, during the 1877-79 alterations by Drew, was a battle which took place over the elaborate new reredos by A.P. Sharpe. It was to have had the *Emblems of the Evangelists* and a gradine. According to Bourke, parishioners described it as 'objectionable' and demanded it be removed. At a special hearing the bishop decided on a compromise involving the removal of the *Emblems* and alterations to the gradine so that nothing could be placed on it. Cherubs were also to be removed and finials altered so as not to resemble crosses. There were similar disagreements in 1891 in connection with the iconography of the east window, to be given by the 4th Earl of Rosse, and in particular over a proposed depiction of the Crucifixion.

The gallery also houses a pleasing Heaton, Butler & Bayne Ascension, dating from the end of the nineteenth century. Largely in glowing golds and whites, it has strongly conceived figures, executed with characteristic boldness. It is to this studio that we turn next.

Heaton, Butler & Bayne of London

Twelve of the windows seen in the diocese of Limerick & Killaloe are from one of the most prolific of all the nineteenth-century London studios, Heaton, Butler & Bayne. The partnership between Clement Heaton (1824-1882) and James Butler (1830-1913) was established in 1855. In 1862 Robert Turnhill Bayne (1837-1915) joined them, and the windows which he designed are some of the finest of the High Victorian period. Amongst these is the set of five apse windows of around 1860 at Holy Trinity Church, East Ferry, county Cork. During the 1870s the studio adopted an 'Aesthetic' style, and continued to produce strikingly beautiful work, characterised by a gentler approach and less adherence to the rules of the Gothicists, with more naturalistic figures, the backgrounds and foregrounds incorporating flowers and foliage. All this adds up to 'art for art's sake', the defining quality of the Aesthetic movement.

There are no examples of Heaton, Butler & Bayne's High Victorian work in the diocese, and just one Aesthetic window – at Valentia. This good-quality chancel-and-nave church by Joseph Welland was probably built around 1860.[79] It stands in an enviable position on Valentia Island at the top of the little street sloping down to the quay at Knightstown. There are memorials to the Knights of Kerry who lived nearby at Glanleam, with its extensive sub-tropical gardens. Possibly the FitzGeralds were behind the endowment of the interior with rich details. The floors throughout have encaustic tiles, and there are steps up into the chancel in red marble and into the sanctuary in white marble. This upward progression, together with the dignified length of the chancel, are in the manner favoured by Welland. His east window, consisting of three separate tall and narrow lancets, has pleasing glass by Heaton, Butler & Bayne, with three sturdy female allegorical figures of Faith, Charity and Hope, and backgrounds of richly coloured fruit and leaves. Charity has a vase of flowers in the foreground, highly characteristic of the era. In the west gable, Welland has placed a plain-glazed rose window of interesting configuration.

The other Heaton, Butler & Bayne windows in the diocese date from the last decade of the nineteenth century and the first of the twentieth; these are at Adare, Birr, Killarney, Woodlawn and Limerick (both St Mary's and St Michael's). During these decades, the sheer volume of output from this studio had the consequence that the early work was seldom matched in originality. Nevertheless, although the style did not move on and the studio failed to embrace the new movements in art, it maintained unfailingly high standards of drawing and craftsmanship, and invariably took a professional and fluent approach. Typical of the studio's work at this time are the four windows of 1889 to 1895 at St Michael's, Limerick: eight solemn Old Testament kings and prophets are executed in Heaton, Butler & Bayne's polished, if unexciting manner. In contrast, the large Mayer east window depicting ten parables is colourful, youthful and lively. The church (1838-44), by James Pain, stands in a leafy and elegant Georgian district of the city.[94] Some record of the introduction of stained glass and of internal re-ordering and furnishing was given in 1888 in *The Irish Builder*:

William Francis Dixon for Mayer & Co

25 – Detail from east window at Clontuskert church, near Ballinasloe, county Galway
(see page 132)

opposite

26 – Detail from east window at Borrisokane, county Tipperary

St Michael's, Limerick, in which the east window has been recently filled with stained glass, has had a bequest of £300 for a similar object left by the widow of the late Archdeacon Jacob. Other effective improvements have been carried out – viz the fixing of additional choir stall, prayer desks, chancel and vestry-room furniture, the placing of the organ on the north side and the pulpit on the south side, the fixing of a brass memorial tablet, communion rail and porch light. The walls have been decorated and the aisles laid throughout with encaustic tiles.[80]

All the enrichments listed in this piece have survived, mercifully unaltered by passing liturgical fashions. There is fine stencil decoration to the chancel arch and a magnificent wooden roof.

Dixon for Mayer & Co of Munich

In contrast to the pedestrian work coming out of Heaton, Butler & Bayne at this time, Mayer & Co were producing bewitching work in a romantic style. It was the year 1894 that marked this change of direction, the year that they were joined by the English artist William Francis Dixon (1848-1928). He had trained at Clayton & Bell and then set up his own studio, Dixon & Vesey, before moving to Germany to work at Mayer's. The arrangement was a happy one – the marrying of Dixon's strength of designing and drawing, in a manner influenced by the late pre-Raphaelites, with Mayer's rich colours, attention to detail and perfection of craftsmanship. He has been described as 'Clayton & Bell's most original pupil'.[81]

Windows which can with certainty be attributed to Dixon are to be found at Dungarvan, county Waterford, Balbriggan, county Dublin, and Sligo. Four more can be added to the list in the diocese of Limerick & Killaloe: at Ardrahan, Borrisokane, Clontuskert and Drumcliffe. Like the Dungarvan and Balbriggan windows, these four are in the romantic style which Dixon and Mayer produced, with a sweetness of drawing, softness of painting, and beautiful tapestry-like details. It is apparent that Dixon was able to dictate his own choice of colour to Mayer.

The church at Ardrahan, county Galway, is a late eighteenth-century single cell, with a small apsidal sanctuary and rare hexagonal tower. In the graveyard are the remains of an earlier church and the site of a round tower, and nearby are the remains of a moated castle. The 1908 *Resurrection* is a good example of Dixon's work, with his immediately recognisable and attractive faces and luxurious colour-choice. A characteristic detail is Dixon's drawing of feet with very clearly defined toes and toenails. The elaborately patterned drapery is in rich dark browns and red-purples, and the cloak of the sleeping soldier is painted on a green-yellow streaky glass.

The simple single-cell First Fruits church at the centre of the village of Borrisokane, county Tipperary, was greatly enriched by introducing a Dixon window rescued from Conger in 1991. Its interior is flooded with light from six original clear windows. Dixon's *Mary and Martha* window has a refined beauty, and the heads are especially sensitive (Plate 26). A ruby glass, varying in tone from pale pink to deep burgundy, is used for the drapery of the figure of Christ, and a finely decorated umber for Mary. The distant Gothic landscape is particularly pleasing.

The little Church of St Matthew, Clontuskert, is set in a magnificent and remote part of county Galway. Nearby are the ruins of Clontuskert Abbey. The early nineteenth-century church occupies the site of, and possibly incorporates parts of an early thatched preaching house. Its interior is brilliantly lit from four large clear windows, and everything exudes a feeling of a building in good health. The deep chancel, reached by a total of three steps, is the setting for another perfect example of Dixon's work (Plates 1, 25). It dates from 1908, the same year as the Ardrahan window. The drawing, painting, execution and craftsmanship are of the highest quality. Dixon's predilection for large eyes is readily apparent here. There is a good choice of colour, and the details are sumptuous and exquisitely conceived. Particularly fine is the detail around the hem of the cloak of Christ: the glass used is red, laminated onto yellow; parts of the red are removed with acid-etching, and then details of line and shade are painted and fired. At least half a dozen variants of brown and violet glass have been selected, in a highly original way, to create the group of buildings amongst which the figures stand. The foliage is lush and the landscapes are romantic. The delights of this building are made complete by a rare example of a coal stove, still in use in the nave amongst the pews.

Shrigley & Hunt of Lancaster

Kinnitty church in county Offaly has a rare and beautiful collection of windows by the distinguished Lancaster firm, Shrigley & Hunt. Sadly they are not seen at their best due to the presence of discoloured and light-reducing screens, needlessly fitted to the outside of the window openings. Kinnitty is one of the many first-class churches which Joseph Welland built for the Church of Ireland.[82] The church is on the site of a sixth-century monastery. A ninth-century High Cross stands nearby, and an early Christian inscribed stone is stored in the church. The present church, built in 1851 in the Early English style, is cruciform, but, unusually for Welland, has only a nominal shallow chancel, extending the full width of the nave and under the same roof. The crossing has stone arches to the transepts but not to the nave or the chancel, which are formed by trusses. The shallow chancel and the presence of a west gallery suggest that Welland underplayed the ecclesiology to suit local sensibilities.

28 – Detail from east window by O'Connor & Taylor at Castleconnell
opposite 27 – Detail from CHRIST HEALING THE BLIND MAN *window*
by Shrigley & Hunt at Castleconnell, county Limerick

Nevertheless, there are three marble steps up to the chancel, which has a pavement of encaustic tiles.

The materials and detailing throughout are of excellent quality, and the fenestration, based on simple Early English lancets, is interesting and varied. The nave has some singles and some pairs; each transept has a widely spaced pair with a small rose above; there is a small west rose, high up above the porch; the east window consists of three separate lancets. A quaint detail is the bell-cote, which incorporates a flue for the small fireplace in the family pew at the west end. The pew, beneath the gallery, was presumably for the Bernards of Castle Bernard. Confusingly, a font now stands there. The three Shrigley & Hunt windows, dating from 1907 to around 1910, have between them seven lancets and a rose. They are delicately drawn and have a restrained use of colour. There are dainty, small square quarries with stained and painted motifs. The figures have noble and dignified heads and each stands before a characteristically 'dipping' arras, richly coloured and decorated and with gold braids and ropes.

Shrigley & Hunt was established in Lancaster in 1874. This successful studio produced windows, mosaics and tiles to a consistently high standard well into the twentieth century. The chief designer at this studio was the Swedish-born Carl Almquist (1848-1924). He was a pupil of Henry Holiday and a man of considerable abilities. The Kinnitty windows seem to make use of some cartoons by Almquist and some by other designers at the studio influenced by his work.

Another Shrigley & Hunt can be seen at Castleconnell, county Limerick. As always, the drawing is sensitive and refined and there is an overall fifteenth-century feeling (Plate 27). Above and below the central *Christ Healing* scene are small diamond quarries of perfect proportion, decorated with silver-stained motifs. There is much use of silver-staining elsewhere, giving the whole its characteristic golden-white character, with patches of olive green, burgundy red and slate blue. The window is signed with a good example of the 'S&H' rebus.

O'Connor & Taylor of London

Castleconnell is also home to two windows by O'Connor & Taylor. The Irish artist Michael O'Connor (1801-1867) was an important figure in the early days of the Gothic Revival in stained glass, working with such eminent figures as Pugin and Butterfield. He set up his studio in Dublin, and subsequently moved it to London. Although his career was prematurely cut short by blindness, the studio in London continued working, in the tradition he had founded, in the hands of his sons. In 1873 William George Taylor joined the practice, and by 1877, he had taken over control. The earliest of the three O'Connor & Taylor windows at Castleconnell consists of large areas of grisaille with a richly coloured Ascension in the centre (Plate 28). It dates from around 1877, but the style still shows the influence of Michael O'Connor. The same design appears at Kilpipe, county Wicklow. Another reuse of a cartoon is the *Charity* window at Castleconnell, which appears again at Ardrahan, with slight changes: the basket of bread has become a baby!

Alterations to the church at Castleconnell during the nineteenth century clearly reflect the changing attitudes to architecture in the Church of Ireland at the time, especially in the eventual reversal of an earlier liturgical re-ordering. In 1826 the architect James Pain enlarged the existing simple single-cell building with the addition of a porch and north transept, complete with gallery. Then, in 1842, he re-ordered the interior arrangements by converting this transept into a nave and siting the sanctuary against the south wall of the former nave, with seating facing it from three sides. However, in true form, Welland & Gillespie re-established the correct orientation in 1863. They re-sited the sanctuary by creating, internally, a 'chancel' at the east end of the nave. They were skilfully able to imply a chancel by making use of Pain's transverse nave to suggest a crossing, emphasised by the diagonal bracing of a new roof. They also provided new east-facing seating and put in first-pointed Gothic window-openings.[83]

All of this was in place for twenty years before O'Connor & Taylor came along with glass which can be counted as a good response to Welland & Gillespie's achievements. Unfortunately, when two further windows eventually appeared – one by Shrigley & Hunt and one of unidentified provenance – there were then five stained-glass and two coloured ornamental windows leading to an unnecessarily dark interior. The only light comes from three small clear windows beside the west gallery and one small clear window in the transept. This somewhat oppressive feeling is emphasised by the presence of over thirty wall monuments to local families – the Massys, Vandeleurs and FitzGibbons.

Another O'Connor & Taylor Ascension is to be found at Woodlawn estate church, Kilconnell, county Galway. It has this studio's characteristic palette and stylistic inconsistencies. Nine architectural drawings, signed by James Forth Kempster (1816-1893) and dated 1861, are kept at the church.[84] They show a proposed building with more elaborate fenestration, including a three-light decorated west window with three sexfoil tracery-lights, and two-light windows throughout the nave. The building, as executed, retains the same plan – notably the slim tower and spire unconventionally set against the north wall of the nave – and just one of the elaborate windows, as drawn. This is the triple-lancet east window with its engaged marble shafts with foliate capitals and with a marble reredos below, the ornamental stained glass also being by O'Connor & Taylor. In the south-west corner there is a pretty little Heaton, Butler & Bayne war memorial window. The interior is surprisingly plain for an estate church, although possibly the walls, now painted over

29 – ANNUNCIATION window by Mary Lowndes at Drumcliffe church, Ennis

opposite

30 – Surviving detail from ANNOUNCEMENT TO THE SHEPHERDS window by Mary Lowndes at Aghancon church, near Clareen, county Offaly

Behold·the·handmaid of·the·Lord

in a domestic eau-de-Nil, were once decorated with stencil work. It remains for the three stained-glass windows and the encaustic-tiled floor to provide any richness.

H.M. Barnett of Newcastle-Upon-Tyne

Just a few metres from the huge and richly decorated Roman Catholic church at Nenagh, built in 1894 by Walter Doolin, stands the excellent and more modest Church of Ireland church by Joseph Welland, begun in 1858 and completed in 1861 by Welland & Gillespie. It consists of an Early English chancel and nave, with a south aisle and north-west tower. At the west end there is a gallery for the Telford & Telford organ, with pipework arranged to frame the small west rose in the gable.[85]

Doolin succeeded in outdoing Welland in size and elaboration, but not in quality: Welland's church is one for the connoisseur – a perfect example of Early English Revival and a lesson in restraint and quiet strength. It is a textbook example of the new ecclesiology, the emphasis being diverted away from the Word and directed to the Sacraments. His distinct broad and deep chancel is reached from the nave by three steps, and the sanctuary by another step. The climax is the sizeable altar table with an arcaded reredos, decorated with modern paintings of Celtic-inspired symbols by Anne Tower. The pavements are of elaborately patterned encaustic tiles.

The baptistry has been moved to an uncomfortable location at the east end of the south aisle, but otherwise the interior remains largely as Welland intended, if rather dominated by poor stained glass. There is ugly ornamental glass in the triple east lancets. Two of the four south-aisle windows, which would have given good light, have stained glass of no particular merit. However, on the north side, is a most interesting and unusual window by Henry Mark Barnett (1832-1888), depicting St Paul and St Luke. Barnett's father and grandfather were both in the stained glass business, and Henry started his own studio in Newcastle in 1858. Most of Barnett's windows are to be found in Roman Catholic churches, especially in the north of England, and, true to character, the Nenagh window looks as if it were intended for the Roman Catholic church next door.

R.W. Winfield of Birmingham

In 1882, R.W. Winfield purchased the Camm Brothers studio in Smethwick, Birmingham, which had been set up by Thomas William Camm (1838-1912). According to Alan Crawford, Winfield's had a 'high reputation for craftsmanship and design in glass-work'.[86] A rare example of Winfield's work is to be found at

Kiltinanlea church, Clonlara, county Clare. In 1892 *The Irish Builder* reported 'extensive alterations and improvements' to the First Fruits church of St Senan.[87] In addition to a well-proportioned new chancel, organ chamber (now sadly without an organ) and vestry, there was a memorial window to Lady Dillon Massy 'in Bath and Portland stone by Messrs. Harrison, Great Brunswick Street'. This is a rare example of a memorial consisting not only of stained glass (by Winfield), but also the magnificent stone opening.

The stone-carving is as elaborate as could be imagined. Above, there is freestanding, so-called 'double' tracery in the form of a five-cusped arch. The inner order of the opening is a simple Gothic point, and the outer order is ogee with crockets and finials. The two orders are separated by an arch of deeply incised carvings of vines and grapes. Sunk deep into all of this is a small window-opening with a five-cusped head and delicate quatrefoil above. The stained glass is a most restrained and tranquil depiction of Christ with Mary and Martha, and there are panels of decorated quarries above and below. The window makes use of subtly shaded glass in a painterly way, giving moulding and lightness to the drapery. This little-known studio has come up with a window of the highest quality, equivalent in every way to the unique and elegant stonework.

Watson & Co of Youghal

In his doctoral thesis on twentieth-century Irish stained glass, Dr Michael Wynne referred to the existence of over fifty small studios in Ireland in the nineteenth century.[88] Very little research has been done on these, but as far as Church of Ireland churches are concerned, the most frequently occurring name is that of Watson & Co of Youghal, county Cork. The first known window by Thomas Cox Snr (1840-1873) dates from about 1860, and his studio continued to operate under his sons Edward and Thomas Jnr, eventually in partnership with Michael Buckley.[89] No later than 1880, an Irish branch was opened in Youghal, trading initially under the name Cox & Buckley (or Cox, Sons, Buckley & Co), but in the early 1890s it was taken over by Watson & Co, and the London branch was taken over by Curtis, Ward & Hughes. It would not be unfair to describe the work of Watson & Co as variable in quality, and, like many of the trade firms, they made use of cartoons from a wide range of freelance artists as well as from their own staff.

One of the most anomalous of all church buildings began life as a mill in 1820, but as the millstream could not provide sufficient power, the mill was closed and, in 1842, the first floor was converted to become Christ Church, Corbally, near Roscrea. The choice of architectural style for the conversion of the Georgian mill building was extraordinary: the tower takes the form of an Italianate campanile, and the ceilings, especially at the crossing, are baroque. The inadequate millstream still passes by the entrance. A memorial tablet to John Dawson Hutchinson (d.1881) gives the background:

> During many years when there was no church here, he defrayed the expenses of divine service held in a mill on his property, including the stipend of a clergyman, and maintained a day school and Sunday school at his own expense. The mill having been subsequently altered and consecrated became the parish church of Corbally and he, by his will, liberally endowed the benefice.

In addition to the elaborate ceilings, decoration takes the form of three ornamental windows by Watson in the apse and a three-light window, also by Watson, in the south transept. Two of the lights have ornamental designs – work which this studio did rather well – and the centre light, *Christ as Good Shepherd*, was cartooned by the important freelance English stained-glass artist, George Measures Parlby (1857-1944). When the studio had access to drawings of this quality the standard is much elevated. It seems that Parlby did, from time to time, send cartoons down to Youghal: there are, for example, two Watson/Parlby windows at Blackrock, county Cork.

In most cases, the addition of chancels to existing churches was done during the 1860s, but as late as 1906 Joseph Fogerty added a chancel and transepts to the 1825 nave at Borrisnafarney.[90] The church stands in remote and unspoilt countryside adjacent to the Lougton demesne in county Offaly, seat of the Pepper family and later, by inheritance, the Barons Bloomfield. The transepts emanate from the chancel, the south housing the vestry and the north providing a private entrance and family pew for the Peppers. Beneath the original west gallery is a baptistry dating from the period of the enlargements. The spacious chancel is reached by two marble steps, and one further marble step leads up to the sanctuary. The floors throughout are in terracotta tiles, lending a warmth to the interior, echoed by the well-chosen earth-pink colour-wash to the interior walls. Watsons have risen to the challenge of this fine setting with an excellent two-light window, *Christ Blessing Children*, no doubt contemporary with the new chancel. The broad lancets have a busy and lively composition and there is a good choice of glass.

Lowndes & Drury of London

The motivation for the founding, in 1903, of An Túr Gloine, was entirely from within Irish culture, but the model for its realisation was found in the London Arts and Crafts movement, and specifically in the philosophies of its leading figure, Christopher Whall (1849-1924).[91] Whall rejected the hierarchical structures of the large studios and believed that individual artists should be able to have access to

31 – Woodlawn church by James Forth Kempster

32 – Woodlawn, Kilconnell, county Galway
the seat of the Barons Ashtown

shared facilities to design and paint and make their own windows, or at least to supervise closely all stages in the manufacture. A highly influential figure, Whall taught at the Central School and the Royal College of Art, and was responsible both for far-reaching artistic developments and for technical innovations in the richness, colours and textures of glass. One of the types of glass developed, sometime around 1889, was very thick and irregular, known as 'slab' glass. It was made by the London firm Britten & Gilson at Whall's suggestion, and it became one of the hallmarks of Arts & Crafts windows. In 1895 he set up a studio at his London home, but he remained, at first, closely involved with Britten & Gilson, who continued to manufacture his windows using the slab glass.

At this time, Mary Lowndes (1857-1929), a pupil of Henry Holiday (1839-1927), was working at Britten & Gilson and was greatly influenced by Whall's beliefs.[92] In 1897 she and the studio foreman, Alfred John Drury (1868-1940), left the firm and set up an Arts & Crafts stained-glass studio in Chelsea, which was to provide facilities for stained glass artists to make windows according to Whall's principles. Lowndes & Drury was the model for the founding of the 'Tower of Glass' in Dublin in 1903, and it was Alfred Ernest Child (1875-1939), Whall's assistant and pupil, who joined Sarah Purser there as manager and teacher. Three years later, in 1906, the similarly named 'Glasshouse' was purpose-built in Fulham as the new premises for Lowndes & Drury.[93]

There is a notebook in existence giving the location of some Lowndes windows,[94] but it was rewarding to find an Annunciation, dating from about 1900, at Drumcliffe, which had not previously been documented (Plate 29). It has an Art Nouveau character, especially in the foliate border which frames the figures, and is made of Britten & Gilson's slab glass. Lowndes used the same cartoon for a window at Lamarsh, Essex.[95]

Drumcliffe was built in 1871 by Lanyon, Lynn & Lanyon. It is in an Early French Gothic style and is all-of-a-piece. The east end has unfathomable masses of masonry and roofs, consisting of a tower, polygonal apse, nave gable – complete with chimney, resembling a Celtic monastic round tower – south-aisle gable with a rose window and organ chamber gable beneath. All is built in a cold grey stone. The interior is spacious, with its wide nave and wide aisle, and the considerable height is emphasised by the soaring chancel arch. The granite columns of the south arcade have acanthus-form foliate capitals. Three steps lead up to the deep and richly adorned chancel, and a further three steps to the apsidal sanctuary, with its exceptional reredos consisting of three ranges, each of eight niches and each with a figure of a saint. The work, by Catherine O'Brien (1881-1963), is executed in a mosaic-like medium known as *opus sectile*, closely related to stained glass.

Aghancon church, near Clareen, county Offaly, is a simple early nineteenth-century single-cell building in a remote hilly setting, and has connections with nearby Leap Castle, seat of the Darby family. Its unhappy fate is to have become a graveyard for the scarcely recognisable remains of an important collection of Mary Lowndes windows. These are all that remain of several commisioned by the Lloyd family of Gloster for the nearby church at Ettagh.[96] When it was closed, the set of Lowndes windows was removed and fundamentally altered by discarding the backgrounds and setting the figures in crass commercial glass. With this deliberate act of mutilation, a valuable collection of English Arts & Crafts glass – unique in Ireland – was rendered meaningless and worthless. In just one small area of the *Announcement to the Shepherds* window, in which a part of the background has survived, some idea of the quality of the original work can be judged (Plate 30). The consequences of the iconoclasm are appalling, not only for these works of art but also for Aghancon church, the character of which has been compromised. A small panel from another of the Ettagh windows is kept within the Shinrone parish. Although damaged, it was not submitted to the process of alteration and it is to be hoped that it will be repaired and put on public view.

CONCLUSION

THE RANGE OF CHURCHES HAVING NINETEENTH-CENTURY STAINED GLASS IN THE diocese of Limerick & Killaloe is as varied as could be, as are the settings, including a massive medieval cathedral in a busy city centre; a small mid-nineteenth-century chancel-and-nave church on an offshore island; a complete early fourteenth-century abbey church; a Georgian mill converted into an Italianate church in remote countryside; a tiny First Fruits church on the shores of Tralee Bay. The legacies of the land-owning families and their relationship to the Church of Ireland live on in the great houses that stand and those that no longer stand, and in the churches that they built and adorned. Birr, Regency, galleried and dignified, stands at the gates of the great demesne of Birr Castle, home to the Earls of Rosse. Woodlawn is the remote estate church for the seat of the Barons Ashtown, now forlorn and empty (Plates 31, 32); a carriage drive, now overgrown, brought the members of the family to church, and their private railway station, still in use, stands nearby. Ballyseedy, desperately in need of a major investment in conservation, is the epitome of the Irish estate church, and the house, although now a hotel, still stands. Kilfergus, on the edge of the demesne of Glin Castle, the seat of the Knights of Glin, is an exceptional building by a gifted and original Irish architect. Abington, alongside the demesne of Glenstal Castle, is as elaborate as any small Church of Ireland church, and nothing short of Tractarian; the exterior is in subtle and understated polychromy and the interior is a riot of colour.

The writer visited his first Church of Ireland church, St Nicholas's in Cork, in

1991, and since then has recorded the stained glass in about 350 Irish churches and cathedrals. Whilst it has to be accepted that the memories of some of the buildings and some of the windows merge into a blur, others are the subjects of abiding memories, and there were several in the diocese of Limerick & Killaloe. Unaltered early thirteenth-century cathedral churches, with not even any later fenestration, are rare anywhere. Killaloe, with its Warrington windows, is one such and is an extraordinary survivor in a country with a troubled history. The long vista from the west wall of Adare, beneath the tower and into the extensive chancel, with Hardman's magnificent five-light east window in the far distance, must be one of the most memorable in any church in Ireland.

There are mixed memories of Limerick. Clayton & Bell's great south window is arguably the most magnificent nineteenth-century stained glass in Ireland, but the juxtaposition of their refined and elegant work with the crude rubble walls serves to diminish it. The ruins of Clontuskert Abbey include highly original fifteenth-century elements – a vaulted rood, a west door with extensive stone-carvings and the most elegant of cloisters, built to a small scale, with ogee arches. The little Church of Ireland church matches the excellence of the abbey in its tranquillity and with its exemplary stained-glass window by Dixon for Mayer.

Architecturally and historically, the churches discussed represent a microcosm of the ever-fascinating story of the Church of Ireland. The stained glass, too, is a microcosm of the story of Irish and English nineteenth-century stained glass.

———

ACKNOWLEDGEMENTS

I wish to thank the Representative Church Body of the Church of Ireland (RCB) and the Heritage Council, who jointly funded the research on which this article is based, and also the RCB for permission to reproduce the photographs. I wish also to thank Peter Cormack, Dr Nicola Gordon Bowe, Dr Dennis Hadley, Martin Harrison, Dr Michael Kerney, Meg Lawrence, Dr Raymond Refaussé, Dr Stanley Shepherd, Trevor Stacey, Jean Turner, the Bishop, the deans, rectors and churchwardens of the churches mentioned in the article, and the staff of the Irish Architectural Archive and the British Architectural Library.

ENDNOTES

The following abbreviation is used:
RCB   Representative Church Body, Dublin

[1] A. Acheson, *A History of the Church of Ireland 1691-2001* (Dublin 2002) 112.
[2] M. Craig, *The Architecture of Ireland from the Earliest Times to 1880* (London 1989) 288.

[3] A. Rowan, *The Buildings of Ireland, North West Ulster* (Harmondsworth 1979) 64.

[4] *ibid.*

[5] For example, 'Chancel windows, Munich Glass, one date of commemoration 1867. Terrible anyway'. I. Nairn and N. Pevsner, *The Buildings of England, Sussex* (Harmondsworth 1985) 566.

[6] D. Lawrence, 'Stained Glass in the United Diocese of Cashel, Ossory & Ferns', report for the RCB, Dublin, 2001; copies at RCB library and Irish Architectural Archive.

[7] R. Fenn and J. Sinclair, *The Parish Church of St. Mary the Virgin, Kington*, church guidebook (1998) 12.

[8] D. Verey, *Shell Guide to Herefordshire* (London 1955).

[9] N. Pevsner, *The Buildings of England, Herefordshire* (Harmondsworth 1963) 209.

[10] M. Harrison, unpublished letter to the author, 2001.

[11] M. Harrison, *Victorian Stained Glass* (London 1980).

[12] A.W.N. Pugin, *The True Principles of Pointed or Christian Architecture* (London 1841).

[13] C. Brooks, *The Gothic Revival* (London 1999) 246.

[14] A. Acheson, *A History of the Church of Ireland 1691-2001* (Dublin 2002) 153.

[15] *ibid.*, 170.

[16] *ibid.*, 154.

[17] C. Forster, *The Life of John Jebb* (London 1837) 160.

[18] *ibid.*, 161.

[19] *ibid.*, 174.

[20] *ibid.*, 308.

[21] Quoted in D. Lawrence and A. Wilson, *The Cathedral of Saint Fin Barre at Cork* (Dublin 2006) 77.

[22] K. Milne, *The Church of Ireland, A History* (Dublin) 20.

[23] S. Lewis, *A Topographical Dictionary of Ireland*, I (London 1837) 18.

[24] C. Winston, *An Inquiry into the Difference of Style Observable in Ancient Glass Paintings, Especially in England, with Hints on Glass Painting* (Oxford 1847).

[25] E. Baily, *Kilnasoolagh Church* (Newmarket-on-Fergus 1992); Warrington trade list, *c.*1865, ex. inf. Michael Kerney.

[26] D. Lawrence, 'Stained Glass in the United Diocese of Kilmore, Elphin & Ardagh', 2005, RCB library, Dublin

[27] *The Ecclesiologist*, 1849, 81-97.

[28] An account of the work of James and George Pain is given in D. Lee and C. Gonzalez, *Georgian Limerick 1714-1845*, 2 vols (Limerick 2000) II, 216-54

[29] Details of the Warrington windows cited in this paragraph can be found in D. Lawrence's reports on the dioceses of Dublin & Glendalough; Cashel, Ossory & Ferns; Kilmore, Elphin & Ardagh, RCB library.

[30] *The Irish Builder*, 29, 15th May 1887, 134.

[31] House of Lords Record Office, collection 304, letter 327, letter from A.W.N. Pugin to J. Hardman.

[32] S. Shepherd, 'Hardman's Stained Glass and the Transfer from Pugin to Powell', *True Principles – The Voice of the Pugin Society*, II, 4, 2002, 25.

[33] Countess of Dunraven, *Memorials of Adare* (Oxford 1865) 27; Special Collection, University of Limerick library.

[34] P. Stanton, *Pugin* (New York 1971) 206.

[35] R.H. Brash, *The Ecclesisatical Architecture of Ireland, to the Close of the Twelfth Century; Accompanied by Interesting Historical and Antiquarian Notices of Numerous Remains of that Period* (Dublin 1875).

[36] Harrison, *Victorian Stained Glass*, 36.

[37] *The Ecclesiologist*, 1857, 196.

[38] Harrison, *Victorian Stained Glass*, 36.

[39] *ibid*., 26.

[40] M. Harrison, unpublished papers read at Glaziers Hall, London, 2004, and Art Workers Guild, London, 2005.

[41] Craig, *The Architecture of Ireland*, 315.

[42] Details of all windows in Church of Ireland churches referred to in this article can be consulted in D. Lawrence's reports, some of which are cited above. Copies are kept at the RCB library and the Irish Architectural Archive.

[43] *The Dublin Builder*, 3, 15th September 1861, 633-34

[44] *ibid*.

[45] Lawrence Collection, reproduced in L. Mulvin, 'St Mary's Cathedral, Limerick: unpublished correspondence', *Irish Architectural and Decorative Studies*, 4, 2001, 196-99.

[46] This refers to St Michael's Church, Limerick; *The Irish Builder*, 19, 1st December 1877, 357.

[47] N. Ellerker, *Stained Glass Windows in St Mary's Cathedral, Limerick*, cathedral guidebook; summary of material in M. Talbot, *The Monuments of St Mary's Cathedral* (Limerick 1976).

[48] Some of the component panels in this window have been inadvertently interchanged so that in places the iconographic sequence has been lost.

[49] Martin Harrison, unpublished letter to the author, 2006.

[50] Lawrence and Wilson, *The Cathedral of Saint Fin Barre at Cork*, ch.7.

[51] RCB library, drawings, signed and dated 1868, f.2.

[52] Quoted in J. Williams, 'William Atkins – a Forgotten Cork Pre-Raphaelite' in A. Bernelle (ed.), *Decantations in Honour of Maurice Craig* (Dublin 1992) 247.

[53] J. Williams, *A Companion Guide to Architecture in Ireland 1837-1921* (Dublin 1994) 224.

[54] *The Irish Builder*, 3, 15th June 1889, 161.

[55] 'Thirteen windows under R. Mannix', *Building News*, 45, 1883, 868.

[56] Leaflet for visitors at church; also quoted in A. Hewson, *Inspiring Stones* (Limerick 1995) 132.

[57] The trade catalogue of the Alexander Gibbs studio of 1878 has 'Protestant Church, Tralee, all the windows'; *The Builder*, 13, 1855, 570 has 'Protestant church, sixteen memorial windows by Gibbs.'; *Building News*, 47, 1884, 1058 has 'Protestant church, St John the Baptist window in memory of the Dean of Kerry, by Barnett & Son of Leith'. Unless all of these windows have been removed, these references would seem to refer to another church. The matter remains unresolved at present.

[58] *The Dublin Builder*, January 1859, 12.

[59] *The Dublin Builder*, April 1860, 239.

[60] M. Wynne, *Irish Stained Glass* (Dublin 1977) 11.

[61] National College of Art & Design library, Dublin, Earley Collection.

[62] RCB library, drawings, signed and dated 1865 and 1879, f.20.

[63] P. Howell, 'Who was "Rogers, A Pupil of Woodward"?', *Irish Arts Review*, 13, 1998, 105-11; B. Grimes, 'The Church Architecture of James Edward Rogers (1838-1896)', *Irish*

Architectural and Decorative Studies, II, 1999, 175; F. O'Dwyer, *The Architecture of Deane & Woodward* (Cork 1997) 395-401.

[64] Drumcondra Church of Ireland church, vestry minute book.

[65] *The Irish Builder*, 12, 15th November 1870, 281.

[66] RCB library, contract drawings, signed & dated June 1869, f.17.

[67] *The Irish Builder*, 16, 15th February 1874, 63.

[68] *ibid.*

[69] Report of sermon in the *Limerick Chronicle*, 10th November 1870.

[70] RCB library, drawings, f.4.

[71] *The Dublin Builder*, January 1859, 48.

[72] *The Dublin Builder*, October 1861, 650.

[73] The London journals also record various other commissions, including (a) Clonmore, 'Sillery of Dublin, design given by Mr. J. Welland, architect', *The Builder*, 15, 1857, 706; (b) Clonmacnoise, *Building News*, 3, 1857, 1300; (c) Attea, *The Builder*, 17, 1859, 15.

[74] *The Irish Builder*, 38, September 1896, 191.

[75] *Building News*, 78, 16th February 1900, 248.

[76] RCB library, drawings of pews, pulpit, desks by Welland & Gillespie, 1862, f.2.

[77] F. Bourke, *Church and Parish of St Brendan* (Birr 1966) 8.

[78] *The Irish Builder*, no. 19, 1st June 1877, 161, 165; no. 29, 1st February 1887, 46; no. 41, 1st December 1899, 373.

[79] RCB library, drawings, f.2.

[80] *The Irish Builder*, 30, 1st November 1888, 278.

[81] Harrison, *Victorian Stained Glass*, 61.

[82] RCB library, drawings by Joseph Welland, 1851, f.19.

[83] Church also known as Stradbally; RCB library, drawings, f.19.

[84] Kempster was County Surveyor for the East Riding of county Galway and built a large number of secular public buildings. He is described in *The Dublin Builder*, 8, 1st June 1865, 144, as 'diocesan architect', but Woodlawn is the only church in the list of commissions in the Irish Architectural Archive Index. Kempster also extended and remodelled Woodlawn (the house).

[85] *The Builder*, 19, 23rd February 1861, 129. RCB library, drawings, f.19; also RCB MS 139.

[86] A. Crawford, *By Hammer & Hand: The Arts & Crafts Movement in Birmingham* (Birmingham 1984) 33.

[87] *The Irish Builder*, 34, 1st October 1892, 211.

[88] M. Wynne, 'Stained Glass in Ireland 1760-1963', Ph.D. thesis (Trinity College Dublin 1975).

[89] J. Little (ed.), *Stained Glass Marks and Monograms* (London 2002) 34.

[90] *The Irish Builder*, 48, 17th November 1906, 928.

[91] P. Cormack, *The Stained Glass Work of Christopher Whall* (Boston 1999).

[92] P. Cormack, *Women Stained Glass Artists of the Arts and Crafts Movement*, exhibition catalogue (William Morris Gallery, London, 1986) 5-6.

[93] Harrison, Victorian Stained Glass, 67-68; photograph of the Glasshouse, fig. 79.

[94] B. Forbes, unpublished notebook, 17th October 1945, transcribed in Ann O'Donoghue, 'Mary Lowndes – A Brief Overview of her Life and Work', *The Journal of Stained Glass*, 24, 2000, 38-52.

[95] Ex. inf. Peter Cormack.

[96] Forbes, unpublished notebook, 50

1 – St Patrick's steeple, 1749-50, by George Semple

(all photos by the author unless otherwise stated)

Chapel Royal and symbol of the Church militant: the iconography of Christ Church and St Patrick's cathedrals, Dublin, *c*.1660-1760

ROBIN USHER

W ORKS OF ARCHITECTURE OF MEDIEVAL ORIGIN FEATURE ONLY OCCASIONALLY in *Irish Architectural and Decorative Studies*,[1] and were generally absent from its predecessor, the *Quarterly Bulletin of the Irish Georgian Society*. However, this essay, exploring the iconography and State uses of Christ Church and St Patrick's cathedrals in the late seventeenth and early eighteenth centuries, is an adaptation rather than a contradiction of the rule, as the two buildings in question had a long and important afterlife in the early modern capital. In the period 1660 to 1760, the city's pair of Anglican cathedrals were structurally consolidated, re-ornamented inside and out, and otherwise adapted to facilitate Irish Protestant worship and supplementary commemorative activity.[2] In what follows, the interfaces between architecture, ritual and symbol are explored in an attempt to chart the meanings inherent in and ascribed to Dublin's premier places of worship during an era usually characterised as one of political, social and religious stabilisation.[3] There are two motives behind this approach: first, it will allow for a preliminary survey of the most significant of the architectural changes made to the cathedrals; secondly, as the essay progresses, it shall demonstrate how the study of the ritual deployments of particular buildings can be used to investigate some of the cultural dimensions of urban ecclesiastical authority in Stuart and Georgian Dublin.

The symbolic power of Dublin's cathedrals was well understood by their seventeenth- and eighteenth-century custodians, even if their bad material condition frequently led to complaints. In May of 1713, the formidable Archbishop of Dublin, William King, wrote a letter of welcome to Jonathan Swift following his elevation to the deanery of St Patrick's, and issued a set of instructions about the maintenance of the place. Swift is advised that the previous dean, John Stearne, 'did a great deal to his church and house', and is now asked to contract with workmen to build a brick spire on the cathedral's bare fourteenth-century tower. Done soon, King argues, the work will create employment and win the esteem of the indigents, in addition to the visual enhancement it would give to the cathedral. Swift's reply procrastinates about the costs involved, and King's subsequent response urges him to waste no more time. In the end, the spire was not constructed until 1749-50, five years after Swift's death and twenty-one after King's, but it is noteworthy that one of the dean's first responsibilities, as the Archbishop saw it, was to ensure that St Patrick's – the cathedral of which King, himself a prolific and opinionated church-builder, had once been chancellor – cut the right figure in its locality.[4] As the second of the most senior places of worship in Dublin, it was also the capital's largest, and, to roughly the same degree as its companion cathedral Christ Church (so King recognised), it represented an important part of the city's religious iconography.[5] Just as revealingly, when King entered a dispute with the chapter of Christ Church about corruption and disobedience in the cathedral administration, a key indictment was that 'They squander away economy, have turned their chapter-house into a toy-shop, their vaults into wine-cellars ... their cathedral is in a pitiful condition.'[6]

Such complaints about the condition of Christ Church (Plate 2) were exaggerated but not unjustified. Later, in 1777, Thomas Campbell, a somewhat prim Ulster clergyman, dismissed it and St Patrick's as 'mean Gothic buildings', and most contemporary commentators wrote in a similar vein.[7] However, the decay of Dublin's elder churches ran against their distinguished heritage. Thanks to a valuable essay collection edited by Kenneth Milne, the basics are now well known.[8] Christ Church had been established in the middle of the eleventh century and raised to cathedral status prior to the Norman conquest. The medieval fabric mostly dated to c.1200-35. Positioned on a spine of high ground in the core of the old, walled city (Plate 3), it was, in legal terms, the premier church of the diocese and archdiocese of Dublin, and was used by the viceregal court as the country's Chapel Royal.[9] Moreover, it had a string of local connections, containing the chapel of the Merchants' Guild and pews for the Lord Mayor and the Lord Lieutenant.[10] In addition to the freeholds of the dean's estate, the cathedral was also ensconced by a liberty of approximately one acre, technically immune to the jurisdiction of the corporation of Dublin.[11] With its multiple roles, the position of Christ Church as the leading ecclesiastical foundation in the capital was never in question, even if its building presented a somewhat miserable spectacle.

St Patrick's (Plate 4), a far more imposing edifice, began as an Anglo-Norman collegiate church and achieved cathedral rank at an unknown point. The chapter did not have the same litany of privileges as that at Christ Church, though it too had a small municipality of its own (Plate 5).[12] Topographically, the main draw-

P. 371.

2 – *Christ Church Cathedral, Dublin*

from Walter Harris, THE HISTORY AND ANTIQUITIES OF THE CITY OF DUBLIN, FROM THE EARLIEST ACCOUNTS *(1766)*

3 – *Christ Church and its environs*

from John Rocque, AN EXACT SURVEY OF THE CITY AND SUBURBS OF DUBLIN *(1756) (courtesy NLI)*

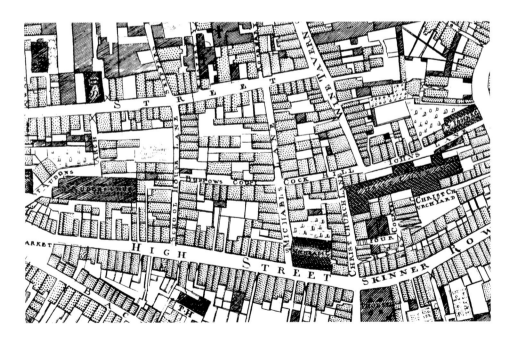

4 – St Patrick's Cathedral, Dublin, from the southeast

from Walter Harris (ed.), THE WHOLE WORKS OF SIR JAMES WARE CONCERNING IRELAND, REVISED AND IMPROVED
3 vols (2nd edn., Dublin, 1764) I

5 – St Patrick's and its environs, from Rocque, AN EXACT SURVEY (courtesy National Library of Ireland)

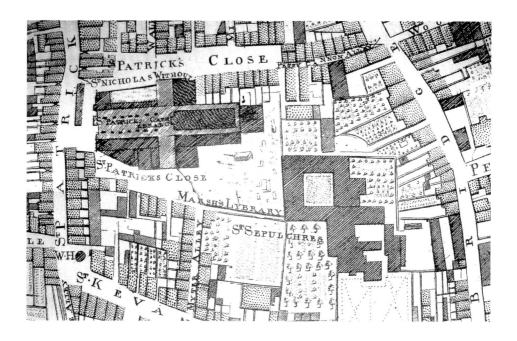

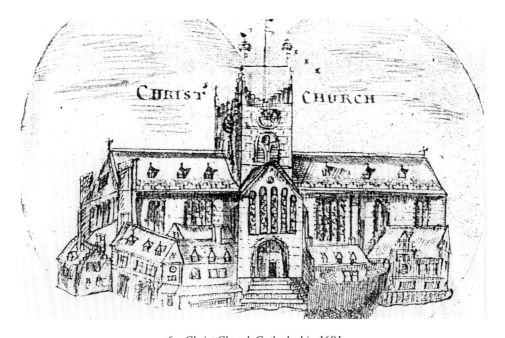

6 – Christ Church Cathedral in 1681

from Thomas Dineley, 'Observations of a Tour in Ireland', 1681 (courtesy National Library of Ireland, MS 392)

back of St Patrick's was that it had been built on a sunken plateau outside the old, walled city centre. Flooding was common.[13] The social milieu was also troublesome. The liberty of St Patrick was more industrial than the mainly commercial area around Christ Church, meaning that the economic lapses of the 1720s and 1740s turned the locality into one of the most poverty-ridden parts of the capital. Deprivation soared in Swift's quarters.[14]

Regardless, a visitor to Dublin in 1660 – or, indeed, 1760 – would have had some difficulty in perceiving the exact material extent of its cathedrals, though far more so in one case than in the other. Christ Church once dominated the skyline of the city as a reminder of its colonial past, but in the period studied it was encircled by a cluster of commercial premises and houses of uncertain vintage.[15] A drawing made in 1681 by the English lawyer Thomas Dineley shows the cathedral's northern flank, probably viewed from the depressed area at the foot of Winetavern Street (Plate 6). Even from this vantage point, a welter of roofs huddle around the carcass of the building. The other side, to Skinner's Row, was worse. Since the early seventeenth century, the courts of King's Bench, Common Pleas, Chancery and Exchequer occupied the site of the ruined cloisters, badly obscuring the cathedral's south side.[16]

Behind this jumble of ramshackle secular structures, Christ Church itself was a pastiche of old and new. In 1562 the vaults collapsed, necessitating the total rebuilding of one side of the nave. The north elevation retained its original appearance, consisting of a clerestory and a triforium passage on top of a stocky arcade. The damaged south elevation was resurrected as a solid masonry wall, divided into three strips and perforated at triforium and clerestory levels by round-headed windows (Plate 7). During the same campaign, the vaulting was substituted for an exposed timber roof and the long choir became the principal liturgical space. With its interior divided into two parts, separated by an arch at the crossing, only a fragment of the cathedral was actually used for worship.[17] The disparity was less jarring on the outside, where the roofline was uninterrupted and the neighbouring domestic infrastructure concealed the disorder behind. Tellingly, the leases issued between c.1660 and c.1700 insist that tenants of the chapter must not do anything that might prevent light from reaching the cathedral's windows.[18]

The single exterior fixture that proclaimed the cathedral's presence on a city-wide basis was its battlemented Jacobean tower (Plate 8), built in rubble masonry and originally ornamented with clock faces and a wind vane.[19] A peal of bells, renewed in 1670, was hung inside, and sounded on Sundays and holy days as well as State festivals, such as the arrival of the Viceroy and royal deaths and marriages. The tower was evidently among the more noticeable iconographic signifiers of the city, as William King's aggressive polemic, *The state of the Protestants of Ireland under the late King James's government*, published in 1691, states that the dean and chapter had been imprisoned by the Jacobite Lord Mayor, Sir Thomas Hackett, for failing to ring in the birth of the alleged son of James II with sufficient vigour.[20]

The architectural history of the eighteenth-century cathedral is mostly uneventful and may be passed over quickly. The chapter acts record repainting and routine maintenance.[21] Substantial repairs were considered in 1745, the canons requesting that 'the Proctor do order the west End of this church to be Propt, and when done that the same be pulled down, in order to be rebuilt, and that Mr [Arthur] Nevil[le] Jones [the Surveyor General] be applied to for a plan for the same.' It would take further investigation to establish whether or not Jones accomplished anything, but Roger Stalley has ascertained that the blocky additions to the exterior walls at the north-west corner, visible in topographical prints (for example, Plate 9), were constructed in a long campaign beginning in the early 1730s, meaning that the unstable fabric was probably consolidated rather than replaced.[22] The Victorian engravers who captured the cathedral *in extremis* depict a piece of Tintern Abbey dropped into the city centre, but, ignoring their picturesque affectations, these images show with appalling clarity the effect of years of half-hearted patching-up.[23]

The only real instance of architectural innovation at Christ Church was the new deanery, built in 1731-33 by Sir Edward Lovett Pearce (Plate 10). This, entered from Fishamble Street, ingeniously concealed three houses – one each for the dean,

7 – Interior of Christ Church before the 1870s restoration, from THE DUBLIN PENNY JOURNAL, *1835 (courtesy NLI)*

8 – The early seventeenth-century tower of Christ Church

9 – A picturesque rendition of the north and west sides of Christ Church
from Richard Cromwell, EXCURSIONS THROUGH IRELAND (London, 1820)

10 – Christ Church deanery, by Sir Edward Lovett Pearce, (1731-33), from THE GEORGIAN SOCIETY RECORDS OF EIGHTEENTH-CENTURY DOMESTIC ARCHITECTURE AND DECORATION IN DUBLIN, 5 vols (Dublin, 1909) IV, plate cxxi

chancellor and chanter – behind a single brick-and-stone façade, distinguished by aggressively modelled window and door surrounds. The frontage, more than any edifice in Dublin, invoked the Palladianism of the English Office of Works. But unfortunately, because of the existing topography, this grand mask had no significant role in the structural formation of the streetscape. The main approach was concealed at the end of a long, trapezoidal yard with a narrow entrance, as can be seen in Rocque's *Exact survey of the city and suburbs of Dublin* of 1756. And, for obscure reasons, the deanery seems to have been regarded as a nuisance to live in. The third dean to reside there, the politically ambitious George Stone, a future Archbishop of Armagh, moved out in 1743 on the pretext that the building was 'inadequate'. By the 1760s it had been let to an apothecary.[24]

Christ Church and its mongrel hinterlands were far from splendid, yet the ritual activities associated with the cathedral could transform it from a mouldering wreck to a setting for high ceremony. The Dublin service in celebration of the coronation in 1661 centred on a long train of knights, gentlemen and personnel from the viceregal household, in the middle of which walked the members of the Privy Council. The leaders of the procession began the proceedings by greeting the Lord Mayor at the Tholsel, or city hall, and listening to a laudatory speech by the City Recorder. The train then marched to Christ Church, where it was welcomed by a group of singing choristers dotted around the cathedral yard.[25]

It was not only the exceptional events in the ritual calendar that weaved Christ Church into the broader symbolic web of the metropolis. The Corporation of Dublin was required to accompany the viceregal court to Sunday service every week of the year. Writing in 1678, the cantankerous and conservative antiquary Robert Ware noted how a firm distinction had, until recently, been made between the government and the City Fathers. The civic representatives would follow the Lord Lieutenant and Privy Council to Skinner's Row, salute it from the steps of the Tholsel, and enter the cathedral through a door in the south transept. The government would normally go in through the great west door on Christ Church Lane. Ware, a stickler for tradition, was annoyed that in recent years the municipality and the viceregal court had taken to entering the cathedral as 'one body', all using the larger door, thereby blurring the social and political distinctions between the two institutions.[26] However, later sources show that the Viceroyalty's ritual protocols in regard to Christ Church were generally static. The pattern of the Restoration period appears to have been firmly established by the time John Dunton left an account of the arrival of the lords justices at Sunday service in 1698:

> When they go to church the streets from the castle gate to the church door, as also the great isle [i.e. nave] of the church ... are lined with soldiers; they are preceded by the pursuivants of the council chamber, two maces, (and on state

days) by the [Ulster] king [of Arms] and pursuivant at arms[,] their chaplains, and gentlemen of the household, with pages and footmen bare-headed; when they alight from their coach (in which commonly the Lord Lieutenant and one of the prime nobility sits with them) the sword of state is delivered to some lord to carry before them; and in the like manner they return back to the castle, where the several courses at dinner are ushered in by kettle-drums and trumpets.[27]

Elsewhere, Dunton states that the Privy Council had a raised gallery over the entrance to the choir, entered via two 'large stair cases' on either side.[28] In 1721 and 1724, the government, irritated and insulted by the presence of petty hangers-on, ordered that worshippers were not allowed to intrude on a space reserved exclusively for the King's deputies.[29]

After the Williamite wars of 1689-91, Dublin's ceremonial life again flourished. The place of Christ Church in Williamite and Georgian public ritual is fully documented in the diary of the Ulster King of Arms, the official responsible for regulating heraldic grants and viceregal ceremonial. Every 23rd October, the Irish rebellion of 1641 was commemorated with a sermon, usually of a kind that emphasised the past iniquities of Irish Catholics and the need for Protestants to be both vigilant in their leadership roles and impeccable in their personal morals lest the country be victim to further signs of divine displeasure.[30] The anniversary of Charles II's restoration was assiduously observed in April;[31] and, depending on the attitude of individual lords lieutenant, the 'martyrdom' of Charles I was marked by another special sermon on 30th January.[32] Guy Fawkes' festival, which had some popular appeal (perhaps because it was on the day after William III's birthday), was similarly celebrated.[33] Christ Church Cathedral, evidently, was where official Dublin extolled peace, authority and good order.

The rites of state were not the only large ceremonies to converge in Christ Church. The cathedral was also the most exclusive burial place in the capital. The FitzGeralds, the earls of Kildare, had their family plot in the chancel. In general, the earls and countesses and their heirs were granted elaborate heraldic funerals arranged by the Ulster King of Arms. A typical procession contained the entire family of the deceased, in addition to a collection of the lords, knights and gentry of the realm; these were required to march in order of social rank. Before its disposal, the body (or a specially prepared wooden mannequin with a wax face) would be displayed in a canopied bier with armorial flags at the corners, set up in the home of the deceased. During the funeral march, four of Ulster's assistants would carry to the cathedral a crested helm and surcoat, and a sword and shield painted with the arms of the dead. Following the burial, a heraldic hatchment was normally hung over the grave.[34] But not all of the FitzGeralds got such a colourful send-off:

Ulster's funeral notes for Robert, a younger son who died in 1699, merely mentions that he was privately buried at night 'in the antient burial place' belonging to the family.[35]

The FitzGeralds had had a connection with Christ Church for centuries. However, burial was also permitted for figures that had been active in public life, and this tended to underscore Christ Church's status as a sort of mausoleum for the country's Protestant governors.[36] Charles Coote, the first earl of Mountrath, died in 1661, and 'being one of ye Lord Justices' was buried in the cathedral, having been accompanied there by an enormous crowd of mourners.[37] Mountrath's eldest son got a similar send-off in 1672, but the procession commenced at the Inns of Court on the north bank of the Liffey where he had been a senior member of the judiciary.[38] Variations on the standard funeral were minor. The retainers at the funeral of Archbishop John Bramhall of Armagh in 1663 carried a mitre and staff instead of the military accoutrements usually accorded to men.[39] Conversely, for the funeral of General Henry Ingoldsby in 1712, the martial iconography was accentuated. The props included cannon and 'bomb carts', and when Ingoldsby's body was removed from the hearse in Christ Church yard, salutes were fired by troops from the Dublin garrison.[40] Clodagh Tait's important study of death in early modern Ireland has touched on the representations of family honour in funerary customs, and these are manifest in the examples described here,[41] but for our purposes it matters more that grandiose public ritual may have involuntarily functioned to make the physical decay of the cathedral building seem irrelevant, whilst simultaneously confirming its place as the senior church of the capital.

Judging from the rich yield of monuments it contains, it would obviously be wrong to presume that St Patrick's lacked ritual activity beyond the normal functions of a cathedral. The best-documented heraldic funeral at St Patrick's during this period was in 1665, for the Lord Chancellor Sir Maurice Eustace. Robert Armstrong's piece on Eustace in the *Oxford Dictionary of National Biography* speculates that his body may already have been buried in county Kildare, suggesting that the funeral accorded to him by the Lord Lieutenant may have been primarily symbolic.[43] According to the records of Ulster's office, Sir Maurice's (or a dummy's) bier was transported to Christ Church in a vast procession from Eustace House on Dame Street.[43] As an aside, it is unclear why St Patrick's was selected as the resting place. It may have been that the pavements in Christ Church could take no more, as the registers mention that the grave slab of a certain John Preston, buried twenty years later, was proving difficult to identify because of the size and number of some of the recent memorials.[44] We do know, however, that the rest of the funerals at St Patrick's were less splendid than the Chancellor's, and the list of tombstones compiled by Victor Jackson suggests that it in terms of power and prestige, its interrees were usually marginal figures or had some vague familial connection to the area.[45]

St Patrick's, like any early modern cathedral, was not a free-for-all, but the criteria for admission were less stringent than in the decaying but socially and constitutionally superior church that stood only a couple of hundred yards in the distance.

Correspondingly, St Patrick's was rarely favoured for State ritual between 1660 and 1760. In the first half of the seventeenth century, incoming governors received the Sword of State in the cathedral, and the opening of parliament was normally preceded by a service featuring a preacher nominated by the Speaker of the House of Commons. The viceregal connection ended during the controversial rule of Sir Thomas Wentworth (1632-41), apparently because of a squabble with the chapter, and, as a possible consequence, the number of grand State occasions at the cathedral was allowed to dwindle, fading completely during the civil wars and the Cromwellian protectorate. With the disintegration of the latter, however, St Patrick's was put to occasional use, but this was thinly spread. Twelve bishops were consecrated on the same day in January 1661, having been chosen by the government for their 'conspicuous loyalty to the Anglican cause' during the interregnum.[46] The train gathered at Christ Church and walked to St Patrick's 'with silent, solemn grace', where it was viewed by large throngs of onlookers who seem to have been solicited for the purpose.[47] Dougal Shaw, the author of a groundbreaking dissertation on British and Irish monarchical culture in the Stuart era, contends that the Irish Privy Council engineered the spectacle as a kind of public relations exercise in the wake of the political instability and religious extremism of the 1650s.[48] If this is correct, then it may have been the case that St Patrick's was chosen as the location for this highly contrived display purely because it had a more spacious setting than Christ Church, which, on constitutional grounds, should have been the venue.

The State uses of St Patrick's in the Williamite and Hanoverian periods only occurred, once again, at major historical fulcrums where Christ Church was, for some reason, deemed unsuitable. In 1690 the lords justices gathered for a sermon on 23rd October, which undoubtedly chimed with the prevailing political currents. But little else followed. In 1729 Swift described St Patrick's Day as 'our only festival in the year', implying that the chapter had few ceremonial responsibilities beyond commonplace funerals and daily worship.[49] Then, in the 1750s and 1760s, the Friendly Brothers of St Patrick, a Masonic-style fraternity that opposed libertinism and duelling, celebrated the feast day of the saint with a service. Regular non-standard use of the cathedral would not return until 1783, when a new order of chivalry, the Knights of St Patrick, included an annual sermon on their list of incantations.[50] In terms of ceremony, the eighteenth century had not had a very extensive catalogue.

Nonetheless, what St Patrick's lacked in ceremonial splendour it compensated for through architectural immensity, and its sheer presence as a building strongly affected how it was interpreted. As Michael O'Neill has discovered, the cathedral's

11 – John Cruise
THE NAVE OF ST PATRICK'S
CATHEDRAL
1838, oil on canvas
(courtesy National Gallery of Ireland)

interior, far larger than the dim, asymmetrical nave of Christ Church, was white-washed in 1559, fixing the building's internal character for the next three centuries. The only identifiable visual image of it is an unusual painting of 1838 by the little-known John Cruise (Plate 11). In addition, a lath-and-plaster wall displaying the Ten Commandments closed off the cathedral choir, and in 1681-85 the chancel vault was decorated with blue paint and gilded stars. Structural changes were mostly a matter of subtraction. After the nave vaults collapsed in 1547 and 1555 (a fate shared by Christ Church), the cathedral was roofed in timber and reroofed again in 1671-72. The most drastic alteration was a set of flying buttresses and battlemented parapets along the flanks of the building, masking the junction between the roof and the weathering courses.[51] These alterations mutilated the old fabric but did have aesthetic advantages. The engraving of St Patrick's included in Walter Harris's *History and*

12 – St Patrick's Cathedral
from Harris, History and Antiquities (1766)

Antiquities of the City of Dublin of 1766 shows a clean silhouette that would not be out of place in an English provincial city (Plate 12).

The siting of St Patrick's, despite the seasonal floods, was also scenographically beneficial. It had the biggest green enclosure of any ecclesiastical building in Dublin, and, as shown in Rocque's *Exact survey* of 1756, was mostly uninhibited by nearby residential buildings (Plate 5). It was claimed earlier in 1729 that good views could be had on the cathedral's northern side, facing the city, and it appears from another sketch by Thomas Dineley that the main (west) front, with its recessed door and traceried window, could almost be taken in at a single glance.[52]

The evidence suggests that in the eighteenth century the cathedral became structurally unsound but managed to sustain its external visibility.[53] Swift's predecessor as dean, as seen above, had planned a steeple for the tower. Swift defaulted, Archbishop King got impatient, and the project lapsed. But in 1749 the deanery agreed to a proposal for an octagonal spire by the prodigious Dublin builder and architect George Semple (Plate 1), the funds coming from a bequest by Dean Stearne.[54] Whether or not the work enhanced the dean's personal reputation is a matter for conjecture, though corroborative sources imply that it may have boosted the cathedral's appearance by acting as a symbolic hub for the sunken region to the southwest of the city. A letter from Lady Elizabeth Germain to Swift indicates that in 1733 a bonfire was lit on top of the tower to mark the defeat of Sir Robert

Walpole's unpopular excise bill, presumably in the expectation that the blaze would be clearly seen throughout the vicinity.[55] It was probably well appreciated that the tower was a potent visual anchor; Semple's long, tapering steeple would give it greater, more enduring force (Plates 11, 12).

But imposing though it was, St Patrick's was not the only emblem of ecclesiastical authority in the area. The cathedral liberty adjoined the Archbishop's personal jurisdiction, the manor of St Sepulchre (Plate 5). Territorial disputes were recurrent. The Archbishop's attorneys claimed that the deanery was answerable to the diocese, with the implication that taxes imposed in St Sepulchre's could be collected in the precincts of the cathedral and criminals apprehended and sentenced without the chapter's knowledge.[56] Hence, in 1731, an irate Swift quipped that

> I am Lord Mayor of 120 houses, I am absolute Lord of the greatest Cathedral in the Kingdom: am at peace with the neighbouring Princes, the Lord Mayor of the City, and the A. Bp. of Dublin, only the latter, like the K. of France sometimes attempts encroachments on my Dominions, as old Lewis did upon Lorrain.[57]

These battles did not have an iconographic dimension per se, but the medieval palace of St Sepulchre did constitute a potent symbolic presence (Plate 13). An article by Danielle O'Donovan has fleshed out its history. Built by Archbishop John Comyn in the late twelfth or early thirteenth century, it consisted of three irregular ranges wrapped around a courtyard, the open part facing towards Kevin Street. Successive archbishops, the most influential being Michael Boyle (1663-78) and Francis Marsh (1681-93), undertook repairs but left the exterior mostly as they found it. William King, unsurprisingly, set about more far-reaching renovations, the most striking of which was a perimeter wall pierced in the middle by fluted gate piers, which created a threshold between the publicly shared streetscape and the official, semi-private residence of the city's chief ecclesiastic.[58] Under King, the palace itself was coated in rendering and sashes were put in place of the old-fashioned mullion-and-transom windows, thus replacing medieval disarray with a homogenising Georgian skin.[59] The exterior profile, shown in a print in *The Gentleman's Magazine* in 1771 (Plate 14), was still dreadfully asymmetrical, but the Archbishop's Dublin mansion did not need another overhaul until 1785, when the incumbent, Robert Fowler, called on the government to foot the bill.[60]

It was not King, however, who first brought architectural classicism to St Sepulchre's. Famously, Archbishop Narcissus Marsh had founded a library prior to his translation to the primacy in 1703, and this, designed by the distinguished and experienced English architect William Robinson, was a rectangular block over a basement. At the end of the decade, Thomas Burgh, Robinson's less corrupt successor as Irish Surveyor General, added a second range, making the library L-shaped in

13 – St Sepulchre's Palace, Dublin (various dates from c.1200; gate piers added in about 1712)

opposite 15 – Marsh's Library, Dublin (1701-10),
by Sir William Robinson and Thomas Burgh (with nineteenth-century refacings)

14 – St. Sepulchre's Palace
from THE GENTLEMEN'S MAGAZINE, 1771, after a drawing by Gabriel Beranger (courtesy National Library of Ireland)

plan.[61] The Caroline-style exterior, now partly refaced in flat nineteenth-century red-brick to the front end, and limestone rubble to the churchyard side, is extremely plain (Plate 15). A tall hipped roof sits on stone corbels, and the walls are perforated with unjambed sash windows, while the corners of the building are defined by masonry quoins. Presumably, an architraved doorcase (not the current porch reached by stairs) ornamented the main entrance at basement level.[62] The visual outcome, impossible to experience today, was that when viewed from the cathedral close the library made the palace look bigger, an effect that was totally spoiled by the conversion of St Sepulchre's to a barracks of the Royal Irish Constabulary in the early nineteenth century.

Swift, we know, had taken umbrage at the building of Marsh's Library because the number of Archbishop's appointees on the library board (two of which were annexed to the deanery) would give the senior clergy greater sway over the proceedings of the cathedral chapter.[63] Nevertheless, the run-ins between the personnel of St Patrick's and the Archbishop of Dublin had no obvious topographical manifestations, and the only physical evidence for the rival jurisdictions was the fence separating the cathedral yard from the Archbishop's garden. For a majority of Dubliners, the run-ins were probably not of much consequence. St Patrick's was considered, above all, a place for Protestant devotion, symbolic of the established church rather than any other authority. In a mock dialogue published in about 1719, following a parliamentary bill that guaranteed Irish dissenters freedom of worship, the cathedral is thus used as a metaphor for haughty Anglicanism, engaged in dialogue, with the supposedly purer form of Christianity represented by a nonconformist conventicle. The humble 'Meeting-House' opens the deliberations by acknowledging the intimidating scale of the cathedral:

> Tell me great Fabrick! tho' Our Distance seems,
> Something Remote, why should our Converse cease.
> Altho' thy Spire attempts [tries to reach] the distant Skie,
> And thy high Rood does o're our Houses rise
> Altho thy Pomp and gilded Altar shine,
> By Holy Sanction and a Right Divine,
> Submissive People tremble at it's Nod,
> And Worship it, tho' they profane their God,
> Yet suffer me that I enquire the Cause,
> Why thus thou'rt raised and by what mighty Laws,
> Some are by force unto thy Altars brought,
> Compelled to bow or Impiously you break,
> What your faith calls the Stiff and Stubborn Neck,
> You're strength is like some Whale upon the Sea,

That makes the trembling Fishes to obey,

Or else you execute pretended power,

The Right Divine is given to you to Devour.

The conversation quickly turns to accusations and counter-accusations of idolatry, mob rule, and the appropriate style of worship for a modern church (and, needless to say, the indomitable meeting house has the last word).[64] It is significant that the pamphlet, attributed to the contentious pastor of the Wood Street Presbyterian congregation, Joseph Boyse, selected St Patrick's as the icon of Restoration Anglicanism at its most obnoxious; where the confections of State were concerned, Christ Church had a near monopoly, but for some, at least, it was the lesser (if physically bigger) cathedral that represented the favoured denomination of the Protestant nation *in toto*.

From the restoration of the monarchy to the middle of the eighteenth century, Dublin's cathedrals were among the city's most richly symbolic buildings. This was in spite of the fact that their architectural development was largely shaped by expediency, and lagged far behind the ceremonial functions of the places. (The exceptions, of course, were Semple's steeple at St Patrick's and Pearce's Christ Church deanery, which could both claim some measure of architectural refinement.) Yet between them there were some very strong contrasts in meaning. Christ Church, though in many ways unsatisfactory as a work of architecture, was regarded as a symbolic fulcrum of the State. Its role as Chapel Royal and its connection with the Irish executive and Dublin Corporation ensured that it occupied a far higher place in the symbolic hierarchy of the capital than its slightly younger and more remote neighbour. As a totem of authority, then, Christ Church, the destination of regular official ritual, invoked the power and supremacy of the Protestant establishment, presided over by the Lord Lieutenant. Its symbolic meanings, in turn, owed more to this linkage than to its existence as a place of devotion in the care of the established church. At St Patrick's, where the bond with the post-Restoration polity was intermittent, the building was, in consequence, less governmental than ecclesiastical in its connotations. Ironically, when it did become a 'national' cathedral in 1870, it stood at the apex of a weakened church, whose disestablishment was intended to pacify a majority that did not belong to the denomination that one of its greatest architectural legacies had long represented.

———

ACKNOWLEDGEMENTS

My Ph.D. supervisor, Dr Lawrence E. Klein, was the first to read the part of my thesis on which this article is based. His recommendations were received most gratefully. As always, valuable suggestions came from Alex Dougherty and John Montague. For allowing me access to his files and indexes, I thank Dr Edward McParland, as well as the keepers of the repositories cited here.

ENDNOTES

The following abbreviations are used:
DCLA   Dublin City Library and Archive
NLI   National Library of Ireland
TCD   Trinity College, Dublin

[1]   An example is A. Dolan, 'The Large Medieval Churches of the Dioceses of Leighlin, Ferns and Ossory: a story of adaptation and change, part I', *Irish Architectural and Decorative Studies*, II, 1999, 26-65.

[2]   The art and architecture of Christ Church in the period 1500 to 1850 is studied in detail in a forthcoming TCD Ph.D. thesis by Stuart Kinsella, which locates the post-medieval cathedral within contemporary aesthetic discourses. Although much of the cathedral's architectural history is covered in the present essay, its objectives are different to Kinsella's work.

[3]   Despite the many alternatives, the best survey remains S.J. Connolly, *Religion, Law and Power: The Making of Protestant Ireland* (Oxford 1992).

[4]   King to Swift, 16th and 25th May 1713, and Swift to King, 23rd May 1713, in H. Williams (ed.), *The Correspondence of Jonathan Swift*, 5 vols (Oxford 1963-65) I, 349, 354, 357, discussed in J. McMinn, 'A Reluctant Observer: Swift and Architecture', *Irish Architectural and Decorative Studies*, VI, 2003, 90-119, 105-06.

[5]   King's activities as a church builder are detailed in R. Usher, 'Power, Display and the Symbolic Terrains of Protestant Dublin, c.1660-1760', Ph.D. dissertation (University of Cambridge 2007) ch.2.

[6]   King to Francis Annesley, 4th February 1724, quoted in R.T.C. Kennedy, 'The Administration of the Dioceses of Dublin and Glendalough in the Eighteenth Century', M.Litt. dissertation (TCD 1968) 148-49.

[7]   T. Campbell, *A Philosophical Survey of the South of Ireland, in a Series of Letters to John Watkinson, M.D.* (London 1777) 18.

[8]   K. Milne (ed.), *Christ Church Cathedral, Dublin: A History* (Dublin 2000).

[9]   'Annals' of Christ Church, c.1875, reproduced in C. Lennon and R. Refaussé (eds), *The Registers of Christ Church Cathedral, Dublin* (Dublin 1998) 127.

[10] DCLA, Gilbert MS 62, 11, W. Monck Mason, 'Collections for a History of Dublin', c.1820, transcribed by J.T. Gilbert; DCLA, Gilbert MS 78, 119, Minutes of the Merchants' Guild, 27th May 1648, in 'Charters and Documents of the Holy Trinity or Merchant's Guild of Dublin', transcribed by J.T. Gilbert.

[11] DCLA, Gilbert MS 229, f.6, E. Haines, 'On the Matter of the Perambulation of the City boundaries',1683.

[12] N.T. Burke, 'Dublin, 1660-1800: A Study in Urban Morphogenesis', Ph.D. dissertation (TCD 1972) 62.

[13] DCLA, Gilbert MS 132(9) 85, 215-16, 365, anonymous, 'A Diary of the Weather and Winds for 19 years Commencing with An. Dom. 1716 & Concluding with 1734'.

[14] J.S. Price, 'Dublin, 1750 to 1850: Spatial Distribution and Organisation of Economic Activity', M.Sc. dissertation (TCD 1980) 35-37.

[15] K. Milne, 'Restoration and Reorganisation, 1660-1830', in *idem* (ed.), *Christ Church Cathedral*, 255-97: 276-78.

[16] E. McParland, 'The Old Four Courts at Christ Church', in C. Costello (ed.), *The Four Courts* (Dublin 1996) 23-32.

[17] This section is based on R. Stalley, 'The 1562 collapse of the nave and its aftermath', in Milne (ed.), *Christ Church Cathedral*, 218-36.

[18] M.J. McEnery and R. Refaussé (eds), *Christ Church Deeds* (Dublin 2001) 366, 404.

[19] Stalley, 'The 1562 collapse', 232.

[20] Milne, 'Restoration and Reorganisation', 260-61, 269.

[21] Representative Church Body Library, C.6/1/8/5, 108, Christ Church Cathedral Chapter Acts, 14th April 1735.

[22] Representative Church Body Library, C.6/1/8/6, 27, Christ Church Cathedral Chapter Acts, 28th March 1745; Stalley, 'The 1562 Collapse', 235.

[23] A. Bonar Law and C. Bonar Law (eds), *The Prints and Maps of Dublin*, 2 vols (Dublin 2005) I, 144-45, 148-49, 150-51.

[24] E. McParland, 'Edward Lovett Pearce and the Deanery of Christ Church, Dublin', in A. Bernelle (ed.), *Decantations: A Tribute to Maurice Craig* (Dublin 1992) 130-33.

[25] NLI, GO MS 6, 59-61, Richard St George, Ulster King of Arms, to the Lords Justices, 18th April 1661.

[26] DLCA, Gilbert MS 74, I, 177-78. Robert Ware, 'The History and Antiquities of Dublin', 1678, transcribed by J.T. Gilbert (original in Armagh Public Library).

[27] J. Dunton, *The Dublin Scuffle* (1699), ed. A. Carpenter (Dublin 2000) 174.

[28] J. Dunton, *Teague Land, or a Merry Ramble to the Wild Irish* (1698), ed. A. Carpenter (Dublin 2003) 132.

[29] NLI, GO MS 6, 5-7, 9-11, Orders of the Privy Council, 1721 and 1724.

[30] NLI, GO MS 10, Ulster's Diary, entries for 23rd October, 1698-1784, *passim*; Milne, 'Restoration and Reorganisation', 260; T.C. Barnard, 'The Uses of the 23rd of October 1641 and Irish Protestant Celebrations', in *idem*, *Irish Protestant Ascents and Descents, 1641-1779* (Dublin 2003) 111-42.

[31] NLI, GO MS 10, ff.20v, 28, 32v, Ulster's Diary, entries for 29th May 1734, 1742, 1744.

[32] NLI, GO MS 10, ff.23, 24, 26, Ulster's Diary, entries for 30th January 1737, 1738, 1741.

[33] NLI, GO MS 10, ff.19v, 22. 10, Ulster's Diary, entries for 5th November 1733, 1735.

[34] NLI, GO MS 656, funeral entries relating to the FitzGeralds, 1861, *passim*.

[35] NLI, MS 73, 203, funeral entry for Robert FitzGerald, d.31st January 1698.

[36] Lennon and Refaussé (eds), *Registers of Christ Church Cathedral*, 87-98.

[37] NLI, GO MS 73, 31, funeral entry for Mountrath, interred 6th February 1662.

[38] NLI, GO MS 74, 4-5; NLI, GO MS 76, 126-27; NLI, GO MS 347, ff.37-38.

[39] NLI, GO Ms. 19, 3-5, funeral entry for Bramhall, d.10th July 1663.

[40] NLI, GO MS 302, 30-31, funeral entry for Ingoldsby, buried 9th February 1712.

[41] C. Tait, *Death, Burial and Commemoration in Ireland, 1550-1650* (Basingstoke 2002).

[42] R. Armstrong, 'Eustace, Sir Maurice (1590x95–1665)', in H.C.G. Matthew and B. Harrison (eds), *Oxford Dictionary of National Biography*, 60 vols (Oxford 2004), XVIII, 657.

[43] NLI, GO MS 19, 93, funeral entry for Eustace, d.20th June 1665, 93; NLI, GO MS 78, ff.101-2

[44] Funeral entry for Preston, 1686, in Lennon and Refaussé (eds), *Registers of Christ Church Cathedral*, 121.

[45] V. Jackson, *The Monuments in St. Patrick's Cathedral, Dublin* (Dublin 1987).

[46] D. Shaw, 'The Coronation and Monarchical Culture in Stuart Britain and Ireland, 1603-1661', Ph.D. dissertation (University of Cambridge 2002) 214, 219, 224; J. McGuire, 'Policy and Patronage: The Appointment of Bishops, 1660-1', in A. Ford and K. Milne (eds), *As By Law Established: The Church of Ireland Since the Reformation* (Dublin 1995) 112-19: 112.

[47] B. Boydell, *A History of Music at Christ Church Cathedral* (Woodbridge 2004) 65.

[48] Shaw, 'The Coronation', 233-35.

[49] J. Kelly, '"The Glorious and Immortal Memory": Commemoration and Protestant Identity in Ireland, 1660-1800', *Proceedings of the Royal Irish Academy*, C, vol. 94, no. 2, 1994, 25-52: 29; B. McCormack, *Perceptions of St. Patrick in Eighteenth-Century Ireland* (Dublin 2000) 71.

[50] M. Casey, 'The most illustrious Order of St Patrick', *Dublin Historical Record*, vol. 44, no. 2, 1991, 4-12.

[51] M. O'Neill, 'St. Patrick's Cathedral, Dublin, and its Place in Irish Medieval Architecture', Ph.D. dissertation (TCD 1995) 26-41.

[52] Isaac Butler, 'The Antiquities of St. Patrick's Cathedral', 1729, reproduced in O'Neill, 'St. Patrick's Cathedral, Dublin', 233-41: 234; NLI, MS 392, Thomas Dineley, 'Observations of a Tour in Ireland', 1681.

[53] Thomas Cooley, survey of St. Patrick's, 22nd November 1769, reproduced in O'Neill, 'St. Patrick's Cathedral, Dublin', 243.

[54] George Semple, 'Proposals for Building a Spire', 1749, reproduced in O'Neill, 'St. Patrick's Cathedral, Dublin', 242; M. Hanna, *The National and Collegiate Church of St. Patrick, Dublin: Conservation Plan* (Dublin 2006) 23.

[55] Williams (ed.), *The Correspondence of Jonathan Swift*, IV, 150 (1st May 1733).

[56] National Archives, Dublin, M.2545, 27-52, Christopher Robinson, 'The Case of the Enclosure Liberty Claimed by the Dean and Chapter of St. Patrick's Dublin...', 15th November 1757; DCLA, Gilbert MS 31, 1-19, Robinson, 'A State of the Case Between the Archbishop of Dublin & the Dean and Chapter of St. Patrick's, Dublin...', 1753; DCLA, Gilbert MS 31, 20-27, W. Fowke, 'An Answer to the State of the Case Drawn up by Mr. Robinson Relateing to the Liberties of St. Patrick's Close'.

[57] Swift to Alexander Pope, 8th July 1733, in Williams (ed.), *The Correspondence of Jonathan Swift*, IV, 171.

[58] D. O'Donovan, 'English Patron, Irish Building? The Importance of St. Sepulchre's Archiepiscopal palace, Dublin', in S. Duffy (ed.), *Medieval Dublin IV* (Dublin 2002) 253-78: 259-64.

[59] William King to Robert King, March 1706, in C.S. King (ed.), *A Great Archbishop of Dublin* (Dublin 1906), 45; TCD, MS 2531/206, William King to Lady Lanesborough, 7th October 1710; TCD, MS 1995-2008/1352, John Stearne to William King, 18th February 1710; TCD, MS 1995-2008/1387, Stearne to King, 11th March 1710; TCD, MS 1995-2008/1366, Stearne

to King, 22nd April 1710; TCD, MS 1995-2008/1456, Stearne to King, 16th June 1713; TCD, MS 1995-2008/1482, Stearne to King, 2nd July 1713; TCD, MS 1995-2008/1465, Stearne to King, 14th July 1713.

[60] NLI, MS 8135, Thomas Orde, Certificate of Repairs, 26th July 1787.

[61] E. McParland, *Public Architecture in Ireland, 1680-1760* (New Haven and London 2001) 165-66.

[62] C. Casey, *Dublin: The City within the Grand and Royal Canals and the Circular Road, with the Phoenix Park* (New Haven and London 2005) 638.

[63] M. McCarthy, 'Marsh, Narcissus (1638-1713)', in Matthew and Harrison (eds), *Oxford Dictionary of National Biography*, XXXVI, 805.

[64] Joseph Boyse (attribution), *Ecclesia & Reformation* (Dublin [1719?]), reproduced in R. Gillespie, 'Presbyterian Propaganda', in K. Herlihy (ed.), *The Politics of Irish Dissent, 1650-1800* (Dublin 1997) 105-20: 109.

———

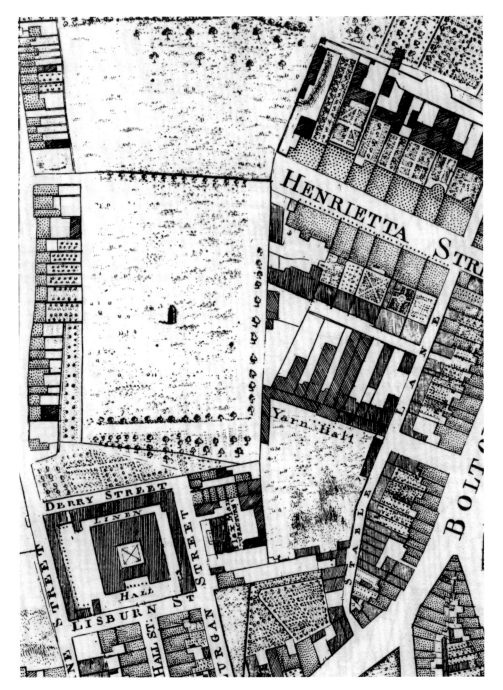

1 – John Rocque, EXACT SURVEY OF DUBLIN (1756)
detail showing dotted symbols at the Linen and Yarn Halls and on Henrietta Street, Dublin
(courtesy Harry Margary Publishers)

A shopping arcade in eighteenth-century Dublin: John Rocque and the Essex Street 'piazzas'

JOHN MONTAGUE

J OHN ROCQUE'S FOUR-SHEET *EXACT SURVEY OF THE CITY AND SUBURBS OF DUBLIN*, (1756), was the most comprehensive and detailed mapping of any city in these islands before the establishment of the Ordnance Survey in Ireland in the early nineteenth century.[1] Rocque was responsible for maps of cities throughout Europe, including plans of Rome, Paris and London. However, despite their considerable detail and large scale (the London map comprised twenty-four sheets and measured almost seven-by-thirteen feet), all of Rocque's previous maps had been limited to a depiction of the city block. His Dublin map, by contrast, was the only one which claimed to provide a detailed plan of 'the Ground Plot of all Publick Buildings, Dwelling Houses, Ware Houses, Stables, Courts, Yards &c' within the precincts of the mid-eighteenth-century city. Something about the intensity of the detail in this Dublin map, the linear idiosyncrasies, and the irregular, generally unrepeated shapes of many of the buildings depicted, tends on first view to suggest a level of accuracy we generally associate with a satellite photograph, or, indeed, of the early nineteenth-century OS maps. For the most part, Rocque delivered on the claims, quoted above, which he made in the title of the map. As a result, the 1756 map is the first port of call for historians and archaeologists in their efforts to reconstruct the city or decipher its excavated remains, whether they be medieval, early modern or eighteenth-century. Nevertheless, Rocque's limitations need to be considered.[2]

One aspect of the intense detail on display in Rocque's work is the manner in which he used the types of linear shading available to the engraver – parallel lines, hatched or cross-hatched, or stippled dots and spots in various patterns – to augment the information of the plan itself. Besides the limited number of hachures used to suggest the nature of the ground relief on the outer areas of the map, Rocque used these engraved micro-lines as symbols to indicate the function of the buildings

2 – John Rocque, Exact survey of Dublin *(1756): detail showing the care taken by engraver Andrew Dury over modulated stippling (courtesy Harry Margary Publishers)*

3 – John Rocque, Exact survey of Dublin (1756): detail showing dotted symbols at the Linen and Yarn Halls and on Henrietta Street, Dublin (courtesy Harry Margary Publishers)

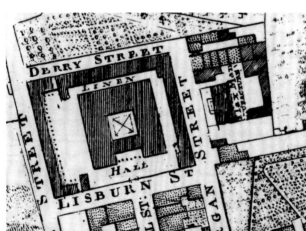

4 – Charles Brooking, A Map of the Cty and Suburbs of Dublin *(1728): elevation of the Linen Hall, Dublin*

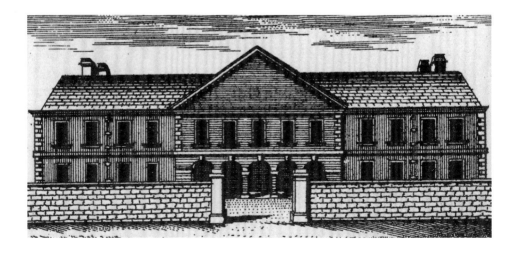

delineated.[3] So the utility building, outhouse and stable were shaded with a series of parallel lines; domestic or dwelling houses were stippled; public buildings were described by a more intense parallel diagonal line, and Church of Ireland churches by a cross-hatch. Roman Catholic chapels and meeting houses of various denominations were also included, and although they were for the most part labelled by initials, we might perhaps not read too much into the fact that they have the same diagonal hatching as the stable or outhouse![4] The close control exercised over these discriminating ciphers is one of the factors which makes this map so potentially exciting as a repository of historical information. The care taken by Rocque's engraver – on this project Andrew Dury – to, for example, modulate the stipples inside every single house to give a slight hint of modelled three-dimensionality suggests to us the possibility that equal care was taken with the micro-lines which depicted function (Plate 2), with all of the social and historical information that this implies.

However, a slightly different type of stippling, or series of differently shaped or sized dots, was used to depict other subtle topographical and architectural features. A quick survey of examples will show the range of possible meanings of these dotted patterns, and the consequent difficulty in some cases of their interpretation. For example, in Rocque's depiction of the Linen Hall (Plates 1, 3), we might be forgiven for thinking that its entrance was marked by a row of six columns, while the more careful illustration in Brooking's elevation drawing indicates that this was an arcaded entrance loggia with four piers (Plate 4).[5] The series of dots to the west of the Linen Hall entrance portico, with their suggestive shading, we might more confidently assume to be an arcaded loggia of the type found in the Royal Hospital or Royal Barracks. If we are to take it, for example, that the five dots in front of the Yarn Hall (Plate 1) represented a portico of some sort, what should we assume to be the meaning of the equally prominent dots in front of the terrace of houses just to the north of it on Henrietta Street? No doubt, its context, and our knowledge of the buildings which survive, suggest the probability of bollards, demarcating a pedestrian zone of the type also seen on Rocque's Sackville Mall, and confirmed as such by the near contemporary Oliver Grace view.[6] However, this does not help us when we look at the wobbling line of dots on the east side of Liffey Street, or when we come to interpret the even more obtuse significance of the line of dots in the yard of the Roman Catholic St Mary's Church on Liffey Street, mysteriously hidden from view behind the street façade on a site now occupied by Marks & Spencer's (Plate 5). Then, just to confound our expectations, Rocque used an axonometric 3D depiction of the bollards at the front of the Church of Ireland St Mary's nearby. A similar three-dimensional approach was also used for the bollards in front of the private dwelling house (Langford House), which was on the same block as the city's main Roman Catholic chapel. Some deference by the cartographer to social significance, shown by his choice of marks, may be assumed.

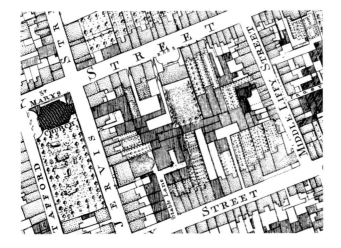

5 – John Rocque, Exact Survey of Dublin (1756): detail showing block between Jervis, Henry, Liffey and Abbey streets, featuring St Mary's Roman Catholic and Church of Ireland churches (courtesy Harry Margary Publishers)

6 – John Rocque, Exact Survey of Dublin (1756): detail showing Custom House Quay (courtesy Harry Margary Publishers)

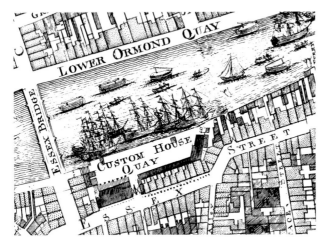

CUSTOM HOUSE

An interesting case, and the principal subject of this article, is brought to our attention by the series of dots used by Rocque and his engraver to describe the layout of the old Custom House (Plate 6), for which we are well served by comparative contemporary or near-contemporary images. This building was constructed between about 1704 and 1707 by Thomas Burgh, architect of the Old Library in Trinity, and of the Royal Barracks and Linen Hall already mentioned.[7] This Custom House was the third such building on a quay which had been laid out in the early seventeenth-century for the receipt and inspection of all goods being imported into or exported from the city.[8] There are three lines of dots on Rocque's map here: one (to the north) in front of the Custom House proper; a very light line of dots directly to its rear (on the south side); and a much more prominent set (also to the south) at the front of a terrace of houses facing onto Essex Street. In between is a heavy-handed depiction of the Custom House Gate, which appears on Rocque to involve a pair of vaulted passages separated by a wall.[9] The nearest contemporary image of the Custom House is Joseph Tudor's marvellous 1753 *A Prospect of the Custom House and Essex Bridge* (Plate 7). This seems to represent a far longer and thinner building than the one shown on the 1756 map. The existence of the ground-floor loggia, albeit of up to thirteen bays, is greatly curtailed on Rocque's map. Nevertheless, the robust nature of the arcade is given expression on what otherwise would be an unforgiving scale for such descriptive detail. Brooking's 1728 view is also very instructive (Plate 8). It includes the detail of the wider opening for the Custom House Gate, as well as the returns of the terrace of houses to the east, which Rocque had also indicated on his plan.

As noted already, there are two lines of dots to the south of the Custom House on either side of what was its city-side main entrance. Those on the east are of much greater girth than those on the west – which we might guess, based on the evidence already cited, were a line of bollards, or some indication of a separation between the spaces of the pedestrian and that of vehicular traffic. It is the dots on the right (east) which are the most interesting and which point to the structure which is the subject of this article. Based on previous examples, the fairly substantial dots, square in plan, combined with the shading to the rear, almost certainly must have represented a loggia of some sort, albeit one that connects a line of domestic dwelling houses, as indicated by the stippled code. However, we have other and more conclusive evidence for this. The restriction of the arcade to one side only of the Custom House Gate is at least confirmed by the line of faint dots on what is believed to have been George Semple's published *Plan for Opening and Widening a Principle Avenue to the Castle* of 1757.[10] However, a far more telling image, and one closely contemporary to both the Rocque map and Semple's drawing, is the Wide Streets Commissioners' map shown in Plate 9, which sketches out the proposed location of the newly planned Parliament Street.[11] On this carefully measured survey drawing, a very definite set of square-planned elements (smaller in girth than those which held up the loggia at the front of the Custom House) can be seen clearly on the east side of the Essex Street entrance. We might have been left to believe, without Rocque's depiction of the dwelling houses, that this was a continuation of the Custom House complex and was some kind of arcade which gave access to public offices, which we might have assumed existed somewhere here. As we shall see, there is enough contemporary documentary evidence to show that this range combined both domestic and commercial functions, but was not at all part of the official zone of the Custom House.

However, none of this made complete sense until the recent discovery in Australia, and publication in Ireland soon after the volume was returned to this

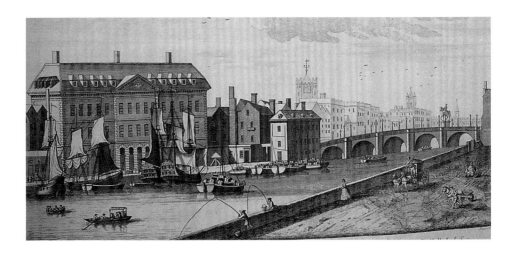

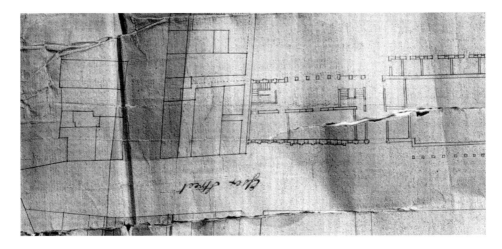

country, of Hugh Douglas Hamilton's *The Cries of Dublin*, an album of descriptive and closely observed drawings of street traders which can be dated to around 1760.[12] Rich with new evidence of mid-eighteenth-century social and cultural history, there are few images amongst the drawings, however, which contain any architecture. One, called *Hard Ware* (*The Cries of Dublin*, pl.51), is not place-specific, but does give us an impossibly phallic representation of a bollard – one of those, perhaps, which Rocque suggested were located in some of the grander streets such as Sackville Street or Henrietta Street. However, another of Hamilton's drawings to include architecture is certainly identifiable, and it brings to life a location in the city which had long since disappeared from the visual record.[13] This is Hamilton's *A Shoe Boy at Custom House Gate* (Plate 10). Here we see a shoeboy or shoeblack standing in a distracted fashion in the middle of Essex Street, holding his pot of lampblack mixed with rotten eggs. Behind him a dray is pulled towards the gates of the Custom House, and beyond this we see a ship on the quay and a great weighing scales set on a tripod.[14] Behind the main figure is another shoeboy placed towards the rear of the picture, bent at his work blacking the shoe of a man with a cane, who leans against a square post of some sort, belonging to a remarkable structure. The image shows what can only be the beginning of a ground-floor walkway, slightly raised above the level of the street, with a first floor projecting over it. The face of the first floor is carried on a straight timber lintel, supported by the square post at the corner and by what appears to have been a colonnade of Corinthian columns beyond it. That the colonnade continues eastwards is confirmed by the Rocque and Wide Streets Commissioners' maps. Rocque's stippled pattern asserted that these were separate dwelling houses of some kind, albeit all connected by this remarkable colonnade.

PIAZZAS

From references in contemporary newspapers and from other sources, it can be asserted that these houses with the colonnaded ground floor were commonly known as 'piazzas'. For example, in the November 16th edition of *Faulkner's Dublin Journal* in 1754, we hear that Robert Lewis 'Mathematician and Land Surveyor, having removed from the Piazza in Essex-Street, has furnished a [new] house ... in

7 – Joseph Tudor, A Prospect of the Custom House and Essex Bridge (1753)
(courtesy Board of Trinity College Dublin)

8 – Charles Brooking, A Map of the City and Suburbs of Dublin (1728): elevation of Custom House

9 – Wide Streets Commissioners' map showing Custom House
c.1757 (photo Peter Pearson; courtesy Dublin City Archive)

10 – Hugh Douglas Hamilton, A SHOE BOY AT CUSTOM HOUSE GATE
(from THE CRIES OF DUBLIN, 1760)

11 – Commissioners of Revenue 1775 survey of Custom House
(courtesy National Library of Ireland)

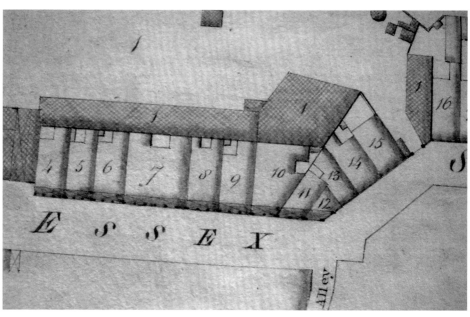

Temple Lane'. On 28th August 1762, also in the *Dublin Journal*, we hear that 'the widow McCormick, Paper-stamper, being obliged to quit her house in Essex-street, has opened shop lower down the said street opposite the middle of the Piazzas'.[15] While Robert Lewis was leaving the 'piazza', and Mrs McCormick was moving in across the street from the 'piazzas', the following advertisement in the *Dublin Journal* of January 1756 gives a graphic and clear account of the commercial nature of the piazzas themselves, when a house to be let was said to be:

> ...known by the sign of the Black Lyon at the Piazzas in Essex Street ... one of the best situations in the city of Dublin for public business, particularly for a hosier, most of the houses in the Piazzas being occupied by persons of trade.[16]

That the piazzas survived at least until 1775 is confirmed by the finest plan illustration of the covered space to emerge so far, in a Commissioners of Revenue survey drawing of that date (Plate 11).[17] This survey drawing shows the arcade in place still. Each house is labelled with the name of the occupant or whomever held the lease there. Of these named occupants of the nine houses in the piazzas proper, evidence for only three in the corresponding edition of *Wilson's Street Directory* emerged; it is otherwise extremely difficult to establish from that source on what side or part of the street any trader was located. The following, matching those recorded on the 1775 Commissioners of Revenue maps, were found: Richard Pattison, Hosier, at newly numbered 3 Essex Street; Widow (in *Wilson's* named as Martha) Windas/es, Hosier at No. 7; and Daniel O'Brien, also Hosier, in No. 9 Essex Street.[18] What emerges here then is a colonnade with shops, or a 'shopping arcade', dominated at least at the time of Hamilton's drawing and the Rocque map by the profession of hosiers. This explains, therefore, at least one of the house signs illustrated on the Hamilton drawing, depicting a pair of legs, above the lintel on the southern wall of the piazza building. The other shop sign visible on the same drawing may depict a bishop's mitre, although that name has not emerged amongst the house signs listed in leases or in Henry Berry's valuable list of house signs in the *Journal of the Society of Antiquaries*.[19]

Some significant evidence has also been found in the Registry of Deeds. Of those houses which can be categorically associated with the piazzas – i.e. where the piazzas (or on one occasion 'the pizzas') were named – we find a number of other hosiers such as Joseph Piercy, his wife, formerly Mary Power, and her father John Power (also hosiers), as well as an Andrew Keating, publican, and a Patrick Geoghegan, victualler, amongst others.[20] Geoghegan may well have been the tenant who answered the ad for the Black Lyon, already cited as a place eminently suited for business, because in 1757 he took out a lease on that premises from John Rogerson on a relatively short-term thirty-one-year agreement at a cost of £45 sterling per year.[21] Rogerson's grandfather, Sir John, the former Lord Mayor, had owned a great deal of property in this area, much of which he divested himself of around 1718, although his grandson is seen leasing a number of houses here throughout the 1750s and 1760s.[22] However, it is not clear from this evidence who was responsible for the unusual development, at least as it appeared in the Hamilton illustration and on the Rocque map and other plans. There is a suggestion in one mid-century lease that the arcade as it appears here might have been in existence as early as 1712, and the details of the window – flush to the wall and with a shallow segmental head – would seem to confirm an early date, possibly coeval with the construction of Burgh's Custom House itself.[23]

CLOISTERS

However, one could not help but speculate on whether the colonnade, which could be interpreted as expressing or being part of a high-status processional space, might have been part of Arthur Capel's newly planned Essex Street of 1674-75, which was terminated at the old city walls by the equally new Essex Gate.[24] This is despite the fact that the actual houses represented on Rocque's and Hamilton's images appear to have been completed with, or after, the construction of Burgh's Custom House in the early eighteenth century.[25] That an arcade or colonnade of some sort was part of Essex's late-seventeenth-century development can, in fact, be proved by evidence that has only recently come to the attention of the present author.[26] During the 1680s, a Thomas Denton of Cumbria visited his son who had settled in Dublin, and, in fact, worked in the Custom House. Denton has left us an accurate and first-hand description of Dublin, based on this visit, which he included in his much more substantial historical topography of Cumberland and Westmorland, the Isle of Man and Ireland, commissioned by Sir John Lowther (1655-1700), a local land owner and MP for Westmorland, and later Viscount Lonsdale.[27] Included in this was a superb description of Denton's approach to the city. After landing at Ringsend, he was carried across its strand towards the city by the chariot-like three-seater 'Rings-end coach' for a penny fare, up 'Lazy-hil' [sic] (Townsend Street), before entering 'into Temple-barr-street, along the southside the river, and so into Essex Street, reedified in a very uniform manner, with cloyster on each side, when the earl of Essex was deputy'.[28] That the word 'cloister' was used to mean a colonnade or arcade is confirmed by the fact that Denton used the exact same term to describe the arcades in the courtyard of the Royal Hospital at Kilmainham.[29] The structures in Essex Street must certainly have existed from the 1680s at least, the period when Denton visited, and in his opinion they were part of the work carried out by the Lord Deputy in the previous decade. Denton would appear to be best placed amongst our sources to make such a pronouncement. Most remarkable, perhaps, is the fact that the cloisters, or piazzas as they were referred to in the eighteenth century at least, existed in the late-seventeenth century on both sides of Essex Street, north and south.

This was one of the pre-eminent zones of the city, including as it did at this time the Council Chamber on the south side of Essex Street, in the location of the later Dolphin Hotel on the east corner of Crane Lane;[30] the Horse Guard, consisting of stables and a guard house, also on the south side, close to the Council Chamber, built by John Payne in 1663-65;[31] the Custom House on the north side of the street, with its great gate decorated by the city arms, as recorded in the Hamilton image; and west of these was the principal entrance to the city, which Essex had marked by his new gate constructed in 1674. This arcaded street was the culmination to the approach from overseas into the heart of post-medieval Dublin. Having made their way, just as Denton described it in his own trip, from Ringsend via Lazer's Hill and Temple Barr, newly arriving lords lieutenant first paid their respects at the Council Chamber (destroyed by fire in 1711), where they were 'sworn into office' to great ceremony before finally entering the old walled city.[32] As late as 1763, on the occasion of the King's birthday, a celebration was held by Speaker Ponsonby at the Custom House. 'On this occasion the front of the building next to Essex-street was covered with most elaborate devices, and illuminated with about two thousand lights.'[33] The particular grandeur of the arcades on both sides of the street, that appear to have been introduced under the instigation of the Earl of Essex some hundred years earlier, would have been entirely in keeping with this iconography of State.[34]

The 1775 map, already referred to, shows that the piazzas survived until the last quarter of the eighteenth century at least. Another survey drawing, also by the Commissioners of Revenue, first drafted in 1769 but copied and annotated in 1799, refers to the 'Old Piazza Ground'.[35] The word 'ground', and the blank space on the survey drawing where the houses were located, might suggest that the buildings were no longer extant in this closing year of the eighteenth century.[36] But a Wide Streets Commissioners' map that may date to the early nineteenth century, and that shares the footprints of the 1775 map, appears to hint, by means of a strange overlap of some of the houses, that parts of the piazzas could have survived into the early nineteenth century. It is difficult to be certain (Plate 12).[37]

The late eighteenth-century survival of the piazzas is, however, corroborated by a number of complaints and generally negative reports regarding them, as well as a number of attempts to have them removed. For example, in an attempt to divert the plans to move the Custom House to the location on which Gandon's building was eventually constructed, a note in the minute book of the Dublin Society of Merchants (in the Royal Irish Academy), dated 17th April 1769, recorded:

> That it is our Opinion that while private property and the General Interest of Trade would Suffer, no public Utility can be pretended for removing the

12 – Wide Streets Commissioners(Map 507)
depicting Essex Street and the Custom House complex (courtesy Dublin City Archive)

Custom House from its present situation, as the insufficiency of the Ground can [be] easily & amply supplied by purchasing the Houses called the Piazzas, and a line of Houses which extend to Temple Lane slip, and adding the Ground on which they stand to the present Custom House Quay.[38]

On 3rd November 1770 it was reported that the merchants and traders of the city requested 'that the lord mayor take notice of the billiard tables in the Piazzas in Essex Street'. The following week the Lord Mayor ordered the closure of that establishment. But in December it was reported that 'Joe's billiard table had evaded closure', and the following January requests were renewed for 'the billiard tables at the Black Lion in Essex Street' to be removed.[39] It is not clear whether the anti-gaming lobby had any success in this instance. However, only three years later, in 1774, a correspondent to the *Freeman's Journal* felt himself competent to announce 'that the Piazzas in Essex-Street, with the houses leading to the Ballast-office, will be taken down, in order to enlarge the Custom-house quay.' [40] However, the piazzas were still very much in place ten years later, when, in 1784, it was reported that 'A strange man from Liverpool under the piazzas ... was robbed for what cash he had about him ... in one of those destructive night houses kept there.' [41] A further call was made in 1786 to the high sheriffs of the city that the 'houses condemned in Essex Street be taken down' because they had

> become the open and licentious receptacle of robbers and prostitutes, particularly that dreadful rookery which is in hourly danger of falling down, called the Golden Bottle, and two other ruins which have been condemned, in the range of the piazzas.[42]

However, the piazzas still stood at least as late as 23rd September 1788, when, on a

> Monday night, between the hours of twelve and one o'clock, a number of
> drunken buckeens reeling red-hot from the tavern ripe for sport paraded thro'
> Essex-street ... and at the end of the piazzas having met an oyster woman ...
> knocked the poor unoffending creature down...[43]

MEANING

So what is to be made of the word 'piazzas' which was applied to the colonnaded
structure indicated by Rocque and Hamilton? The *Oxford English Dictionary* is very
helpful in this regard. In its second or alternative definition to the word piazza, it
states the word was '[e]rroneously applied to a colonnade or a covered gallery or
walk surrounding an open square or piazza proper, and hence to a single colonnade
in front of a building'. It goes on to say that '[it] appears to have begun with the vul-
gar misapplication of the name to the arcade built after the designs of Inigo Jones on
the north and east sides of Covent Garden, London, instead of to the open market-
place or area'.[44] This exactly explains the case at Essex Street, where the word has
nothing to do with an open space or square, but is a misappropriation (or corruption)
of its original meaning to a new context – the colonnaded or arcaded walkway.
Indeed, we find the word being used in the same way for the area under the colonnade of Edward Lovett Pearce's Parliament House, as shown in Rowland Omer's
plan of 1767;[45] in a proposal for a colonnade or piazza between two gateways north
of Dublin Castle on the Semple plan discussed above;[46] and in the area under the
loggia on the river side of the Custom House itself.[47] One of the latest uses of the
word in this context was in the great Dublin historian, J.T. Gilbert's own mid-nineteenth-century description of Essex Street in the eighteenth century. Indeed, Gilbert
seemed to have been quite aware of the existence of some kind of gallery in this
location, although his use of the since-obsolete colloquial term for it had perhaps
left his account of the colonnade somewhat opaque to later readers until now.[48] It
seems less likely, as Gilbert claimed, that the arcade spanned both sides of the
Custom House Gate in the mid-eighteenth century, despite the ambiguous evidence
of Rocque's map. An arcade on the eastern side only is very clearly marked in on
the 1775 Revenue Commissioners' map, and on the even clearer *c*.1757 Wide
Streets Commissioners' map (Plates 9, 11).[49]

The word, and the use of columns to reserve a space separated from the
street, evokes, and must have partaken to some extent, in the meaning and status of
the piazza in Italy, or the Plaza Mayor in Spain, all ultimately derived from the
Roman forum and the colonnaded stoas of the Greek agora.[50] However, its direct

source in this country was perhaps more modest. Some of the so-called 'rows' in Chester, the first coach stop on the road from Holyhead to London,[51] are of this exact type (Plate 13), although the majority of the other rows in Chester were a distinct species of first-floor passage raised above half-basements.[52] There are some rare images, however, of what really might have been a very general type throughout England from the seventeenth century. One of the finest of these is Thomas Sandby's image of colonnaded spaces for shopping in eighteenth-century Nottingham (Plate 14).[53] Another is a still-surviving ground-floor loggia in front of a terrace of shops in Winchester.[54] A later-eighteenth-century example is the pantiles in Tunbridge Wells, Kent. Far more of these seem to have existed, but documentary or archaeological evidence for them is sometimes sparse.[55]

Whatever of their broader iconographical meaning and their likely architectural sources, this present impression, from the images of Rocque and Hugh Douglas Hamilton, as well as the documentary evidence of the colonnaded walkway, providing a type of stage or covered promenade in front of a succession of dwellings of mixed domestic and commercial function, is an extremely important addition to our very limited stock of knowledge of how shops appeared in Dublin at this time. There are the images in Malton of a type of shop – at least in terms of the arrangement of their façade – we might properly believe only emerged in the later decades of the eighteenth century.[56] A type of structure which could be a more primitive cousin of that shown on Hamilton's drawing can be found in the lean-to shambles illustrated in *West Front of St. Patrick's Cathedral*, also by Malton.[57] One remarkably late survival of this type of structure were the shambles at Castle Market, photographed just before their demolition in 1878.[58] Shops without fenestration, protected only by shutters which went up at night, were common, and indeed we have no idea whether or not the shops inside the piazzas were glazed.[59] Finally, the strange lean-to fenestrated projections to houses on College Green illustrated in Joseph Tudor's image of that area could be an early seventeenth-century type of shop front; there is nothing, at least in an Irish context, with which to compare them.[60]

There seems to be little evidence that an arcade or walkway such as the piazzas existed anywhere else in Dublin in the eighteenth century. In the nineteenth century, Dublin, like Paris, Milan and London, would make its own gesture to the craze for arcaded life in the passageway which existed briefly between Suffolk Street and

_____

13 – Lower Bridge Street Rows, Chester (1817) by George Batenham
(courtesy Board of Trinity College Dublin)

14 – Nottingham: detail of image by Thomas Sandby showing ground-floor colonnade
(courtesy Nottingham City Museums & Galleries: Nottingham Castle)

15 – Wide Streets Commissioners' elevation of Thomas Sherrard's design for Westmoreland Street, featuring a ground-floor colonnade referred to as 'piazzas' (courtesy Dublin City Archive)

College Green.[61] Before this, however, in May 1799, the Wide Streets Commissioners had requested a design from Thomas Sherrard for a colonnade in Westmoreland Street, which not only replicated in an elaborate classical scheme the form, but also the very nomenclature of the Essex Street piazzas. The minutes of 25th May 1799 record that the Commissioners:

> Resolved that the Buildings to be erected in said [Westmoreland] Street shall stand upon a Calonade [sic] of Twelve feet Wide & fifteen feet high ... so as to form an Extended piazza for the length of the Street on either Side the Super structure to be supported on Stone Pillars of the Doric order the said Piazza to be vaulted underneath & Flagged & to occupy the space of the footway...[62]

This statement is reflected by Sherrard's surviving design for the scheme, which is remarkably similar, albeit in a classicised guise, to that of the piazzas in Essex Street upon which Sherrard's scheme must have been modelled (Plate 15).[63]

Although the Westmoreland Street design proposals were never carried to fruition, their vision of shopfronts included within an integrated architectural scheme would be some decades in advance of the type of 'designed shopping street' which Summerson had suggested only emerged in a modest fashion during 'the Regency and after' in London.[64]

CONCLUSION

All vestiges of Dublin's eighteenth-century shopping arcade have now disappeared. Nevertheless, there is some persistent quality in architecture, and the development of cities generally, reminiscent of the persistence of tracks made by goats on a mountainside, which has resulted in the great door of the Clarence Hotel today being situated in almost the exact same place as the gate into the Custom House in the mid-eighteenth century. The place of the eighteenth-century shoeboy with his pot of black paint, however, is now taken by a twenty-first-century bootboy with a mobile phone.

———

This article has emerged from research for my Ph.D. dissertation on John Rocque's map of Dublin, which I am carrying out under the generous supervision of Edward McParland. I am very grateful to him for his relentless enthusiasm and optimism, and his caring and expert guidance throughout. I am in the debt of Robin Usher for his many helpful leads and for the numerous discussions we had on the architecture of Dublin in the seventeenth and eighteenth centuries. I also received welcome advice and encouragement throughout the preparation of this work from Anna Moran. Others who gave assistance or offered suggestions include Catherine Delano-Smith, Paul

Ferguson, Lisa-Marie Griffith, Patricia McCarthy and Niall McCullough. I am also grateful to Giles de Margary of Harry Margary Publishers; to Sarah Skinner and Nottingham City Museums & Galleries, Nottingham Castle; Peter Boughton, Keeper of Art & Architecture, Grosvenor Museum, Chester; Mary Clark of Dublin City Archive; Elizabeth Kirwan of the National Library of Ireland; Charles Benson, Keeper of Early Printed Books at TCD; as well as the Board of Trinity College, Dublin. Finally, I would like to thank Finola O'Kane and Gillian O'Brien who gave me my first chance to air this topic at the Bare Bones of a Fanlight conference in 2006.

ENDNOTES

The following abbreviations are used:

DCLA	Dublin City Library & Archives
NLI	National Library of Ireland
RD	Registry of Deeds, Dublin
WSC	Wide Streets Commissioners

[1] John Rocque, *An Exact survey of the city and suburbs of Dublin in Which is Express'd the Ground Plot of All Publick Buildings Dwelling Houses Ware Houses Stables Courts Yards & C By Iohn Rocque Chorographer to Their Royal Highness the Late & Present Prince of Wales 1756* (Dublin 1756).

[2] Bill Frazer, 'Cracking Rocque?', *Archaeology Ireland*, XVIII, 2, 2004, 10-14, has made a considerable contribution in this regard in his recent critical interpretation of Rocque's accuracy and surveying techniques in the Liberties area of the city.

[3] Catherine Delano-Smith, in a paper entitled 'From diagram to portrait: recognising the reader in the map image' at *The Images of Maps: Maps of the Imagination* conference, Ashmolean Museum, University of Oxford, 12th May 2006, used the expressions macro-lines and micro-lines to distinguish, respectively, the lines used to outline the subject of the map and those used for the content of the map, such as map signs and words.

[4] Another distinction is that Church of Ireland churches, like public buildings in the city, were given their full title, for example, St Mary's Church or St Andrew's Church, while the equivalent Roman Catholic churches were marked simply with a cross without being named.

[5] Charles Brooking, *A Map of the City and Suburbs of Dublin and also the Arch Bishop and Earl of Meaths Liberties with the Bounds of each Parish. Drawn from an Actual Survey. Made by Charles Brooking* (Dublin 1728), including inset 'The Custom House'.

[6] Oliver Grace, *A Perspective View of Sackville Street and Gardiner's Mall Dublin...* (Dublin, n.d.; *c.*1756), reproduced in Andrew Bonar Law and Charlotte Bonar Law, *A Contribution Towards a Catalogue of Engravings of Dublin. Originally by E. MacDowel Cosgrave: Revised and Expanded, to which is added volume 2, a similar contribution towards a catalogue of: the maps and charts of Dublin city and county*, 2 vols (Shankill, Co Dublin, 2005) I, pl.41. The function of these bollards or posts is made clear by a published complaint in a contemporary newspaper regarding the practice of shortening them to 'stumbling blocks'. Proper posts of about three feet in height had been put in place, it was argued, 'to guard the Foot Passengers from Carriages and Cattle [and] are set up in Streets and Highways, in every well regulated Country...', the *Freeman's Journal*, 82, 16th-19th June 1764, 327. I am grateful to Lisa-Marie Griffith for bringing this reference to my attention.

[7] Rolf. Loeber, *A Biographical Dictionary of Architects in Ireland 1600-1720* (London 1981) 35.

[8] R.M. Gilbert (ed.), *Calendar of the Ancient Records of Dublin*, 19 vols (Dublin 1889-1944) V, 546-60.

[9] This depiction of a paired entranceway at the Custom House Gate is not corroborated by any other contemporary plans or by the Hugh Douglas Hamilton image discussed below.

[10] DCLA, Gilbert Library, WSC/Maps/329.

[11] The lines on the map which indicate the proposed location of the new Parliament Street suggest that this drawing dates to soon after 1757, the date of the establishment of the Wide Streets Commissioners, when such a survey would have been drafted.

[12] William Laffan (ed.), *The Cries of Dublin &c: Drawn From the Life By Hugh Douglas Hamilton, 1760* (Dublin 2003).

[13] There are two other images with some suggestion of an architectural backdrop in Hamilton's album: plate 4, *Oyster Carrs at Ormond Market Gate*, shows two horses standing before the open door and window of a dwelling house, and plate 66, *A Travelling Cutler*, shows the cutler of the title standing before a cobbler's display of shoes. It is not clear whether this was a permanent stall to the front of a shop or one belonging to an itinerant tradesman.

[14] It just might be possible that the gate shown here represents one of two vaulted entries side by side, as suggested by Rocque, although there is nothing in the drawing to suggest as much (cf. note 9 above).

[15] See also the *Freeman's Journal*, 6th August 1768, when the same business had just imported 'at their Paper Warehouse, opposite the Piazzas in Essex-Street, a new curious Assortment of Paper for hanging Rooms, Ceilings, Stair-cases, Chimney-boards...' However, they were also manufacturers of 'all Kinds of Irish Paper, and [were willing to] finish plain Rooms in the neatest Manner'.

[16] Jenny Price, 'Dublin 1750 to 1850: Spatial Distribution and Organisation of Economic Activity', MSc thesis (Trinity College Dublin 1980) 37, fn.17, quoting from *Faulkner's Dublin Journal*, 17th January 1756.

[17] NLI, 16 G 16 (15), Commissioners of Revenue Map of Essex Street, 1775.

[18] *Wilson's Street Directory* (Dublin 1762), *passim*. There is only one house on the 1775 survey between Richard Pattison's (which must only recently have been assigned as No. 3), and the Custom House, which therefore must have been considered, from the rear façade facing south at least, to have been No. 1 Essex Street.

[19] Henry F. Berry. 'House and Shop Signs in Dublin in the Seventeenth and Eighteenth Centuries', *Journal of the Royal Society of Antiquaries of Ireland, Papers and Proceedings*, Part II, XL, 1910, 81-98.

[20] RD, for example, Memorial nos 292.216.190193, Piercy to Keating, 4th March 1772; 290.392.192716, Power to Butler, 4th May 1772; 290.392.192716, Power to Butler, 4th May 1772.

[21] RD, Memorial no. 190.297.126844, Rogerson to Geoghegan, 3rd May 1757.

[22] RD, Memorial no. 21.369.11841, 'All Sr. John Rogerson's houses in Essex Street', 1718. For the activities of Sir John Rogerson's grandson, cf. lease to Geoghegan cited in fn.19 or, for example, Memorial no. 219.134.142955, John Rogerson to John Power, 29th September 1761.

[23] RD, Memorial no. 97.63.67295, Camak to Black, 13th October 1739, which refers to the piazzas on Essex Street, refers also to a parent lease dated to 1712 (not actually recorded in the memorials), of which this 1739 lease was possibly a direct copy.

24 Arthur Capel, Earl of Essex, was Lord Lieutenant from May 1672 until June 1675, and again from May 1676 until May 1677; see T.W. Moody, F.X. Martin and F.J. Byrne (eds), *A new history of Ireland IX: maps, genealogies, lists* (Oxford 1984) 489-90. His order to Dublin Corporation 'that a highway [Essex Street] be made from the Custome house lane [Crane Lane?] through the garden in the possession of Alderman Lovett, at the Blind Key' is recorded in Gilbert (ed.), *Calendar of the Ancient Records of Dublin*, V, 30; cf. 'The Seventeenth Report of Sir Bernard Burke, C.B. Ulster King of Arms, Keeper of the State Papers in the Record Tower, Dublin Castle, dated 1st February, 1885', *House of Commons Parliamentary Papers, 1884-85*, Appendix III, XL (London 1885). For an extended discussion of Essex Street and Essex Gate, see Robin Usher, 'Power, Display and the Symbolic Terrains of Protestant Dublin, *c.*1660-1760', Ph.D. dissertation (University of Cambridge 2007)

25 The segmented-headed windows as shown on the Hamilton drawing is one clue to their early eighteenth-century date. For a full exposition of the early development of this zone from the beginning of the sixteenth century, see Nuala T. Burke. 'Dublin's north-eastern city wall: early reclamation and development at the Poddle-Liffey confluence', *Proceedings of the Royal Irish Academy*, LXXIV, section C, 1974, 113-32. I am also grateful to Edward McParland for his suggestions in this regard and others.

26 Angus J.L. Winchester, 'Dublin in the 1680s', *History Ireland*, XV, 1, January-February 2007, 48-51, which in turn refers to the more substantial and complete Angus J.L. Winchester and Mary Wane (eds), *Thomas Denton: a Perambulation of Cumberland 1687-1688 including descriptions of Westmorland, the Isle of Man and Ireland. Record Series: The Surtees Society and Cumberland & Westmorland Antiquarian & Archaeological Society*, CCVII (Woodbridge 2003). Both of these are based on the original manuscript of Denton's topographical work: Carlisle, Cumbria Record Office D/Lons/L12/4/2/2. I am grateful to Robin Usher for bringing the recent article on this subject to my attention.

27 Winchester and Wane (eds), *Thomas Denton: a Perambulation*, 8-9 and *passim*.

28 *ibid.*, 531. The italics are inserted by the present author. Attention should be drawn here to the fact that the word 'cloyster' appears partially in square brackets, i.e. as cl[oyster] in the 2003 publication. According to fn.33 on p.525 of that publication, a linen strip repair had obscured a small section of the manuscript on the sides of pp.182 and 183. The missing material from these pages was supplied by a copy of the manuscript which is in the Manx archives of the Isle of Man. This fact has also been corroborated by a personal communication with Dr Winchester, the editor of that work.

29 Winchester and Wane (eds), *Thomas Denton: a Perambulation*, 537.

30 The exact location of the Old Council Chamber, just prior to the laying out of Essex Street, is indicated on de Gomme's 1673 map of Dublin: Greenwich, National Maritime Museum, P/49(11): *The Citty and Suburbs of Dublin from Kilmainham to Rings-End, werein [sic] the Rivers, Streets, Lanes, Allys, Churches, Gates &c are Exactly described 15th No: 1673*; cf. Edward McParland, *Public Architecture in Ireland 1680-1760* (New Haven and London 2001), 114, quoting John Dunton: Oxford, Bodleian Library, MS. Rawl D71, Dunton's letters, ff.25-26.

31 Loeber, *A Biographical Dictionary*, 83.

32 Robert Pentland Mahaffy (ed.), *Calendar of the State Papers relating to Ireland. Preserved in the Public Record Office. September, 1669-December, 1670* (London 1910) 3, 6, 111-13; McParland, *Public Architecture*, 17, 91; Nuala T Burke. 'Dublin 1600-1800, a study in urban morphogenesis', Ph.D. dissertation (Trinity College Dublin 1972) 149.

[33] J.T. Gilbert, *A History of the City of Dublin*, 3 vols (Dublin 1972) II, 139.

[34] It is also possible that the colonnade had a more modest or mixed inception than this. We have no evidence for the external appearance of the Old Council Chamber, but it was a grand architectural piece, according to John Dunton's description of its great stair and first-floor Council Room. It may simply have been that this building had been constructed with a loggia to the front, and houses opposite picked up on this when Essex Street was laid out.

[35] NLI, 16 G 16 (19), 'A MAP of the Old Custom House Dublin together with the several Offices thereunto Belonging SURVEYED / by Order of the Commissioners of the Revenue / in April 1769 by T Mathews. C.S. [city surveyor] / Copied / By A.R. Nevill City Surveyor / December' [manuscript torn here]. Although the year is missing in the title of this drawing, an annotation within the body of the map refers to an agreement 'bearing date the 28th of Aug.st 1799'.

[36] It seems more probable that it was because the houses and piazzas were outside of the agreement defined by the drawing that they were not delineated.

[37] DCLA, Gilbert Library, WSC/Maps/507.

[38] Royal Irish Academy, MS. 12-D-29, Minutes Book of the Dublin Society of Merchants, 1767-82, unpaginated. I am once again grateful to Robin Usher for this reference.

[39] The *Freeman's Journal*, 3rd and 13th November 1770, 8th and 18th December 1770, 8th January 1771, 13th June 1771 and 20th August 1771. I am grateful to Lisa-Marie Griffith for bringing my attention to these references.

[40] *ibid.*, 31st May 1774.

[41] *ibid.*, 22nd July 1784.

[42] *ibid.*, 16th November 1786.

[43] *ibid.*, 23rd September 1788.

[44] *The Compact Edition of the Oxford English Dictionary: complete text reproduced micrographically*, 2 vols (Oxford 1971) II, 2163; cf., for example, a view of the 'piazzas' by T. Sandby, 1768, reproduced in John Summerson, *Inigo Jones* (Harmondsworth 1966) 94.

[45] *The Plan of the Parliament House Dublin ... R. Omer delin.* (Dublin 1767); see also the complaint in the *Freeman's Journal*, 9th March 1768, about the 'Set of Miscreants, under the Piazzas of the Parliament-house, playing Ball, Pitch and Toss, &c. [the same] Roof, under which All our Laws are framed, [and which provided] a Covering for such Wretches to trample upon all Laws, Divine and Human'.

[46] DCLA, WSC/Maps/329, 'and the Treasury Office, answerable to the present Gate of said upper Yard; with a handsome Colonade [sic] or a Piazze [sic] betwixt said two Gates, for the Guards, &c &c'.

[47] Commissioners of Revenue map, 1769/1799, area marked No. 6, and explained in the reference table as 'The Piazza'.

[48] Gilbert, *History of the City of Dublin*, II, 165. Gilbert also noted the existence here of the hosiers, the billiard tables, and the Black Lion Tavern, amongst others.

[49] Rocque's marks on the western side are of a much smaller girth, and are more likely suggestive of bollards, as noted already.

[50] For a discussion of the persistent Spanish type and its roots in Roman precedents, see Roland Martin et al (eds), *Forum et Plaza Mayor dans le Monde Hispanique: colloque interdisciplinaire – Casa de Vel·squez – Madrid: 28 Octobre 1976* (Paris 1978); for a descriptive evocation of the cultural implications of both the agora and the forum, see Richard Sennett, *Flesh and Stone: the Body and the City in Western Civilization* (London 1994) 52-60, 111-18.

[51] D.M. Beaumont, 'An Irish gentleman in England – the travels of Pole Cosby *c*.1730-35', *Journal of the British Archaeological Association*, CXLIX, 1996, 38; see also the many moaning missives from Chester made by Jonathan Swift in his *Journal to Stella*, ed. Harold Williams (Oxford 1974) *passim*.

[52] Andrew Brown (ed.), *The Rows of Chester: the Chester Rows research project* (London 1999); P.H. Lawson and J.T. Smith, 'The Rows of Chester: two interpretations', *Journal of the Chester and North Wales Architectural, Archaeological and Historic Society*, XLV, 1958, 1-42.

[53] Thomas Sandby, *Market Place*, NCM 1939-64 (courtesy Nottingham City Museums & Galleries: Nottingham Castle). A second image of the market square, also by Sandby, can be found reproduced in Mark Girouard, *The English Town: a history of urban life* (New Haven and London 1990) 16.

[54] An image of this row of buildings, which it is suggested was fourteenth-century in origin, is reproduced in Kathryn Morrison, *English Shops and Shopping* (London 2003) 25. From one perspective, the first floor, carried on a colonnade, was a special case of the jettied building, albeit with strong hints towards an antique, if not, at least, a Mediterranean source as well.

[55] For a discussion of the evidence for other colonnades and arcades associated with commercial premises in towns in the Middle Ages and in the seventeenth and eighteenth century in England, see Morrison, *English Shops*, 24-27, 31, 109, 113.

[56] James Malton, *A Picturesque & Descriptive View of the City of Dublin, Reproduced from the Edition of 1799, with an Introduction by the Knight of Glin* (Dublin 1978) *passim*; cf. Edward McParland., 'Malton's views of Dublin: too good to be true?' in Raymond Gillespie and Brian P. Kennedy (eds), *Ireland: Art into History* (Dublin 1994) 15-25.

[57] James Malton, *A Picturesque & Descriptive View of the City of Dublin*, pl.13.

[58] Millard and Robinson, photographed in 1878, reproduced in Niall McCullough, *Dublin, An Urban History: plan of the city* (Dublin 2007) 208.

[59] Note the shops illustrated on the top right-hand side, in the location of the present Westmoreland Street, on the drawing *A view of the Principal Front of the Parliament House...*, which is ascribed to Edward Lovett Pearce, NLI, Drawing 589 TB, reproduced in McParland, *Public Architecture*, 205.

[60] Joseph Tudor, *A Prospect of the Parliament House in College Green, Dublin* (Dublin 1753).

[61] *The Royal Arcade Dublin*, reproduced in Mairead Dunleavy, 'Dublin in the early nineteenth century: domestic evidence' in Gillespie and Kennedy (eds), *Ireland: Art into History*, 196. The Royal Arcade was also depicted directly after it had been destroyed by fire (on 25th April 1837) by William Turner de Lond, and is reproduced in William Laffan (ed.), *Painting Ireland: Topographical Views from Glin Castle* (Tralee 2006) 196.

[62] Edward McParland, 'The WSC, their importance for Dublin architecture in the late-eighteenth and early nineteenth centuries', *Quarterly Bulletin of the Irish Georgian Society*, XV, 1972, 19, quoting from the WSC' Minutes, 25th May 1799, DCLA, WSC/Minutes/3.

[63] DCLA, Gilbert Library, WSC/Maps/195/1-2, 'Elevation of Westmoreland Street (West side), extending from the Portico of the House of Lords to Fleet Street, and design for New Shops by A. Baker, Architect,1799. Approved 30 Jan 1800 Thomas Sherrard, 1800'; reproduced in McParland 'Wide Streets Commissioners', pl.11.

[64] This point regarding the precocious nature of the WSC' designs for the Westmoreland Street façades was made by McParland, 'WSC', 20, referring in turn to Sir John Summerson, *Georgian London* (London 1945) 250.

1 – Kilbixy church with motte and bailey, viewed from the north

(all photos by the author unless otherwise stated)

A new Wyatt church in Ireland

JENNIFER MOORE

O N 4TH NOVEMBER 1802, CATHERINE MALONE WROTE FROM THE FAMILY home, Baronstown in county Westmeath, to her brother Edmond, the Shakespearean scholar, who was living in Queen Anne Street in London. The Malones were an ancient Irish family, an offshoot of the O'Connors, kings of Connaught, and at one time were the largest landowners in Westmeath. The branch which had acquired Baronstown was an eminent legal family. At one point, four brothers and their father were all practising at the Bar at the same time. Several also served as members of the Irish parliament.[1] In her letter Catherine described a clearly very successful entertainment that had just taken place in Kilbixy church, which lay at the entrance of the avenue to their house. She tells Edmond that they had a band consisting of two violins, two violoncellos, a double bass and a fortepiano, as well as singers and a chorus, and there was 'computed to be near three hundred people' in the audience.[2] This is one of the first documented references to the eighteenth-church at Kilbixy. Slightly earlier, on 4th December 1800, there is a letter from Catherine to Edmond telling him that the church had just been dedicated by the Bishop of Meath, and wishing that he had been present.[3]

The church (Plate 3) stands on a rise of ground just within the walls of the Baronstown estate, which had been acquired by the Malone family some time before 1673.[4] It is a hall-and-tower church of five bays, with a half-bay-projecting chancel (Plate 4). The nave windows have pointed arches with hood moulds and wooden Y-tracery. The chancel window at the west end (since the church is not oriented) was more elaborate, with three lights with subarches and originally a quatrefoiled roundel at the top. Flanking the east window and the entrance tower at the liturgical west end are shallow niches, again with hood moulds and delicate blind tracery. Above them are sunk quatrefoils. The tower, dramatically tall in proportion to the rest of the church, also has niches and quatrefoils to the north and south on the lowest stage. At the next level there are roundels with blind rose tracery on three sides, surmounted by windows like those of the nave. The top of the tower has a frieze of elegant blind arcading beneath a strongly projecting cornice, and, above

*2 – Original interior of Kilbixy Church looking towards the chancel,
with reading desk and pulpit flanking the arch (courtesy Watson Mills)*

that, flat-topped crenellation with pinnacles set diagonally at the corners. The nave is similarly crenellated with pinnacles crowning the buttresses. The materials are of very high-quality ashlar using two different stones, that of the buttresses much bluer and, like the plinth, tooled with a reeded finish.

The interior has sadly suffered grievously from the collapse of the roof in 1960. Lack of funds prevented restoration, and only the two bays before the chancel were reroofed, leaving the other three open to the sky and now planted as a court-yard garden. Originally there was a shallow plaster quadripartite rib vault with foliage bosses and corbels. Two tiers of stalls were ranged under the windows facing one another, and a magnificent pulpit and reading desk stood on either side of the chancel arch (Plate 2). This arrangement was not unusual for Georgian rural churches. It was chosen not to reflect a cathedral choir or college chapel, but to provide an unimpeded view of the altar from every part of the church.[5] The position of pulpit and reading desk looks forward to the regulations of the Commissioners' Churches of the early nineteenth century, although this practice had already had the support of George Herbert ('that prayer and preaching might have equal honour and estimation'), and had been followed by some English eighteenth-century churches.[6]

It has long been known from the inscription over his sarcophagus that Kilbixy church was paid for by Edmond Malone's elder brother, Richard Malone, Lord Sunderlin, who had inherited the Baronstown estate from his uncle Anthony Malone, but the date and the architect have not hitherto been established. Fortunately, the Bishop of Meath, Thomas Lewis O'Beirne, who dedicated the church and was therefore in a position to know it well, made notes on his diocese in 1818.[7] These were based on information gleaned from a questionnaire sent out to all the parishes of his diocese when he was appointed bishop in 1798. O'Beirne was much involved with rebuilding churches and glebe houses, helped, it seems, by a considerable increase in funding. He also pressed for roads to remote and inaccessible churches.[8] He was clearly an energetic and benevolent bishop, even if his original appointment through the Duke of Portland may have been a political one.[9] His concern after the Act of Union over the representation of Irish bishops in the English parliament would, one imagines, have made him sympathetic with the Malones.[10] Another common interest, especially with Edmond Malone, may have been the theatre; O'Beirne had written, in collaboration with the Duchess of Devonshire, a comedy for Drury Lane. He must have known the Malones well as it was he who wrote the epitaph for Edmond's tomb. In O'Beirne's notes on the diocese he wrote:

> In an arrangement agreed on between the late bishop and the late Sir Pigot Piers, a grant was made by the trustees of the First Fruits for building a church in this parish, and Lord Sunderlin having advanced upwards of £3000 in addition to that grant, a church of Gothic architecture has been erected on a plan of Wyatt's and finished both outside and inside in the handsomest manner; with an organ and everything necessary for the moral decent celebration of divine service.

James Wyatt is the most likely member of the Wyatt clan to have furnished this design. He was the most eminent architect of the dynasty, and, as such, Lewis O'Beirne would not have felt the need to give his Christian name. He was, moreover, the only one of the family known to have come over to Ireland, where he had extensive connections and was, of course, involved in several country houses, notably Castle Coole in county Fermanagh.[11]

The late bishop to whom Lewis O'Beirne refers was Henry Maxwell, whom he replaced in 1798. This, therefore, gives us a *terminus ante quem* for Kilbixy, and also indicates a possible precedent for the employment of Wyatt in ecclesiastical circles. Bishop Henry Maxwell had obtained a set of designs from Wyatt in 1773 for his country house, Ardbraccan, outside Navan. Wyatt had also worked for Archbishop Richard Robinson in 1773 when he designed Canterbury Quad in Christ Church, Oxford.[12] The date of Kilbixy is confirmed by *The Third Report of His*

3 – Kilbixy church, county Westmeath, 1793-1798, here attributed to James Wyatt

4 – Kilbixy church chancel from the south-west (photo T.S. Moore)

Majesty's Commissioners on Ecclesiastical Revenue and Patronage in Ireland, 9 May 1836.[13] The Commissioners describe Kilbixy as 'One church capable of accommodating 300 persons rebuilt in the year 1798 at the cost of 10000L, Brit; whereof £8301 15s 4½d. by way of gift was granted by the late board of the First Fruits and the remainder was contributed by the late Lord Sunderlin' – not quite as much in the end as the £3,000 Lewis O'Beirne had suggested.[14] Another piece of supporting evidence for 1798 as a completion date is the carving of 1799 at the base of the left-hand jamb of the doorway. It has more the appearance of graffiti than an official inscription, but at least gives us another *terminus ante quem*, and it is given emphasis by appearing on a single piece of the same blue-grey stone as the buttresses.

The present church at Kilbixy replaced an important medieval church dedicated to St Bigseach, a virgin saint of the early church who gave her name, Cill Bhigsigh, to the town which grew up there.[15] It seems, however, that there was a considerable time lapse, during which the church was largely ruined and unused. Nothing now remains of Kilbixy town apart from the marks of foundations visible from aerial photography.

According to Sir Henry Piers' *Chorographical Description of the County of Westmeath*, written in 1682, Kilbixy was an 'old town of great note' with twelve burgesses who wore scarlet gowns, and a port on Lough Iron, a market and cross which were traditionally believed to have been later transferred to Mullingar. In Piers's time the church still remained, as well as ruins and an old square castle called the Burgage castle, with forty acres attached to it.[16] That has now gone, although there is still an area called the Burgage land, and a motte and bailey castle still survives to the north (Plate 1) as well as the ruins of a possible leper house just below the church. Piers also notes that 'In this town stands the remains of an ancient and well-built church, the mother of many churches and chapels about it, which had at the west end a very well built high tower or steeple.'[17]

Presumably, therefore, the medieval church was oriented. It seems clear, however, that the church was not being used in Piers's day as he mentions earlier, in his description of Temple Cross church, a couple of miles away, that 'this place supplieth the defect of our mother church Kilbixy'. In Bishop Dopping's Visitation Book of 1682-85, the church of Kilbixy is described as ruined, with no curate.[18] In 1745 there is a letter from H. Tuite to Henry Maule, Bishop of Meath, saying that Prime Sergeant Malone offered £100 if Kilbixy, rather than one of its neighbouring churches, was rebuilt, and that he would also enclose the churchyard with a wall at his own expense. He goes on to say that the old church is at the end of Malone's avenue and is the burial place of his family, 'which to be sure is his chief motive for contributing so handsomely to that church'.[19] Three days later the Bishop wrote to William Smythe of Barbavilla enclosing Tuite's letter, and pointed out that it was Sir John Piers who named the curates and that he had reason to believe that he would never consent to the proposal. Tuite had added a note at the end of his letter saying that with his contribution of thirty guineas and a contribution from Mr Smythe in addition to Malone's offer, 'a very decent church might very easily be finished this summer with proper care'. That could only have been achieved, though, if Sir John Piers had been prevailed upon to agree to the new church despite the competition with Anthony Malone that Bishop Maule implies. The memory of the rivalry was still potent enough in the 1940s for John Betjeman to refer to it in his poem *Sir John Piers*:

> I'll build a mighty wall against the rain...
> And from the North, lest you, Malone, should spy me
> You, Sunderlin of Baronstown, the Peer,
> I'll fill your eye with all the stone that's by me
> And live four-square protected in my fear.[20]

If, as seems likely, Sir John held up proceedings for several years, Anthony Malone would not have been in such a strong position financially to honour his original offer. There is a series of letters from Anthony Malone to Nathaniel Clements from 1756 to 1760, worrying about a debt owed to him which precluded him from making any investments, and the series ends with a letter suggesting that he might have to sell his Roscommon estate.[21] His career was also unstable at this period; he had been removed from the position of Prime Sergeant in 1754 for opposing the claim of the Crown to dispose of unappropriated revenue, and then, in 1760, removed from the office of Chancellor of the Exchequer, to which he had been appointed in 1757.[22] Such reverses of fortune might have prevented his financing large building operations. It is likely, therefore, that the proposal to rebuild the church lapsed until Lord Sunderlin took up responsibility in the 1790s.

After 1760 Anthony Malone returned to the Bar, and, as a famously successful advocate, would have been able to restore his fortune.[23] By 1764 there is a record of activity in the vicinity of Kilbixy Church. On 15th September 1764 Malone paid William Cox 'for 7 short days and 18 long days labour at Church wall'.[24] One would not expect a wall to be built unless there were a church. Possibly, though, the wall was built initially to protect the Malone tombs, as well as anticipating an enclosure for the church they intended sooner or later to build there. Twenty-nine years later, however, we have clear evidence of the start of work on the present church. In *Faulkner's Dublin Journal* for 8th October 1793, there is a report from Mullingar.[25] 'A few days ago the labourers in throwing up a fosse round the new church at Kilbixy, now building by the Right Hon Lord Sunderlin discovered a subterraneous passage...'[26]

———

James Wyatt furnished a considerable number of designs for Irish patrons, but as far as we know only came to Ireland once, in 1785 for the completion of Slane Castle.[27] He furnished drawings in 1772 for Major General Cunninghame's house, Mount Kennedy, county Wicklow, although the building was not undertaken for another ten years.[28] He furnished drawings for Abbey Leix in the same year;[29] for Slane from 1773 to 1775;[30] for Ardbraccan House in 1773;[31] for Curraghmore, county Waterford, between 1778 and 1780;[32] for Westport in 1781,[33] and for Castle Coole between 1789 and 1790.[34] Since the Kilbixy foundations were apparently being dug in 1793, the work cannot have been overseen by Wyatt as he is not known to have returned to Ireland after his work at Slane. He must merely have sent drawings which are not known to have survived. There are extremely careful drawings for the mouldings of Lee Priory in Kent between 1785 and 1790,[35] for doorways and windows at Ashridge Park in Hertfordshire from 1806 onwards,[36] and for Mount Kennedy, as well as minute instructions on the Mount Kennedy drawings to a John Doyle, and a note to Mr Gilliard to give 'molds' to Doyle.[37] So Wyatt was capable even at a distance of controlling the details of his designs. Unfortunately, we have no idea who oversaw the work at Kilbixy.

We do not know how Lord Sunderlin arrived at the choice of Wyatt as his architect. It could have been through a knowledge of Slane. William Burton-Conyngham, who had inherited Slane from his uncle, had a brother, Francis-Pierpoint, who, in the course of his Grand Tour, had sailed down the coast of Asia Minor with Lord Charlemont, where they discovered the remains of the Mausoleum of Halicarnassus.[38] Lord Charlemont was a close friend and frequent correspondent of Lord Sunderlin's brother, Edmond Malone.[39] It is also possible that Henry Maxwell suggested Wyatt.[40] There is, however, a more straightforward connection. Edmond Malone and James Wyatt both lived in Queen Anne Street (now Foley Street), London. Edmond, from 1779, lived at No. 55,[41] and Wyatt, after 1783, at No. 42 in the house that he had built.[42] It seems inconceivable that they would not have known one another since both knew Horace Walpole well.[43]

Kilbixy is the only church and one of only two Gothic Revival buildings by Wyatt in Ireland. The other is Slane Castle, where the picturesque silhouette above the Boyne is due to Wyatt,[44] but the medieval details are more tentative than those of Kilbixy. The magnificent decoration of the Round Room is probably by Hopper.[45] It certainly looks much too dense for Wyatt, who always, whether working in a classical or Gothic idiom, has a restraint, delicacy and elegance that is not present in Slane. In England he had already turned to Gothic at Lee Priory between 1785 and 1790, and, interestingly, this seems to have been inspired by drawings of the monastery of Batalha which William Burton Conyngham had visited in 1783, not long before Wyatt's arrival at Slane.[46]

Probably Wyatt's most famous Gothic building is Fonthill Abbey, Wiltshire

5 – The surviving fragment of Fonthill Abbey, Wiltshire, 1796-1812

opposite, top 6 *– Windows of Fonthill Abbey*

bottom left 7 – *Window of Kilbixy church*
bottom right 8 – *Niche and sunk quatrefoil beside the tower of Kilbixy church.
All the niches are decorated with this delicate blind tracery*

9 – Original interior of Kilbixy church showing the organ loft
(courtesy Watson Mills)

(Plate 5), designed for William Beckford, and almost contemporary with Kilbixy church. Engravings of the lost tower of Fonthill show pinnacles set at angles, as at Kilbixy, and the surviving fragments of Fonthill have almost exactly the same hood mouldings around the windows, made up of two fillets with a hollow between them (Plates 6, 7). The drawings for Lee Priory show the same profile for its hood mouldings.[47] There are also drawings for niches at Lee with lines at the back which correspond to the blind tracery in the Kilbixy niches, as well as quatrefoil decoration like that at Kilbixy (Plate 8). The dome of the staircase of Sheffield Park (*c*.1776), is supported by triple shafts with slim, stiff-leaf capitals, which are very close to the supports of the organ loft of Kilbixy (Plate 9).[48] Among the Mount Kennedy drawings there is one of the battlements of a castle which appear to have flat slabs on top of the crenellations, the form that the Kilbixy crenellations take (Plate 10). This is an extremely unusual feature; elsewhere at this date they are almost always pitched.

It is sad that we have so little left of Fonthill and nothing of Lee Priory with which to compare Kilbixy, but there are also similarities with Wyatt's classical buildings – his fondness for alcoves with very delicate decoration, for instance, circular motifs, blind arcading, and even Y-tracery. The alcove at the top of the stairs at

Mount Kennedy has an elegance that looks forward to Kilbixy's alcoves, even though the vocabulary is different. Circles are obvious shapes for ceilings, but Wyatt also uses them on the walls of Mount Kennedy's façade, as he does on the tower of Kilbixy. He also has Y-tracery in the round-arched windows in a drawing of the Mount Kennedy porter's lodge.[49]

The choice of Gothic for the church could have been that of the architect or the patron. Kilbixy is not the earliest Gothic Revival church in Ireland; Hillsborough, county Down, preceded it by twenty years.[50] It is, however, Wyatt's first completely Gothic design for a church. He had restored, remodelled and added to other churches before this, but his own earlier church designs are either classical like Kentish Town Chapel,[51] or a hybrid classical and Gothic building like the church at Amlwch in Anglesey, which is probably based on a design of his of about 1790.[52]

The history of Kilbixy and the surviving medieval ruins could have suggested Gothic as the appropriate style, but when Lord Sunderlin came to erect a mausoleum the style chosen was neo-classical and very much in the spirit of another contemporary Wyatt building in Ireland, Castle Coole. Both Castle Coole and the mausoleum are magnificently severe; both have fluted Doric columns without bases, set *in antis*, in the pavilions at the ends of the Castle Coole façade, and flanking the doorway of the mausoleum.

10 – Crenellation of Kilbixy church showing the crowning flat slabs

*11 – Malone Mausoleum doorway flanked by footless Doric columns in antis,
viewed from the east (photo T.S Moore)*

12 – Rear of Malone Mausoleum with Malone coat of arms (photo T.S. Moore)

13 – Darnley Mausoleum, Cobham Park, 1782-1786 (photo T.S. Moore)

The mausoleum stands rather menacingly, but splendidly, close to the south-east of the tower and entrance to the church, clearly proclaiming the patronage of the Malones. It is a square building topped by a pyramid on a stepped base of a type derived ultimately from the Mausoleum of Halicarnassus (Plates 11, 12). The door tapers slightly at the top and is crowned with the inscription MORS JANUA VIT[A]E. At the rear of the monument is the Malone coat of arms, surmounted by a coronet. It has a Greek cross plan with a central groin vault and barrel-vaulted recesses. One recess contains the door, and, the other three, sarcophagi for Richard Malone, Lord Sunderlin, Anthony Malone and Edmond Malone. Above each sarcophagus were epitaphs; Richard's and Edmond's are still there but Anthony's has gone.

No documents associated with the mausoleum have survived, but an attribution to Wyatt seems reasonable, partly because of stylistic similarity to Castle Coole, partly because of links with other mausolea designed by Wyatt, and partly because there is no reason to suppose the Malones would employ another architect. Wyatt designed the Dawson Mausoleum at Dartrey, county Monaghan, between about 1770 and 1772, the Brocklesby Mausoleum, Lincolnshire, from 1787 to 1792, and the Darnley Mausoleum in Cobham Park, Kent, from 1782 to 1786. All are on rising ground in commanding positions, and each is the cynosure of the landscape it embellishes. The Malone Mausoleum is admittedly not so isolated nor is it in quite so dominating a position, but it does suggest that it might also be part of a designed landscape.

The Malone Mausoleum is smaller and much more severe than the Darnley example (Plate 13). It uses the baseless Greek Doric order rather than Roman Doric, but both have fluted columns *in antis*, both have strongly projecting cornices and, most importantly, are surmounted by pyramids on stepped bases. The Darnley Mausoleum is almost certainly a good deal earlier than the one in Kilbixy,[53] but it is just possible that there was a connection between the Darnleys and the Malones. The Earls of Darnley owned a considerable acreage of land in Westmeath, not all that far from the Baronstown estate.[54] There is also a letter of 16th January 1789 from an unknown writer in Brussels to Catherine Malone at Edmond's house in Queen Anne Street, making rather arch references to Cobham Park and its 'proprietor'.[55]

It is difficult to date the Malone Mausoleum precisely. It could perhaps have been planned along with the church, but we have no hard evidence. Dynastic pride, either at his elevation to the peerage in 1785 or the new patent of 1797 allowing the title to go to Edmond, may have inspired Richard to plan such a monument. The epitaph over Richard's sarcophagus says that he built 'this tomb for his ancestors and dedicated it to his brother'.[56] The death of Edmond on 25th May 1812 could, therefore, have inspired the mausoleum, or if it had only just been completed the death could have provided the dedication. The particular wording of the epitaph makes the latter more probable. If Wyatt was the architect, the mausoleum must have been designed before 1813 when he died in a coach accident.[57] Lord Sunderlin himself died on 14th April 1816, which, in light of the inscription, means that it must certainly have been finished by then. There would have been a shortage of funds after Lord Sunderlin's death as his sisters were involved in a lengthy lawsuit over the inheritance of the estate.

Baronstown House was destroyed by fire at the end of the nineteenth century,[58] and the estate was divided up by the Land Commission, but the church house mentioned in the epitaph as provided by Lord Sunderlin lies across the road from the church and has Wyatt windows, so it seems possible that this too may have been built to a design provided by the architect of the church.[59] It was probably built between 1799, when mentioned in Lewis O'Beirne's list of glebe houses built or purchased since 1799, and 1815, when it was purchased from Lord Sunderlin by the Board of the First Fruits.[60] The estate, even as it is today, shows strong indications that this was a carefully designed landscape. The concern for the landscape may account for the church not being oriented.

If it is accepted that Wyatt was involved here through his neighbour Edmond Malone, the landscape and setting could easily have been described to him in London, and the extraordinarily picturesque harmony of these buildings and their surroundings shows how sensitively Wyatt could design for the *genius loci*, as he had done with his mausolea and with Fonthill and Castle Coole.

———

ACKNOWLEDGMENTS

I am enormously grateful to Richard Hewlings for his enthusiasm and encouragement, without which this would never have been written; to Watson Mills who so generously shared his seemingly endless knowledge of Westmeath with me; to Ann Martha and Alistair Rowan for advice and hospitality and for reading and commenting on earlier drafts of this article; to the Knight of Glin and Dr Edward McParland for also commenting on the article, and to my husband Tim for listening endlessly to the problems as well as driving up and down England and Ireland in search of buildings, sometimes hidden within nearly impenetrable undergrowth, in addition to taking many of the photographs.

ENDNOTES

[1]   *Grand Juries of the County of Westmeath*, 2 vols (Ledestown 1853) II, 172-77; *Dictionary of National Biography*, 60 vols (Oxford 2004) XXXVI, 351-53

[2]   Westmeath County Library, Mullingar, MS P/M/D2.

[3] Bodleian Library, Oxford, MS Malone 37 (29, 147).

[4] *Burke's Landed Gentry of Ireland* (London 1904).

[5] Alan Acheson, *A History of the Church of Ireland 1691-1991* (Dublin 1997) 94.

[6] M.H. Port, *Six Hundred New Churches* (Reading 2006) 99, 295: n.75.

[7] Representative Church Body, Dublin, MS 157.

[8] Anthony Malcolmson, *Archbishop Charles Agar* (Dublin 2002) 278-90.

[9] *ibid.*, 475.

[10] *ibid.*, 559-62.

[11] Armagh County Museum, letter from Francis Johnston to J.N. Brewer, 29th February 1820.

[12] A.P.W. Malcolmson, *Primate Richard Robinson 1709-94* (Belfast 2003) 45.

[13] Published parliamentary paper (Dublin 1836).

[14] The Board of the First Fruits was established in 1711. It spent the proportion of the clergy's first year's stipend that had, before the Reformation, been paid to the Pope to buy back impropriate tithes from lay owners. Any surplus was used to build churches and glebe houses. Gradually this became its primary function. I am very grateful to Ann Martha Rowan for giving me this definition.

[15] Elizabeth Hickey, 'Some Notes on Kilbixy, Tristernagh and Templecross, and the family of Piers who lived in the Abbey of Tristernagh in Westmeath', *Riocht na Midhe*, V11, 4, 1981.

[16] *Chorographical Description of the County of Westmeath*, reprinted facsimile by Meath Archaeological and Historical Society, 1981, 76.

[17] *ibid.*, 77.

[18] 'Bishop Dopping's Visitation Book', transcribed by C.C. Ellison, *Riocht na Midhe*, V, 1-4, 1971-74.

[19] National Library of Ireland, MS 41,589/18. I am extremely grateful to Toby Barnard for bringing this correspondence to my attention.

[20] John Betjeman, *Collected Poems* (London 1958; 1979) 61. Reproduced by permission of John Murray (Publishers).

[21] Trinity College, Dublin, MS 1741-3.

[22] *Dictionary of National Biography*, XXXVI, 351-53.

[23] *Grand Juries of the County of Westmeath*, II, 172-77.

[24] Westmeath County Library, Mullingar, Rent Book from Baronstown Estate, P/M/D1.

[25] I am much indebted to Watson Mills for bringing this report to my attention.

[26] There is, however, one other contradictory piece of evidence. Daniel Augustus Beaufort's Map of the Diocese of Meath of 1st January 1797 shows neither a standing nor a ruined church at Kilbixy. This might be due to the fact that he started collecting material for his map in 1785 and later failed to check its accuracy. This suggestion is supported by the fact that Kilbixy church does not appear at all on his reprinted map of 1816.

[27] Mark Odlum, 'Slane Castle, Co. Meath', *Country Life*, 17th July 1980, 201; 24th July 1980, 278-80; 31st July 1980, 382

[28] John Cornforth, 'Mount Kennedy, Co.Wicklow', *Country Life*, 28th October 1965, 1128-31; 11th November 1965, 1258-59.

[29] John Cornforth, 'Abbey Leix, co. Leix, Ireland', *Country Life*, 26th September 1991, 90-93.

[30] Odlum, 'Slane Castle'.

[31] C.C. Ellison in *Quarterly Bulletin of the Irish Georgian Society*, Jan-March 1975.

[32] Mark Girouard, 'Curraghmore, Co. Waterford', *Country Life*, 14th February 1963, 311; 21st

February 1963, 368.

[33] Mark Girouard, 'Curraghmore, Co. Waterford', *Country Life*, 6th May 1965, 1074-77.

[34] Alistair Rowan, *Buildings of Ireland, North West Ulster* (London 1979).

[35] Victoria & Albert Museum, Prints & Drawings, E 1896-1948. Derek Linstrum, 'The Wyatt Family', *Catalogue of the Drawings Collection of Royal Institute of British Architects*.

[36] *ibid*.

[37] National Library of Ireland, AD 3568.

[38] Maurice Craig, *The Volunteer Earl* (London 1948) 44-70.

[39] *ibid*, 208, 211, 212-14, 255.

[40] See note 31 above.

[41] James Prior, *Life of Edmond Malone* (London 1860) 45.

[42] Howard Colvin, *Biographical Dictionary of British Architects 1600-1840* (New Haven and London 1995) 1110. Antony Dale in *James Wyatt* (Oxford 1936) 26, gives Wyatt's address as No. 69.

[43] Peter Martin, *Edmond Malone* (Cambridge 1995) 70-72.

[44] Christine Casey and Alistair Rowan, *Buildings of Ireland, North Leinster* (London 1993).

[45] Odlum, 'Slane Castle'. Alistair Rowan points out ('Georgian Castles in Ireland', *Quarterly Bulletin of the Irish Georgian Society*, VII, 1964) that Wyatt demolished Robinson's building to ground level and even basement level at the front of the house. So although Robinson had introduced Gothic windows to the round tower, the present ones must be Wyatt's.

[46] Odlum, 'Slane Castle'.

[47] Victoria & Albert Museum, Prints & Drawings, E 1896-1948.

[48] John Martin Robinson, *The Wyatts: An Architectural Dynasty* (Oxford 1979) 63.

[49] National Library of Ireland, AD 3568/25.

[50] Maurice Craig and the Knight of Glin, *Ireland Observed* (Cork 1970) 60.

[51] Terry Friedman, *The Georgian Group Journal*, VII, 1997, 56-70.

[52] Howard Colvin, *Biographical Dictionary of British Architects 1600-1840* (New Haven & London 1995).

[53] The drawing in the Soane Museum is dated 1782.

[54] I am very grateful to Roger Bowdler for pointing this out to me.

[55] Malone MSS, private collection, county Westmeath.

[56] I am most grateful to Jeannine Addinall for her elegant translation of the epitaph: 'In sacred memory of Richard, Lord Sunderlin. Memorials are here to testify to his life as a truly pious and generous man in religious affairs, open handed also in domestic matters, and no less fore-seeing of the public good; Namely, a church built at his expense, as also a church house endowed with a generous sufficiency, the district above it, and a school convenient for the peo-ple's needs, as also this tomb for his ancestors and dedicated to his brother. / Gentle and kindly was he whom in death we mourn. He caused suffering to no-one at any time, and gave the greatest help and service to the largest possible number, relying on Christ his saviour. / He died on the 14th April A.D. 1816, aged 78.'

[57] Dale, *James Wyatt*, 101.

[58] For a description of the houses on the site, see Casey and Rowan, *Buildings of Ireland, North Leinster*, 346-47.

[59] Representative Church Body, Dublin, MS 157.

[60] Deed of Sale, private collection, county Westmeath.

The facades of Nos 3 and 4 Harcourt Street, Dublin, built by Michael Stapleton (1786-88)
(photo the author)

Decoration and property speculation: newspaper advertisements from Michael Stapleton and Charles Thorp

CONOR LUCEY

I N COMMON WITH NUMEROUS CRAFTSMEN ACTIVE IN LATE EIGHTEENTH-CENTURY Dublin, the celebrated stuccodore Michael Stapleton became involved with house-building and speculative development. Beginning at Camden Street in 1778, Stapleton was in sufficient business by the mid-1780s to describe himself as 'Master Builder' on leases and other transactions. By the time of his death in 1801, Stapleton's will, dated 4th August of that year, recorded his trade simply as 'Builder', and outlined a substantial property portfolio, including houses in some of the city's most fashionable residential districts. A newly discovered advertisement in *The Hibernian Journal*, dated 7th July 1788, emphasises the significance of this aspect of his burgeoning practice:

> TO BE LET,
>
> FOR a long Term of Years, in HARCOURT-STREET, near END to STEPHEN's GREEN, TWO HOUSES, completely finished in a neat elegant Stile, (Stable and Coach-House to one House only) commanding a most pleasing View of Lord Earlsfort's beautiful Improvements, and Wicklow Mountains, &c. and esteemed the best Situation for Air in Dublin.
>
> Application to be made at said House, or to Michael Stapleton, No. 80, Marlborough-street.

The houses in question are the present numbers 3 and 4 Harcourt Street (Plate 1), and were built on ground leased to Stapleton in 1786 by the surgeon and developer Gustavus Hume.[1] On 4th August 1788, Stapleton let one house to Thomas Usher Esq.,[2] and thereafter the wording of the advertisement was amended.[3] The remaining house, which included the stable and coach house, was let to Lady Maria Steele in January 1790.[4] Designs in the Stapleton collection of drawings, held at the National

Library of Ireland, correspond to the two houses in question, including an elevation in ink and watercolour of a pair of houses that is virtually identical to those built.[5]

By 1788 very few houses had been completed on Harcourt Street (the reference to 'Lord Earlsfort's improvements' describes the half-acre lawn that lay on the opposite side of the street from Clonmell House (17 Harcourt Street), the residence of John Scott, Baron Earlsfort), and emphasising that the buildings were 'near end to Stephen's Green' may have assisted the potential lessee to locate them within Dublin's ever-expanding streetscape.[6]

Something of a contrast is provided by an advertisement placed by the equally renowned stuccodore Charles Thorp[7] in the *Freeman's Journal*, dated 1st March 1781, announcing the availability of a leasehold interest in two houses built by him at Gloucester Street (now Seán MacDermott Street):

TWO ELEGANT HOUSES,

TO be let, in the East end of Gloucester-street, by CHARLES THARP, No.10, North Cumberland-street, Stucco-plaisterer and painter — Every branch in these buildings are executed in modern taste, and in the most masterly manner; the walls, cielings, &c. ornamented, the painting and staining entirely new, and cannot be excelled in this kingdom. No expence has been spared in finishing them to the highest perfection. As the builder has had the honour of compleating the most capital buildings, in this kingdom, he flatters himself that on inspection, these houses (for convenience and taste) will be found to answer every expectation of the judicious and refined artist.

In 1800 Charles Thorp was deemed to be one of the leading builder/developers in Dublin, described as being in 'very extensive' business and employing up to thirty labourers.[8] Thorp built a number of houses at Gloucester Street throughout the 1780s, and on 10th May 1781 leased one 'new dwelling house' to Sarah Cooley, Widow – almost certainly one of the houses referred to in his advertisement.[9] By 1900 Gloucester Street was 'solidly tenemented', and following extensive redevelopment during the 1980s, no traces of its late eighteenth-century terraces survive.[10]

Compared with Stapleton's somewhat gaunt appraisal of the houses on Harcourt Street as being 'finished in a neat elegant Stile', Thorp's advertisement emphasises the fact that his 'elegant houses' have been 'executed in modern taste'. This particular terminology was often used in late eighteenth-century architectural literature to describe what we now refer to as the neoclassical style, an example being William Pain's *The Builder's Golden Rule* (London 1781), which contained 'the greatest variety of ornamental and useful designs ... in the most prevailing modern Taste'. Thorp also takes the opportunity to inform the potential lessee that, as a 'judicious and refined artist', he had been responsible for 'compleating the most capital buildings', a reference to his stuccowork at the Blue Coat School (now the Law Society of Ireland) and at the Royal Exchange (now City Hall), for which he had been described as 'a proper person to execute the stucco work &c. of that magnificent Building, in Preference of several others'.[11] The extended wording of Thorp's advertisement may also indicate a greater awareness of the marketing opportunities afforded by such notices.[12]

Of particular interest is the fact that Thorp's advertisement makes clear that the houses in Gloucester Street had 'the walls, cielings, &c. ornamented' before being presented for sale.[13] The practice of decorating houses as a concomitant part of a speculative venture in late eighteenth-century Dublin is clearly indicated by houses built in pairs,[14] and by reference to the measurement papers of the Dublin quantity surveyor Bryan Bolger, covering the period c.1787 to 1818.[15] It is further confirmed by referring to photographs of the interiors at 43-45 Mountjoy Square (all now demolished), built by Michael Stapleton from 1789. In these houses, prominent elements of the stuccowork were identical in composition and detail, indicating that they formed part of the original building and decorating programme.[16] In an international context, it is worth noting that No. 5 Royal Crescent in Bath, England, built by the plasterer Charles Coles in the early 1770s, is one of the few houses in that celebrated development to feature ornamental stucco ceilings.[17]

These advertisements highlight the commercial interests of craftsmen associated with the building industry in Dublin at the time. Given that property notices in eighteenth-century newspapers often make reference to houses 'richly finished with Stucco Ornaments',[18] indicating the value of an enriched interior as a commodity, it is perhaps only to be expected that stuccodores should decorate their self-built townhouses in order to solicit the maximum potential revenue.

———

ACKNOWLEDGEMENTS

I wish to thank Dr Christine Casey for her comments on a draft of this article, and Anna Moran and Sarah Drumm for useful references.

ENDNOTES

The following abbreviations are used:
NA   National Archives, Dublin
RD   Registry of Deeds, Dublin
RIA   Royal Irish Academy

[1] RD, 418/263/273407. The houses have been almost entirely rebuilt and now form part of the St Stephen's Green Hotel.
[2] RD, 441/440/284857.
[3] From 6th August 1788, the advertisement is identical save for the fact that it is for 'a house'. This revised notice ran continuously until mid-October of that year.
[4] RD, 419/33/273026.
[5] For further information on Michael Stapleton's house-building practice see C. Lucey, *The Stapleton Collection: designs for the Irish neoclassical interior* (Tralee 2007) 77-86. For drawings specifically related to Nos 3 and 4 Harcourt Street, see pls 14, 52, 80, 100, 139.
[6] An advertisement in *The Dublin Evening Post*, dated 31st October 1795, announces a six-month lease on 'a new and fashionable House' in 'Holles Street, near Merrion-square'.
[7] The stuccodore Charles Thorp is listed in *The Dublin Directory* as Tharp to 1789.
[8] RIA, Haliday Ms4.B.31, 'Report on the Trades and Manufacturers of Dublin', *c*.1834. This manuscript document was compiled by the renowned antiquary Charles Haliday from papers 'presented by representatives of the Tradesmen of Dublin to Mr O'Connell as Materials for Argument to Repeal the Union between Great Britain & Ireland'. The information, compiled in 1834 by practising representatives from numerous Dublin trades, identified the most prominent employers in the city in 1800 in an attempt to outline the alarming degree to which they believed trade had declined in the years following the Act of Union. The description of Thorp's practice outlined in this document further records that he 'realized a good property which he sunk in building houses in Dublin — he died wealthy about 1824 & was succeeded by his nephew Charles Thorpe.' I am grateful to Anna Moran for bringing this document to my attention.
[9] RD, 339/135/227821. Another of Thorp's houses on this street was let to the English cabinet-maker Peter Eglesso in 1783: RD, 355/504/242069.
[10] C. Casey, *Dublin, Buildings of Ireland Series III* (New Haven and London 2005) 120.
[11] *The Hibernian Journal*, 19th June 1776.
[12] *The Dublin Daily Advertiser* for 7th October 1736 announced that 'Advertisements that require no particular Place or Character and are of moderate Length, are taken in at Two Shillings each', adding that 'advertisements may be inserted at a cheap Rate, [which] has been much wanting in this City'. Cited in R. Munter, *The History of the Irish Newspaper 1685-1760*

(Cambridge 1967) 61-63. Munter further observed that advertising costs 'were seldom listed'.

[13] An advertisement in *The Dublin Evening Post,* dated 2nd January 1790, for an 'elegant new house' in 'the best part of Dominick Street', notes that the rooms are 'finished in the best stile, with ornamented ceilings, &c'.

[14] There are numerous examples of identical decorative schemes in late eighteenth-century Dublin houses built in pairs, including the front and rear drawing room ceilings at Nos 64 and 65 Merrion Square, built by Hall Lamb Esq., and leased in 1793 and 1792 respectively: RD, 447/477/290677 and 477/240/302068.

[15] On 21st October 1793, Bolger measured the 'Plasterers work done for John Claudius Beresford Esqr. at his New Buildings in Beresford Place', executed by the undocumented James Higgins: NA, Bryan Bolger measurement papers, bundle 'B'. At this date the work included a 'Stucco flower' on the ceilings of the entrance halls of two houses, as well as ornamented cornices and friezes in their respective drawing rooms and parlours. The houses in question are the present Nos 3 and 4 Beresford Place.

[16] The evidence of what may be termed 'speculative decoration' in Dublin houses contradicts the widely held view that the extent of decorative plasterwork was typically the concern of the lessee. Maurice Craig's observation that 'of two virtually identical houses one will be decorated and the other not, according to the circumstances of their original construction or disposal', represents an intermediate position. M. Craig, *The Architecture of Ireland* (London and Dublin 1982) 242.

[17] The thirty separate lots comprising Royal Crescent were built by individual tradesmen behind a unified palace front designed by the architect John Wood the Younger in 1767-75. See M. Forsyth, *Bath, Pevsner Architectural Guides* (New Haven and London 2003) 146-50, and J. Ayres, *Building the Georgian City* (New Haven and London 1998) fig. 36.

[18] *The Dublin Journal,* 21st August 1762. I am grateful to Sarah Drumm for this reference.

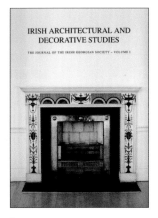

I

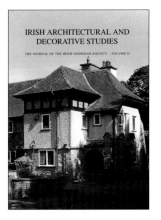

II

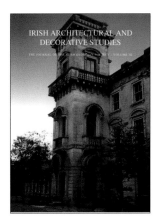

III

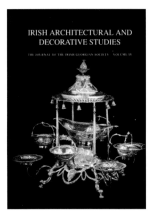

IV

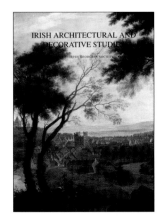

V

VI

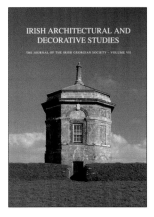

VII

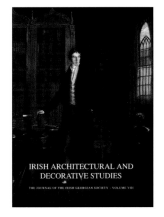

VIII

IX

IRISH ARCHITECTURAL AND DECORATIVE STUDIES

IRISH ARCHITECTURAL AND DECORATIVE STUDIES is the annual journal of the Irish Georgian Society. It is the much-enhanced and dramatically expanded successor to the *Bulletin*, which was published from 1958 to 1997. The journal reflects the Irish Georgian Society's present wider remit, which is no longer concerned solely with Georgian architecture, but acknowledges the importance of the entire spectrum of Ireland's post-medieval architecture and its special need for protection, interpretation, understanding and appreciation. The content of each volume of the journal is wide and varied, testimony to the diversity and scholarship of the series.

■ ORDER FORM   These books can be ordered from any good bookshop
or direct from the Irish Georgian Society or Gandon Distribution.

_____	Volume I	(1998), 224pp, 11 essays, 128 illus	ISBN 978 0946846 160 (ISBN-10: 0946846 162)	€20 pb
_____	Volume II	(1999), 208pp, 8 essays, 110 illus	978 0946846 320 (0946846 324)	€20 pb
_____	Volume III	(2000), 192pp, 6 essays, 143 illus	978 0946846 481 (0946846 480)	€20 pb
_____	Volume IV	(2001), 224pp, 7 essays, 109 illus	978 0946846 726 (0946846 723)	€20 pb
_____	Volume V	(2002), 208pp, 5 essays, 136 illus	978 0946846 962 (0946846 960)	€20 pb
_____	Volume VI	(2003), 240pp, 11 essays, 120 illus	978 0946846 979 (0946846 979)	€20 pb
_____	Volume VII	(2004), 272pp, 10 essays, 159 illus	978 0946846 511 (0946846 510)	€20 pb
_____	Volume VIII	(2005), 272pp, 10 essays, 131 illus	978 0948037 214 (0948037 210)	€20 pb
_____	Volume IX	(2006), 288pp, 9 essays, 203 illus	978 0948037 368 (0948037 369)	€20 pb
_____	Volume X	(2007), 272pp, 10 essays, 148 illus	*clothbound edition* 978 0948037 290	€39 hb
_____			*paperback* 978 0948037 566	€20 pb
_____	Cumulative Index to Volumes I-X (2008), 64pp		978 0948037 641	€5 pb

❑ payment enclosed by € euro / stg £ / US $ cheque for _____   (post free in Ireland, elsewhere at cost)

❑ charge to Laser / Mastercard / Visa __ __ __ __   __ __ __ __   __ __ __ __   __ __ __ __   [MasterCard] [VISA]

expiry date ___ ___ / ___ ___   security code (last 3 digits on signature panel) ___ ___ ___

name _____   date _____   PRINT NAME & ADDRESS

address _____

■ IRISH GEORGIAN SOCIETY   74 Merrion Square, Dublin 2 – T 01-6767053 / F 01-6620290 / E info@igs.ie
■ GANDON DISTRIBUTION   Oysterhaven, Kinsale, Co Cork – T +353 (0)21-4770830 / F 021-4770755
E gandon@eircom.net / W www.gandon-editions.com   (trade orders to Gandon)